CONSTRUCTION SCHEDULES

Contemporary Litigation Series

Consulting Editors for the
CONTEMPORARY LITIGATION SERIES

Professor Stephen R. Saltzburg
University of Virginia Law School

Professor Kenneth R. Redden
University of Virginia Law School

CONSTRUCTION SCHEDULES

Analysis, Evaluation, and Interpretation
of Schedules in Litigation

MICHAEL T. CALLAHAN, ESQ.

H. MURRAY HOHNS, P.E.

THE MICHIE COMPANY
Law Publishers
CHARLOTTESVILLE, VIRGINIA

COPYRIGHT 1983
BY
THE MICHIE COMPANY

Library of Congress Card Number: 83-61658

ISBN 0-87215-642-7

This book is dedicated to Sue Callahan and Jean Hohns. To each of them, we say: "There are many fine women in the world, but you are the best of them all."

Prov 31:29 TLB

TABLE OF CONTENTS

	Page
Dedication	v
About the Authors	ix
Preface	xi
List of Exhibits	xiii

CHAPTER 1.	INTRODUCTION TO SCHEDULES	1
CHAPTER 2.	PROJECT SCHEDULING TECHNIQUES	9
§ 2-1.	Critical Path Method or CPM Schedule	11
§ 2-2.	Precedence Diagramming (PDM)	33
§ 2-3.	Bar Charts	37
§ 2-4.	PERT Charts	41
§ 2-5.	Updating	44
CHAPTER 3.	CONTRACT SCHEDULING REQUIREMENTS	49
CHAPTER 4.	THE LAW AND CONSTRUCTION SCHEDULES	67
§ 4-1.	The Law's View of Schedules	67
§ 4-2.	The Schedule Must Be Complete	74
§ 4-3.	The Schedule Must Be Substantiated	79
§ 4-4.	The CPM Consultant	82
§ 4-5.	The Dates in the Schedule: A Commitment or Guide?	85
§ 4-6.	The Benefit of Float	105
§ 4-7.	Mistakes in the Schedule	112
§ 4-8.	Pre-Bid Schedules	121
§ 4-9.	Mutual Responsibilities Under the Schedule	123
§ 4-10.	Updating the Schedule	128
§ 4-11.	Changes in Scheduled Sequence	131
§ 4-12.	The Schedule as Notice	152
§ 4-13.	Improvements in Contract Scheduling Requirements	157

TABLE OF CONTENTS

Page

CHAPTER 5. USING THE SCHEDULE TO PROVE TIME EXTENSIONS 169

CHAPTER 6. NETWORK SCHEDULES AS EVIDENCE . 197
- § 6-1. Introduction 197
- § 6-2. The Schedule as a Business Record .. 197
- § 6-3. Schedules as Scientific Evidence 205
- § 6-4. The Schedule as an Adversary's Testimony 206
- § 6-5. The Schedule as Expert Testimony ... 208

Appendix 215
Bibliography 289
Table of Cases 291
Index 295

ABOUT THE AUTHORS

H. Murray Hohns, P.E., a thirty-year veteran of the construction industry, a graduate of Tufts University and the Polytechnic Institute of New York, has been retained as a construction consultant in every State of the United States on projects totaling several billion dollars. Since 1965, he has specialized in critical path scheduling for planning new construction and analyzing projects already completed.

Michael T. Callahan, Esq., involved with the construction industry for the past ten years, has a vast background in utilizing various scheduling techniques to prove or repute construction contract delay claims. He is a graduate of the University of Kansas; he holds a J.D. from the University of Missouri-Kansas City, and an LL.M. He is a member of the bar in Kansas, Missouri, and New Jersey.

PREFACE

Courts and administrative boards that are called upon to judge construction industry performance have demonstrated an interpretation of schedules which is not shared by the construction industry. Frequently, misunderstanding of schedules and scheduling techniques has led to decisions which are wrong.

To help construction industry judges (and warn those who are judged), we have set out to capture the real-world, bottom-line meaning of construction schedules. The purpose of this book is not to instruct on how to schedule a project or how to implement a schedule, but rather to alert and to challenge the reader to be aware of the portent of what construction schedules can mean to owners, contractors, users, designers, and bystanders if the project does not proceed systematically. Readers desiring comprehensive instruction in *how* to schedule a project may find the books referenced in the footnotes more than adequate instruction.

The text material reflects two perspectives: Michael T. Callahan's primary background is law; H. Murray Hohns's background is engineering, but both are constantly formulating and offering opinions on *why* and *what* went wrong on late construction jobs. Both men have been contractors and owner's managers; both men's thoughts and experiences are rooted in the real world of construction today.

Whenever possible, we have endeavored to give the reader our opinions along with sufficient reasoning to be convincing. However, the text may raise more questions than provide pat answers. Stereotyped answers don't fit when the distinctive nature of the human element is involved. Everyone on board a project has a destination; everyone proceeds in his own way. In project management, it's the "getting there" that seems to count, not the end result. Or is it the other way around?

This book began with *The Deskbook of Construction Contract Law*, the first book on which we collaborated; *The Deskbook* was author Hohns' second book, author Callahan's first. Our Chapter, "The Law Behind Construction Schedules," generated considerable industry interest and additional questions. In response to this interest, our research and explanation grew —

PREFACE

from a twenty-six page chapter in *The Deskbook,* to the present work, some ten times the original length. The process has yielded *Construction Schedules: An Examination of the Analysis, Evaluation, and Interpretation of Schedules in Litigation.*

We consider this book to be much more than a basic lesson in claims documentation and evidentiary assemblage. We view the text as a significant contribution to the "art of scheduling" and a substantial attempt to interpret schedules. Thus, our introduction to *Construction Schedules,* a book which we believe is important to all serious participants in the construction industry.

Michael T. Callahan
H. Murray Hohns

LIST OF EXHIBITS

Page

Exhibit 1 Partial I-J Diagram 16
Exhibit 2 Example Computer Print Out 25
Exhibit 3 Example Logic Diagram 27
Exhibit 4 Partial Precedence Diagram 35
Exhibit 5 Partial Succeedence Diagram 36
Exhibit 6 Bar Chart Progress Schedule 38
Exhibit 7 Bar Chart Progress Schedule with Critical Path 40
Exhibit 8 Sample PERT Network 43
Exhibit 9 Partial CPM Schedule, Henry Ericsson Co. vs. United States 135

CHAPTER 1
INTRODUCTION TO SCHEDULES

Construction scheduling is not a new phenomenon. For all of recorded history, man has been planning complicated projects. The Twentieth Century may have electronic and environmental features not common earlier, but the concept of someone having to plan out labor, tools, material, and equipment to do a job in some sort of sequence has been with us since Adam gave name to every living creature.

Bar Charts have been used as a scheduling tool for fifty years or more; little is known about how men planned large construction projects before the advent of the bar chart. However, it was not until the development of network diagramming techniques which have the ability to show activity relationships that the scheduling of construction projects began to receive serious attention. For those participating in the scheduling process, this increased use of scheduling as a planning and coordinating tool on construction projects has necessitated legal definitions of the participant's rights, responsibilities, and liabilities.

Perhaps one day the scheduling engineer will combine his talents with the materials-handling, work-flow, work- measurement techniques of the industrial engineer to improve time control and productivity. The assemblage of "high-priced" labor on super projects nets staggering yearly payrolls. For example, in 1980, on any super project in just one area of the United States, 3,000 workers earning an average of $40,000/year contribute a total of $120,000,000 with an accompanying payroll burden of $60-70,000,000 in taxes, unemployment, insurance premiums, union fund contributions, etc. to the local economy. Thus, one project has created, over and over, a laboratory which has proved that the costs of scheduling are insignificant when compared to the project's labor costs but the costs of *not* scheduling are beyond comprehension. Moreover outside influences which interpret the construction industry's schedules are forcing attention to change from "building" the project to the "process of building" the project.

The seed for this text began to germinate in the period of 1956-1958 when E.I. DuPont de Nemours Company in conjunction with the UNIVAC Applications Research Center of Remington Rand developed the Critical Path Method (CPM) to evaluate the potential use of computers to schedule construction projects. The technique was developed by Dr. John W. Mauchly from the UNIVAC Applications Research Center, James E. Kelley, Jr. of Remington Rand, and Morgan Walker of DuPont. CPM was first applied to equipment turnaround on a chemical plant in Louisville, Kentucky, where it was credited with saving DuPont $1 million during the first complete year's use of the technique.[1] The particular equipment involved could not be maintained while the unit was in production. Maintenance was performed when production permitted the equipment to be shut down. Past maintenance had required a shutdown of 125 hours; using the new critical path method for the first time, the maintenance was completed in 93 hours. Subsequent critical path application further reduced the shutdown period to 74 hours.[2]

Then, in 1958, Mauchly formed Mauchly Associates, an organization devoted to solving industrial problems using CPM. Kelley and Walker joined the firm later. It was not until 1961, however, that the scheduling method was applied to construction projects. In that year, Perini-Canada successfully completed the Port-Mann Bridge using a Benota (a French machine that simultaneously drilled and sank caissons) and the critical path method. Mauchly promoted CPM in the early 1960's by presenting seminars across America. The interest shown encouraged A. James Waldron and Lloyd Cathgart of MIT to also promote CPM.

INTRODUCTION

Others, including our partner, William B. Wagner, along with Dwight Zink, and Bill deVos also taught CPM seminars across America in 1962 and 1963. By 1965, the missionary efforts of Mauchly, Waldron, and others led to CPM being specified and required in many government projects and most federal agencies adopted the technique. Major private real estate builders such as Argonaut Realty (General Motors), IBM (CPM needed computers), Ford, and the major telephone companies also specified CPM on their jobs. The market-conscious contractor and design professional began to include statements as to their use of CPM in their advertising brochures.

Amazingly, no dispute involving a construction project with sophisticated construction scheduling was decided by the American legal system until after 1966 (bar chart schedules had been used before, but infrequently). In retrospect, delayed judicial consideration of sophisticated schedules can probably be linked to the so-called Rice Doctrine which made delay or non-direct costs uncollectable in the federal arena until the government changed its rules in the late 1960's. A group of related cases, *United States v. Rice*,[3] *Chouteau v. United States*,[4] *H.E. Crook, Inc. v. United States*,[5] and *United States v. Howard Foley Co.*,[6] were the genesis of what is known as the Rice Doctrine. In summary, the Doctrine interpreted the changes clause (permitting the government to order changes during performance) to give the government the right to take a reasonable time to make such changes. Government delay to contractor performance of the unchanged work for a reasonable time was not considered to permit recovery of additional costs of performance. Expenses for delayed performance of the unchanged work were absorbed by the contractor. The potential of delay for change was known to both parties during the bid stage. However, federal construction contract rules were amended in 1967 to permit contractor recovery of costs of *unchanged* work, including costs for delayed project completion. Subsequently, major federal agencies issued guides to using sophisticated scheduling techniques to measure the effect of change orders on the contractor's *unchanged* work. Until the change in contract forms which eliminated the Rice Doctrine, there was little interest in schedule analysis to determine responsibility for delayed project completion.

Nonetheless, our courts and administrative boards have had less than fifteen years to evaluate the rights and liabilities of the parties involved with construction schedules. There are few cases reported and even fewer law review articles which consider this new development in construction litigation. There is no accumulation of cases or indexes which are grouped together under "schedules" in legal lexicons. Thus, the researcher in construction schedule litigation will find not only a dearth of material, but also no organized way to search for what little information there is. Then too, so many construction disputes are arbitrated, a process which produces no data bank for future cases.

All parties on the building team, including the most important of all, the owner, as well as courts and administrative boards throughout the United States, must deal with construction schedules as an integral part of the construction process. Yet, there is little uniformity in scheduling methods. Specifications, understanding, and use differ. Logic demands that schedules be recognized in the litigation process as schedules are used in the construction process. Indeed the same logic demands and assumes a uniform understanding of scheduling concepts which is often lacking in the construction industry. Not surprisingly, courts and boards have not consistently applied scheduling techniques to construction litigation in the same manner that schedules are applied as a planning tool in the building

INTRODUCTION

and construction industry. This is so despite uniform acceptance of the industry definition of schedules by the court.

The serious student of the construction industry will find this work a worthwhile text. Contractors can see how the law courts have interpreted and applied their "tool" of scheduling and alternately can revise the manner in which they develop and use schedules, or in future disputes show courts how past decisions have erred. Trial lawyers litigating construction cases may use the text in much the same way. Past case law can be used to support present positions or the author's comments can be heeded to influence or change court interpretation of schedules in the past. Contractors will learn the importance of scheduling and see the errors others have made in developing a network diagram. Architects and engineers including scheduling clauses in the contracts drafted for use between the contractor and owner (and even perhaps between designer and owner) may use the illustrated clauses as a guide and perhaps even accept the author's suggestions and modify the clauses to (in theory) eliminate confusion in interpreting the schedules. Designers called upon to resolve disputes which involve schedules between owners and contractors may use the book to assist in reaching an accurate and unbiased decision. Lawyers drafting contracts between owner and contractor or owner and designer may use the text in a manner similar to architects and engineers. Students of all disciplines, professions, and ages will be able to use the book as a guide to learning the proper and improper ways to apply schedules.

The book is not, however, designed to be a text on *how* to produce a network schedule. Rather, it was written to explain the manner in which a schedule should be used and interpreted. Many fine textbooks are available which will instruct on *how* to schedule; the authors have referred to many of them in the footnotes. Few, if any, textbooks are available on how to interpret a schedule and none exist (to our knowledge) on the proper use of a schedule to resolve a construction dispute. This book is designed for the advanced student and industry practitioner to use in the every-day, real world of construction problems.

Schedules are not sacred. There are great schedules and poor schedules. Good schedules can mean successful projects, but good schedules offer no guarantee. Projects can sour despite good schedules because of arrogance, misinterpretation, interference, indifference, ignorance, or ineptitude. Schedules can be ignored, but even if they are obviously wrong, they command a certain amount of respect at the job conference table. Regardless, a project will undoubtedly have a schedule.

This text is intended to both add to the volume of material available to assist those who use schedules in the analysis of construction disputes and to correct the beginnings of misunderstandings and misconceptions which the adjudicative system has shown in some of the cases which have considered schedules. It is hoped this guide will assist courts and administrative boards throughout the United States in using scheduling methods to resolve complicated construction disputes in the same way that the construction industry uses schedules to plan and control the process of building, a manner in which not all courts and boards have heretofor shown a similar ability. The authors reason that

INTRODUCTION

uniformity in court interpretation of schedules will reinforce uniformity of industry interpretation.

---

1. K. Lockyer, *An Introduction to Critical Path Analysis* 2 (1st ed. 1964).
2. J. O'Brien, *CPM in Construction Management* 7 (2d ed. 1971).
3. 317 U.S. 61, 63 S. Ct. 120, 87 L. Ed. 53 (1942).
4. 95 U.S. 61, 24 L. Ed. 371 (1877).
5. 270 U.S. 4, 46 S. Ct. 184, 70 L. Ed. 438 (1926).
6. 329 U.S. 64, 67 S. Ct. 154, 91 L. Ed. 44 (1946).

CHAPTER 2
PROJECT SCHEDULING TECHNIQUES

§ 2-1. Critical Path Method or CPM Schedule.
§ 2-2. Precedence Diagramming (PDM).
§ 2-3. Bar Charts.
§ 2-4. PERT Charts.
§ 2-5. Updating.

The "project schedule" serves different functions and has different meanings to the architects, engineers, contractors, subcontractors, materialmen, owners and most especially, courts of law involved in the construction process. The project schedule may mean the contractually stated final completion date or interim completion dates for phases of the work. It may refer to the process of sequencing and scheduling individual activities or tasks which are required to complete the project.[7] It may also refer to a contractual commitment to complete each element of the work at the date designated in the schedule. It may be written down and studied in great detail. It may be spoken and its essence only the everchanging thoughts of the superintendent. It may be revised constantly. Despite this seemingly wide variety of schedules, there are only a few types of formal construction schedules. The most frequently encountered are gantt (bar) charts and critical path method schedules. PERT charts, a third type, are usually encountered in research and development rather than in construction projects, however these three types of schedules share many characteristics.

Regardless of the type, construction schedules are designed to establish the sequential order in which construction is to be completed. Establishing this sequential order requires an intimate knowledge of construction methods combined with an ability to visualize discrete work elements outlined in the design documents, the physical restraints of the work on the assembly during and after construction and the establishment of the mutual interdependency of these discrete elements. Once sequential order is established, manloading, equipment, material, or other resources may be easily added for greater degrees of control. Their addition may well force changes in the schedule. Unfortunately, many schedules are made without thought to or knowledge of any of the above. The subcontractor system prevents the general contractor from knowing what resources are really required.

Construction scheduling is a time-consuming and difficult task. It is an art as well as a science and it is far from easy. Most construction projects are extensive. They involve thousands of activities with intricate and complex interrelationships which are physical, economical, emotional, or a combination of all. The use of any scheduling technique will produce a schedule only as good as the time invested and the knowledge of the scheduler. If a schedule is based on faulty logic between activity relationship or faulty estimates of activity duration its utility will be limited. Indeed it could easily be valueless. A knowledge shortfall can produce useless logic. Good logic may be ignored by those in charge who think they know better or just don't care.

Construction scheduling is also an attempt to look into the future. This is another characteristic which construction schedules, regardless of type, share. And with battles, bread, riches and favor, time and chance happeneth to construction schedules.[8] Schedules must be continuously revised to reflect present conditions. Without the ability to change, the schedule becomes useless. A construction schedule must be based on the best present information. When earlier assumptions or ideas are changed because of superior information, the schedule must also change. The construction industry has little control over its destiny. It is too often the supplier or manufacturer's schedule and not the job schedule that dictates. A construction job is the ultimate in flexibility; the ingenuity of contractors to work around missing pieces is without equal. Within the ranks of the constructors, all sorts of job inconveniences and cost may be self-imposed to keep the job moving. These costs are almost always absorbed without complaint (unless it is the owner or designer who causes the leaveout or labor shift), then the costs are unabsorbable, documented over and over and the constant subject of polemics and tears. Lack of control, missing pieces, and owner-caused labor shifts all cause changes in the construction schedule which will destroy the schedule unless it is revised to reflect these present conditions. Thus, the constant need to change the schedule based on present, actual information.

The well-informed construction industry member, user, or advisor needs to be well grounded in present scheduling techniques. The same techniques are used worldwide. No country or group has a better way. Papers put forth at Project Management Institute meetings and its European sister, Internet, discuss the same techniques and problems. The common techniques are Critical Path Method (CPM), Precedence Diagramming Method (PDM), Bar or Gantt charts, Program Evaluation and Review Technique (PERT) and the updating of each or any of these.

§ 2-1. Critical Path Method or CPM Schedule.

The critical path method of scheduling has contributed significantly to construction contracting. It reduces the time necessary to complete a project. It is a well-proven, effective tool for planning and scheduling work, directing work, and finally, measuring and controlling work. It permits the work schedule to be understood and thought out well in advance for material procurement, equipment availability, and to some extent, manloading. Preparing the network diagram forces thinking through the job from start to finish, thus permitting early identification of potential problem areas on the project. The CPM schedule is easy to pass to others. The diagram permits efficient communication between field and office forces, and if personnel changes are made during the life of the project, can assist in smooth transition with project management staff. Diagrams make job coordination easier among material suppliers, contractors, subcontractors, owners, and architects/engineers and tell how the planner saw the job logic or work flow. Diagrams often reveal if the planner knows what the job is about, and they always disclose how much the planner understands about construction processes.

Preparing a critical path method schedule requires three steps: (1) determination of most of the elements of construction that must be performed in order to construct the project, (2) ascertainment of the sequential relationships or logic among these activities, and (3) the presentation of this information in the form of a network diagram.[9]

The elements into which a construction project are subdivided for CPM planning purposes are called "activities." An activity is a single work step that has a recognizable beginning and end. Activities are defined as a time consuming task. No standards exist as to the number of activities any CPM schedule should have, but sufficient activities are needed to control the work. No standards exist as to how long activity durations should be; minimum duration for a construction activity is recommended to be no less than one day, but duration can be in hours, or minutes, if needed, depending on the work to be scheduled. For example, some years ago a commercial passenger aircraft turnaround at a typical airport stop was scheduled by CPM to take eight minutes.

The order in which the activities are to be accomplished is called the CPM logic. Logic should be developed with safety, space, and structure in mind. The safety, space, and structure rule reflects the obvious limitation that the start of some activities depends upon the completion of others. An example of a limitation of space is that twelve men cannot wire one motor control center. An example of a limitation of structure is that the roof membrane cannot be installed until the roof deck or fill is complete.

Yet, there are many activities that are independent of one another and can proceed concurrently, although much job logic follows from well-established work sequences that are customary in construction contracting. Nevertheless, there is always more than one way to approach a project; except in the rarest of cases no unique logic exists. There are always many ways to construct a project, consequently many different schedules are possible.

The network diagram is nothing more than a graphical display of job logic, presenting in pictorial form all of the dependencies among activities.[10] The logic diagram may or may not be to a time scale. The experienced scheduler never draws the logic to scale the first time because there is too much to learn as the plan sheets turn. The time scale has to be redone too often. Time scaled logic looks nice, no doubt, makes the schedule easier to read, makes the schedule much larger physically (large walls may be needed on which to hang these schedules), and also makes the redrafting of the time scale a monthly, expensive, and unneeded, but often required exercise.

To be realistic, a CPM schedule must reflect the practical restraints that apply to the job activities. The restrictions of the job logic itself are restraints. The completion of the supporting structure restrains the installation of the roofing membrane. These restraints arise from the necessary order of construction operations and are simply a part of job logic.

There are other types of restraints. Structural steel cannot be erected until it is available at the site, and steel availability depends upon preparation, transmittal, approval of erection diagrams, shop drawings, mill orders, rolling, delivery, steel fabrication at the plant, and delivery to the jobsite. Thus, the start of steel erection is restrained by the all-necessary, preliminary actions of detailing, engineering approvals, steel fabrication, and delivery. These are restraints that must be shown on the schedule (or at least considered) before being possibly dismissed as redundant or as an unnecessary degree of detail.

Restraints or "dummies" are represented on the network as a dotted line. The dummy's purpose is only to explain certain relationships among activities; it does not represent a work activity. Although the activities which restrain the logic can be thought of as time consuming in nature, the restraint for scheduling purposes is considered to require "no time." Thus the dummy itself does not represent performance time.

There are two methods of drawing logic: "I-J" and precedence (PDM). There is a tendency to call "precedence" CPM; many people don't know the difference. I-J was the first technique used, precedence followed. Both methods result in a critical path method schedule.

In I-J, the tail of the arrow is the starting point of the activity; the head of the arrow represents its completion. The starting and ending points of an activity are known as an event or "node." The I node is the beginning point; the J node is the ending point. In a logic diagram, a J node (activity completion) also represents an I node (activity beginning) of the succeeding construction activity. They simply indicate the flow of work and time. Arrows can flow left to right, right to left, up, or down. Some people insist on all arrows flowing from left to right, an insistence which can force the use of a long sheet of paper. For example, an owner's representative in Washington, D.C. once forced us to use 27 feet of paper to chart a CPM. Now retired, only he knows what the value of that 27 feet of continuous flow from left to right was because in the usual network diagram the length and orientation of the I-J arrows have no significance.

Logic diagrams are best drawn free hand on grid paper where the grid does not print in the blue print process. Valuable time can be wasted by using hard line drafting techniques. The best CPM is the one drawn freehand by the scheduling engineer; the idea of a senior consultant transmitting his concept of the logic to a draftsman who then draws the logic usually doesn't work. The scheduler should draw the logic; it's the only way to think the job out.

To illustrate the mechanics of I-J diagramming for the reader who is unfamiliar with CPM, consider a simple project such as the construction of a gas station. A partial I-J diagram illustrating one method of sequencing the construction activities in building a gas station is illustrated in Exhibit 1 [11] which follows.

§ 2-1 CONSTRUCTION SCHEDULES

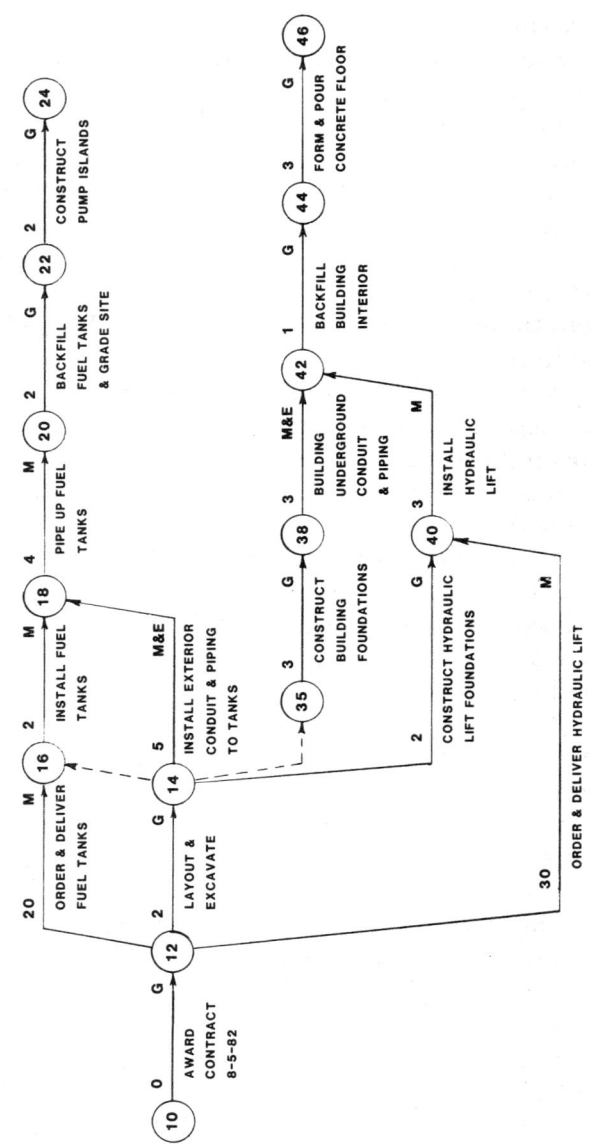

EXHIBIT 1 PARTIAL I-J DIAGRAM

Layout, excavation, and the procurement of fuel tanks and the hydraulic lift are all activities that can begin immediately after the contract is signed. They can proceed independently of one another, since these tasks are usually performed by different people: the layout by the contractor's superintendent, excavation by a subcontractor, and procurement by the contractor's office staff. After the excavation has been completed, construction of the foundations can start. Installation of underground pipes will follow the building foundations but the interior cannot be backfilled until both the hydraulic lift foundations and the hydraulic lift have been completed because both are below the top of the backfill. Concrete floors can be poured after the building interior has been backfilled.

Each arrow or activity is identified by the number located in the I node and J node. For instance, the activity "lay out and excavate" is designated as activity 12-14. The activity "lay out and excavate" has an I node of 12 and a J node of 14. Some I-J diagrams use the same I-J nodes for different but concurrent activities. It is better for each activity to have a unique I number primarily to avoid communication problems. The same I-J number should not be used even if distinctions are only between trades or when more than one trade is scheduled for the same activity.

The I-J method of critical path scheduling is based on the premise that a given activity cannot start until all of those activities immediately preceding it have been completed. In Exhibit 1, "form and pour concrete floor" cannot start until "backfill building interior" has been finished. This is not necessarily true in the field but it is a limitation of the scheduling process.[12] Enough flexibility exists to understand that perhaps 5% or 2% of the preceding activity may hang, and that work following can and will start. The logic diagram is a plan; it is not the erector set instruction book needed for an eight-year-old to assemble his first tinkertoy windmill.

Every activity in the I-J network must have a definite event to mark its beginning. It is not possible to have the finish of one activity overlap the start of the following activity. If the start of one activity overlaps the finish of another, the activities should be further subdivided.

Some computer programs and diagramming techniques will allow the planner to show the lap effect on the I-J diagram. However, in our view, it is better to eliminate lap and lag. They are unnecessary refinements which often prove to be unmanageable in updating the schedule. The scheduling professional seeks to uncomplicate life; the amateur or management information system person sees detail as necessary to protect his domain, but overdetail destroys good scheduling effort. Simplicity is the keyword in scheduling.

The I-J network must be continuous with no gaps, discontinuities, or dangling activities. All activities must have at least one activity following, except those that terminate the project.

In Exhibit 1, the dashed arrow, 14-16, is not a time-consuming activity, but it is an example of a logic restraint. The use of restraints is the most difficult aspect of I-J diagramming. Restraint 14-16 is necessary if job logic is to be correctly portrayed. A correct sequential relationship stipulates that the start of "install fuel tanks" must await completion of "order and deliver fuel tanks." The tanks must be ordered and delivered before they can be installed. But "install fuel tanks" must also await completion of "layout and excavate." The restraint 14-16 shows that the start of "install fuel tanks" depends upon the completion of not only "order and deliver fuel tanks" but also of "layout and excavate." Before the tanks can be installed, they must also have a place to go — the hole must be completed. The direction of the restraint designates flow of activity dependencies.[13]

PROJECT SCHEDULING TECHNIQUES § 2-1

It is customary, but not mandatory, that the I node at the head of the arrow be numbered lower than the activity at its tail, the J node. J is normally greater than I for all activities. This was done originally because of computer program limitations. Although no longer necessary for programming reasons, the practice persists and is preferred because it makes it easier to locate events and activities on the diagram. The experienced scheduler numbers his logic so that it flows from the low numbers at the beginning to the higher numbers at the end. The practiced planner numbers diagrams in bands or areas of logic, so that all activities in a related group (such as all foundation activities) will have the same number group. All foundation activities, for instance, may have a number in the 200 series and only foundation activities will have 200 numbers. The key idea is to number logic in a manner that produces order, not chaos.

In Exhibit 1, the activity description is *below* the line. Although some specifications require the activity description to be *above* the line, the "below the line" technique eliminates physical restrictions on the length of description which may be encountered from the arrow. As to schedule quality, there is no reason why the specification writer or interpreter would insist on the description being above the line. However, the Veterans Administration and others insist on the above line method. One reason given by the VA is that their key punch operators are trained to have the description above the line. Rules, not common sense, seem to run the world, but rules are useless and often self-defeating without common sense application.

Duration is indicated next to the I node on the opposite side of the line of description; contractor responsibility is indicated next to the J node. The activity arrow may also carry additional information. Many CPM specifications require that a dollar and manloading value be assigned to each activity. The more information the activity is required to carry, however, the less useful the CPM schedule becomes to manage and measure time, its original goal. Computers require time to process information. The greater amount of information, the greater the time necessary to process the information. Computers cannot process a great amount of information in a hurry. The more information, the more paper. Production of more information can delay the arrival of the schedule to the field and the volume of material may overwhelm the manager, reducing his effective use of the information.

Once the network diagram has been developed, time, or activity is added to the CPM schedule. Time is generally not considered during development of the logic. The logic diagram is developed using unlimited time and resources. Activity durations are added after the logic is drawn based on equipment, material, and labor limitations. Durations should be reasonably optimistic. Most contractors who have to give the owners a copy of the schedule want to make each activity longer than it should be and still finish two months early. Subcontractors want more time than needed. As durations are added, the planner manually adds them and records the sums over each node. This is called making a forward pass. As time is introduced into the network, it is necessary to redefine certain activities, to condense others into fewer activities, or to expand them into additional ones.

After a time duration has been estimated for each activity of the network, the "critical" or longest path through the network is calculated. The "critical" or longest path through the project determines the period in which the project may be completed and the period of time within which each activity must be accomplished if completion time is to be met.

This calculation involves the determination of four times for each activity. The "early start" (ES) is the earliest time an activity can possibly start after the completion of the proceeding activities. The "early finish" (EF) is the earliest time an activity can be completed and is determined by adding that activity's duration to its early start time. The "late finish" (LF) is the latest that an activity can finish and allow the entire project to be completed within the contract time. It is calculated by working backward through the logic starting at the project's end date and in turn subtracting each activity's duration. The "late start" (LS) is calculated by subtracting the activity's duration from the latest finish time. When the early and late dates are identical and the length of time between start and finish is the same as the activities duration, that activity is on a critical path.

Activity time computations can be accomplished by man or computer. Manually computing the forward pass in sufficient depth to understand and set the schedule and then letting the computer finish the computations enables a scheduler to find errors in computer input and printout.

Using the manual approach for activity time computations, each activity's early start value is determined first. Early finish time is calculated by adding the activity duration to early start. The basic assumption for computation of "early" activity time is that every activity will start as early as possible. As noted above, this process is known as a "forward pass." It starts at the beginning of a project and works forward. Thus, the first activity has an early start time of zero.

Calculation of early activity times indicates the earliest time the last activity will finish. *If* a competent job of planning has been done, *if* activity durations have been accurately estimated, and *if* everything goes well in the field, project completion can be anticipated within the early start times.[14]

The "backward pass" calculates late start and late finish

times by starting at the project end and working backward through the network. During the backward pass, the presumption is that each activity finishes as late as possible without delaying project completion. The backward pass calculation is based on the early completion time for the last activity. Since the scheduler usually thinks the job through from start to finish, backward passes and logic often have errors. Good thinking from the start does not assure that the backward logic is correct. Because backward logic is usually not tied together correctly with restraints, it is almost never totally correct. Backward manual passes are hence passe; let a computer do them. One does not do them. If the user understands CPM, some inaccurate late dates are acceptable. The authors believe such is inevitable. Only the novus or the desperate rely on or argue late dates.

Early and late start and finish times will be the same for some activities. This, and additionally when the period between the early and late start and the activity's duration match, indicates "critical activities," those activities that must begin and end on their early start and finish times for the project to be completed within the contract time.

There are situations when the early and late start and finish times will match but the activity will *not* be critical, when the time period between the start and finish dates does not match the activity's duration. For instance:

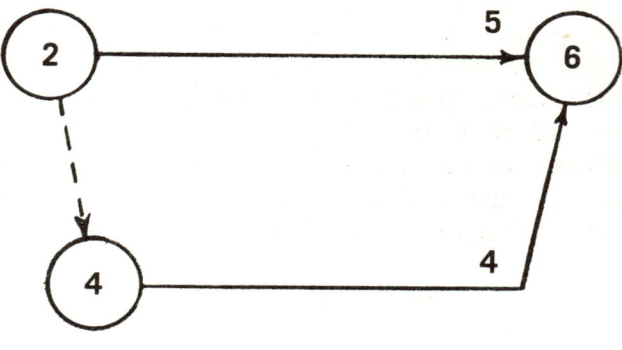

If activities 2-6 and 4-6 have the same early start and early finish dates (remember restraints are not time-consuming activities, so restraint 2-4 does not change activity 4-6's start date) but durations differ, activity 2-6 requiring five days and activity 2-4 requiring four days, 4-6 will not be critical (it takes one day less). Despite the matching start and finish dates only activity 2-6 may be critical.

Critical activities will form a continuous chain through the network known as the "critical path." Critical activities are not necessarily the most difficult or those that may seemingly be the most important job elements; critical activities merely form the longest path. However, the scheduler needs to be able to recognize the real critical path and not be mislead by peculiar idiosyncrasies of his logic. For instance, the critical path will never run through the toilet partitions: they are not necessary for the ultimate use of the building. The critical path calculation will sometimes indicate as critical activities which experience says can never be. The flagpole, although perhaps important to the user is inconsequential to the building and should never be critical. Don't be mislead by idiosyncrasies of logic — look for the real critical path.

Exhibit 2 is the computer printout which shows how the computer has completed a forward and backward pass and calculated the chain of activities which forms the critical path for construction of a gas station. The computer has translated the forward and backward calculations to dates. When the early and late start and finish times and the duration matches the period between the early start and early finish (or late start and late finish) the activity is critical. All critical activities are designated by two asterisks in the far right side of the printout.

§ 2-1 CONSTRUCTION SCHEDULES

Exhibit 3 is the complete logic diagram for the hypothetical gas station. To illustrate the critical path as calculated by the computer, it has been marked with dots on the logic.

PROJECT SCHEDULING TECHNIQUES § 2-1

WAGNER HOHNS INGLIS INC
CONSULTANTS TO THE CONSTRUCTION INDUSTRY

DATE—JUNE 3 1982
RUN NUMBER—INITIAL SCHEDULE

CLIENT—NEWS INDUSTRIAL CORPORATION
PROJECT—CORNER GAS STATION

SORT #1 I-J ORDER

I NODE	J NODE	EST DUR	$ VALUE	PCT CMPL	$ EARNED	BLD LOC	RESP	ACTIVITY DESCRIPTION	EARLY START	EARLY FINISH	LATE START	LATE FINISH	SLACK
1	10	0					G	RESTRAINT	06-03-82	06-03-82	06-03-82	06-03-82	**
10	12	2					G	AWARD CONTRACT 6-3-82	06-03-82	06-03-82	06-03-82	06-03-82	**
12	14	20					G	LAYOUT + EXCAVATE	06-03-82	07-01-82	07-09-82	07-13-82	25
12	16	25					M	ORDER + DELIVER FUEL TANKS	06-03-82	07-09-82	06-25-82	07-26-82	16
12	26	15					M	ORDER + DELIVER FUEL PUMPS	06-03-82	06-24-82	07-16-82	08-20-82	30
12	32	30					E	ORDER + DELIVER LIGHTS + SIGNS	06-03-82	07-16-82	06-03-82	07-16-82	**
12	40	15					M	ORDER + DEL HYDRAULIC LIFT	06-03-82	06-24-82	07-28-82	08-18-82	27
12	54	20					M	ORDER + DELIVER GREASING EQ	06-03-82	07-01-82	07-21-82	08-18-82	38
12	58	3					M	ORDER + DEL AIR COMPRESSOR	06-03-82	06-08-82	08-19-82	08-24-82	33
12	60						G	DELIVER + ERECT FENCE	06-07-82	07-26-82	07-26-82	07-26-82	54
14	16	5					M	RESTRAINT	06-07-82	06-14-82	07-21-82	07-28-82	34
14	18	5					E	INSTL EXT COND + PIPG TO TKS	06-07-82	06-14-82	07-21-82	07-28-82	31
14	32	1					G	INSTL EXT COND + PIPG TO TKS	06-07-82	06-08-82	06-02-82	08-03-82	39
14	36						G	CONSTRUCT LIGHT + SIGN FDNS	06-07-82	07-13-82	07-13-82	25
14	40	2					G	RESTRAINT	06-07-82	06-09-82	07-14-82	07-16-82	26
16	18	2					M	CONST HYDRAULIC LIFT FDNS	07-01-82	07-06-82	07-26-82	07-28-82	16
18	20	4					M	INSTALL FUEL TANKS	07-06-82	07-12-82	07-28-82	08-03-82	16
20	22	2					M	PIPE-UP FUEL TANKS	07-12-82	07-14-82	08-03-82	08-05-82	16
22	24	2					G	BKFL FUEL TKS + GRADE SITE	07-14-82	07-16-82	08-05-82	08-09-82	16
24	26							CONSTRUCT PUMP ISLANDS	07-16-82	07-16-82	08-20-82	08-20-82	25
24	28							RESTRAINT	07-16-82	07-16-82	08-09-82	08-09-82	16

EXHIBIT 2 EXAMPLE COMPUTER PRINT OUT

§ 2-1 CONSTRUCTION SCHEDULES

I NODE	J NODE	EST DUR	$ VALUE	PCT CMPL	$ EARNED	BLD LOC	RESP	ACTIVITY DESCRIPTION	EARLY START	EARLY FINISH	LATE START	LATE FINISH	SLACK
								SORT #1 I-J ORDER					
26	60	2					M	INSTALL FUEL PUMPS	07-16-82	07-20-82	08-20-82	08-24-82	25
28	30	6					G	POUR + STRIP SIDEWALKS	07-16-82	07-26-82	08-09-82	08-17-82	16
30	60	5					G	PAVE SERVICE + PARKING AREA	08-13-82	08-20-82	08-17-82	08-24-82	2
32	20							RESTRAINT	06-24-82	06-24-82	08-03-82	08-03-82	27
32	34	2					E	INSTALL LIGHTS + SIGNS	06-24-82	06-28-82	08-19-82	08-23-82	39
34	60	1					E	HOOK UP POWER + LIGHTS	06-28-82	06-29-82	08-23-82	08-24-82	39
36	38	3					G	CONSTRUCT BLDG FDNS	06-07-82	06-10-82	07-13-82	07-16-82	25
38	42	3					M	BLDG U.G. CONDUIT + PIPING	06-10-82	06-15-82	07-16-82	07-21-82	25
38	42	3					E	BLDG U.G. CONDUIT + PIPING	06-10-82	06-15-82	07-16-82	07-21-82	25
40	42	3					M	INSTALL HYDRAULIC LIFT	06-10-82	06-15-82	07-16-82	07-21-82	25
42	44	1					G	BKFL BLDG INTERIOR	07-21-82	07-22-82	07-21-82	07-22-82	**
44	46	3					G	FORM + POUR CONCRETE FLOOR	07-22-82	07-27-82	07-22-82	07-27-82	**
46	48	8					G	ERECT BUILDING WALLS	07-27-82	08-06-82	07-27-82	08-06-82	**
48	50	5					G	ERECT BUILDING ROOF	08-06-82	08-13-82	08-06-82	08-13-82	**
50	30							RESTRAINT	08-13-82	08-13-82	08-17-82	08-17-82	2
50	52							RESTRAINT	08-13-82	08-13-82	08-17-82	08-17-82	2
50	56	3					G	INSTALL DOORS + HARDWARE	08-13-82	08-18-82	08-13-82	08-18-82	**
52	56	1					G	INSTALL + GLAZE WINDOWS	08-13-82	08-16-82	08-17-82	08-18-82	2
54	60	4					M	INSTALL AIR COMPRESSOR	08-18-82	08-24-82	08-18-82	08-24-82	**
56	54							RESTRAINT	08-18-82	08-18-82	08-18-82	08-18-82	**
56	58							RESTRAINT	08-18-82	08-18-82	08-18-82	08-18-82	**
56	59							RESTRAINT	08-18-82	08-18-82	08-20-82	08-20-82	2
58	60	2					E	INSTL INTERIOR ELEC FXTRS	08-18-82	08-20-82	08-20-82	08-24-82	2
59	60	4					M	INSTALL GREASING EQUIP	08-18-82	08-24-82	08-18-82	08-24-82	**
60	65	2					G	PAINTING	08-18-82	08-20-82	08-20-82	08-24-82	2
60	65	3					G	FINAL TESTS + INSPECTION	08-24-82	08-27-82	08-24-82	08-27-82	**
60	65	3					E	FINAL TESTS + INSPECTION	08-24-82	08-27-82	08-24-82	08-27-82	**
60	65	3					M	FINAL TESTS + INSPECTION	08-24-82	08-27-82	08-24-82	08-27-82	**

EXHIBIT 2—Cont'd

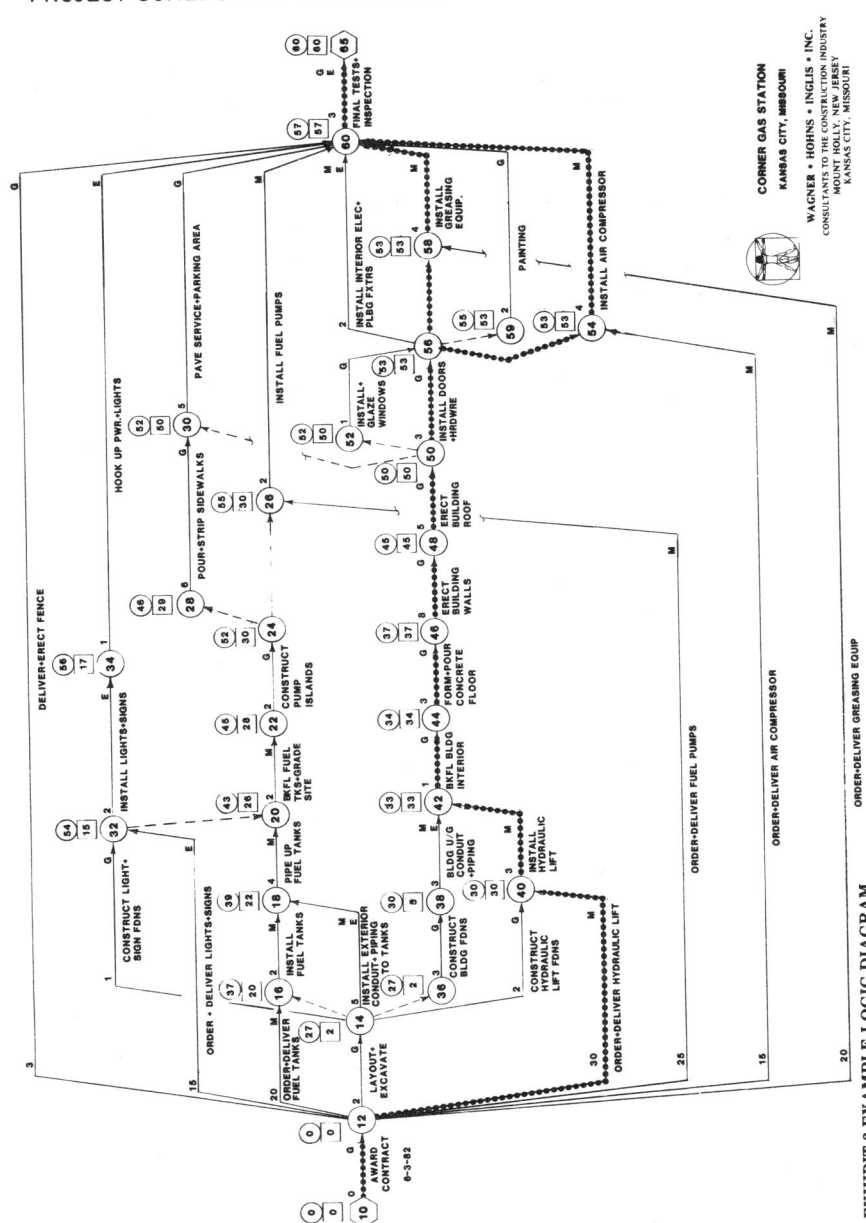

EXHIBIT 3 EXAMPLE LOGIC DIAGRAM

Activities with non-matching early and late start times are flexible; they do not have to begin and end within the *early* start and finish times to meet project completion dates. This flexibility, called "float," is a measure of the capability for a given activity to have its performance extended. Float measures the amount of time an activity can be delayed while still permitting the project to finish on time. Another way to look at float is as a measure of "criticality." The more float the less critical; the less float the more critical. Those activities which have no float are critical and cannot be delayed without delaying the project's completion.

The computer printout at Exhibit 2 has also calculated float time. For activity 18-20, pipe up fuel tanks, the computer has calculated seventeen days float. The seventeen days is the difference between the early start date of July 3, 1975, and the late start date of July 29, 1975 *in work days.* The computer has ignored weekends and holidays in its computations:

I NODE	J NODE	EST DUR	ITEM NO	ACTIVITY DESCRIPTION	EARLY START	EARLY FINISH	LATE START	LATE FINISH	SLACK
18	20	4	M	Pipe Up Fuel Tanks	7/06/82	7/02/82	7/28/82	8/03/82	16

There are many paths or logic chains through a schedule. Not all will be critical, but there may be more than one critical path. Even those paths that are not critical because they contain float, may, however, become critical if the float is eliminated by beginning work later than early start performance once the job is underway.

Two classifications of float are generally recognized. The "total float" of an activity is the difference between its late start and its early start. Subtracting the late finish from the early finish gives the same result.[15] Total float of an activity is the amount of time by which an activity can be delayed without affecting the project's completion date. Total float is a path concept. The activities in the path do not own the float. Activities share total float; using some in one activity will reduce it in all that share it.

For example, look at the series of activities which schedule the installation of fuel tanks in Exhibit 1. The fuel tanks are scheduled to be installed in eight days:

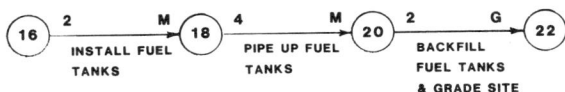

The mechanical contractor is permitted two days to install the fuel tanks and four days to pipe up the tanks. After the fuel tanks have been piped up, the general contractor is given two days to backfill and site grade.

If the mechanical contractor starts to install the fuel tanks a week late, the general contractor's backfill and site grade will similarly be delayed a week (ignoring for the moment the possibility of reducing the actual time it takes to install or pipe up the fuel tanks by increasing the crew or double shifting). The fuel tank installation in our example is a path. Whenever the path is started, it is scheduled to be completed eight days later.

Float is shared among these activities in a similar manner. If the installation of the fuel tanks has ten days float (it can start ten days from its scheduled start date and not delay the project's completion date), piping up the fuel tanks will also have ten days float. But each activity does not have ten separate days of float. It is shared. If the mechanical contractor uses five days of the path's float by starting the fuel tank installation five days after its scheduled start date, the float in the pipe up and backfill activities will be reduced by five days. By delaying its start five days, the mechanical contractor will reduce the general contractor's float which it shares. This is an important concept to understand as it will be used when the various manners in which the ownership of float can be viewed will be discussed.

The second type of float, "free float," is calculated by subtracting an activity's early finish time from the early start time of the subsequent activity. The free float of an activity is the amount by which that activity can be delayed without delaying the early start of the following activity of affecting any other activity in the network. Elimination of free float does not eliminate total float in an equal amount.

In actual usage, free float did not prove itself to be of value. As stated earlier, total float is a path concept; total float is shared by all activities in the chain. Free float, however, is only available when more than one arrow goes into another event. In the case of the last activity in the path, free float usually equals total float. Thus, each activity in a chain may share total float but only the last activity would own free float. As a practical matter, contractors involved with specific activities in a chain are not concerned with free float that is not theirs, but rather are concerned with only total float of which they have a share. The limited value of free float, thus, is for subcontractor planning — the amount of time a subcontractor can delay its work without affecting another activity.

Free float is not an important number in the field. It is a mathematical calculation pertinent only to the last activity or when more than one arrow enters another activity and even that pertinence is reduced since total float usually equals free float and the last activity in a chain may be there by circumstance, rather than design.

PROJECT SCHEDULING TECHNIQUES   § 2-1

To assist project scheduling or to set goals on needed deliveries, "milestone" dates are often established. Milestone dates are points in time identified as being important reference points in accomplishing the work. Milestone events can be dates imposed by the owner for the accomplishment of certain tasks or target dates set by the contractor. Selection of milestones is at the selector's option. Any date can be chosen for special attention. The selector decides what, if any, dates merit closer, interim attention. Milestones are usually identified on the logic diagram by a flag approximately the same size as the activity.

A time scaled network is an I-J network drawn to a horizontal time scale. A time scale is produced by plotting on a horizontal time grid the early start and early finish times for every activity. The length of the connecting arrow is the duration of that activity. Restraints or dummies are also shown; thus float is demonstrated. A time scaled network has several advantages over a logic diagram, but it also has disadvantages. Time scaled diagrams are convenient devices for checking daily project needs of labor, equipment, material, and for the advance detection of conflicting demands among activities for the same resource. A network plotted to a time scale also permits greater ease in making cash flow studies and for recording field progress.[16]

Time scales resemble bar charts and are far more readily accepted by people because unlike the awesome unfamiliarity of arrow network logic, time scales are easily understood. However, a logic diagram is needed before a time scale can be prepared. Setting out first to time scale the CPM logic may result in drawing and redrawing. The time scale should be done last, after the schedule is approved. The computer industry has developed plotters and programs which draw time scales on a large, long sheet of paper. Sometimes these time scales are far too long and with a character which will look useless to the reader. If computer time scales are to have value, an understanding of how the plotters work is essential.

Time scales are probably as a general rule best drawn by hand, by someone who is artistic and understands the purpose of the task at hand. This understanding permits correction of errors in logic and computer input, adjustments to the time scale regarding sensibility, all of which help produce a valuable document. Time scales cost time and money; they must be done last, and they are wanted first. Those who draft specifications usually require the CPM schedule to be done in an impossible time period and require the time scale to be completed before it can and should be. A scheduler can become frustrated if he is required to meet an impossible specification written by someone who has never dealt with a detailed CPM. CPM requirements often include erroneous directions for scheduling work, directions that the reviewer/specification writer insists are correct. For instance, a late start by responsibility sort is a waste of time. It provides no valuable information. One may have to do it, however, if the specification requires it. Stupid requirements abound in the schedule portion of specifications.

Any delay in a critical activity automatically extends the critical path. The length of delay, its cause, the responsible party, and the required willingness to accept these facts are endlessly debated throughout the industry. On nearly every job, the usual move by contractor and/or owner is to debate the issues above and refuse to modify the schedule logic or agree to the modifications. This, of course, renders the logic useless to the builder and owner.

Any delay in the finish date of a critical activity, for whatever reason, automatically extends project completion by that same amount. Identification of critical activities is an important aspect of job scheduling because it locates activities that must be performed timely if the project is to be completed within contract time. Alternately, once identified, critical activities may be rescheduled or have their durations reduced to permit quicker project completion.

To use CPM properly, initial data input must be sensibly accurate and the assumptions upon which this input are based must be reasonable. If the input is introduced carelessly, reluctantly, or with unconcern it will become an added burden to the job which hinders rather than helps.[17]

§ 2-2. Precedence Diagramming (PDM).

Precedence diagramming first appeared around 1964 in the *User's Manual* for an IBM 1440 Computer Program. One of the principal authors of the technique was J. David Craig of the IBM Corporation. Craig was also apparently responsible for naming the technique "precedence diagramming." [18]

In precedence diagramming the nodes represent the activities and the arrows between nodes simply indicate the logic dependencies among the activities. The nodes are typically boxes containing an activity number, description, duration, and all the other information found in a CPM diagram. Each activity has only one number — the I number, drawn by connecting the work activities from either their starting or finishing points, presenting a start-finish sequence without breaking down the activity to eliminate overlap as required in I-J. I-J diagramming assumes that succeeding activities cannot start until preceeding activities have been completed. Thus, there is no overlap in I-J. Other than the difference in the way the diagram is shown, I-J and precedence diagramming are essentially identical, yielding a list of activities with early and late starts, finishes, and floats. A sample box precedence diagram based on the same I-J logic used to illustrate the construction of a gas station is shown at Exhibit 4.

§ 2-2   CONSTRUCTION SCHEDULES

The precedence diagram can also be drawn without the boxes. This technique has been called succeedence, though the name has hardly caught on as a necessary part of one's jobsite vocabulary, and is illustrated at Exhibit 5. The succeedence diagram also illustrates the same gas station logic as previously used.

Precedence diagramming provides more flexibility than I-J. The length and direction of arrows in precedence diagramming also have no significance because they indicate only the dependency of one activity upon another. Precedence diagrams eliminate the need for restraints and extensive details to prevent overlap by utilizing "lag factors" which indicate that an activity cannot start until after the passage of time indicated by the lag factor which may be any amount.

PROJECT SCHEDULING TECHNIQUES §2-2

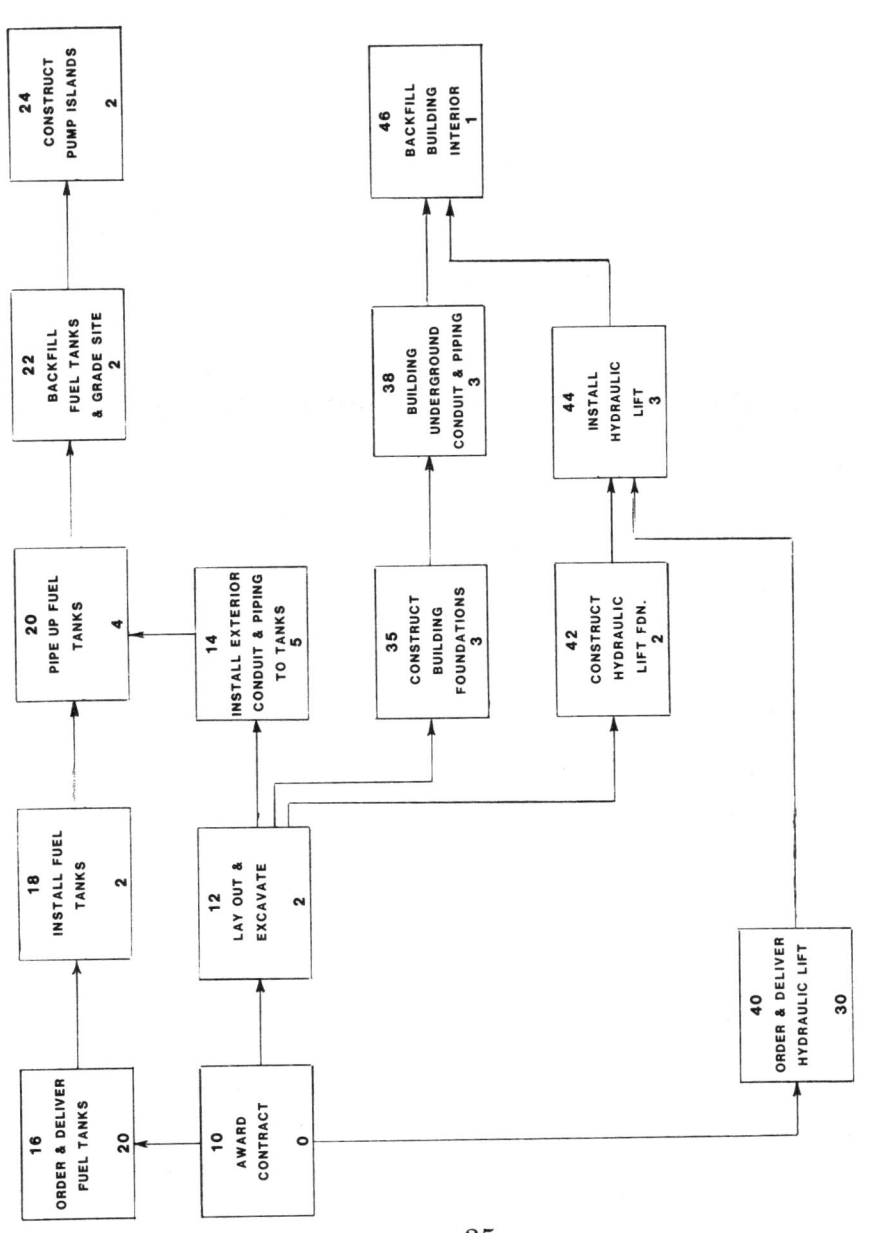

EXHIBIT 4 PARTIAL PRECEDENCE DIAGRAM

§ 2-2 CONSTRUCTION SCHEDULES

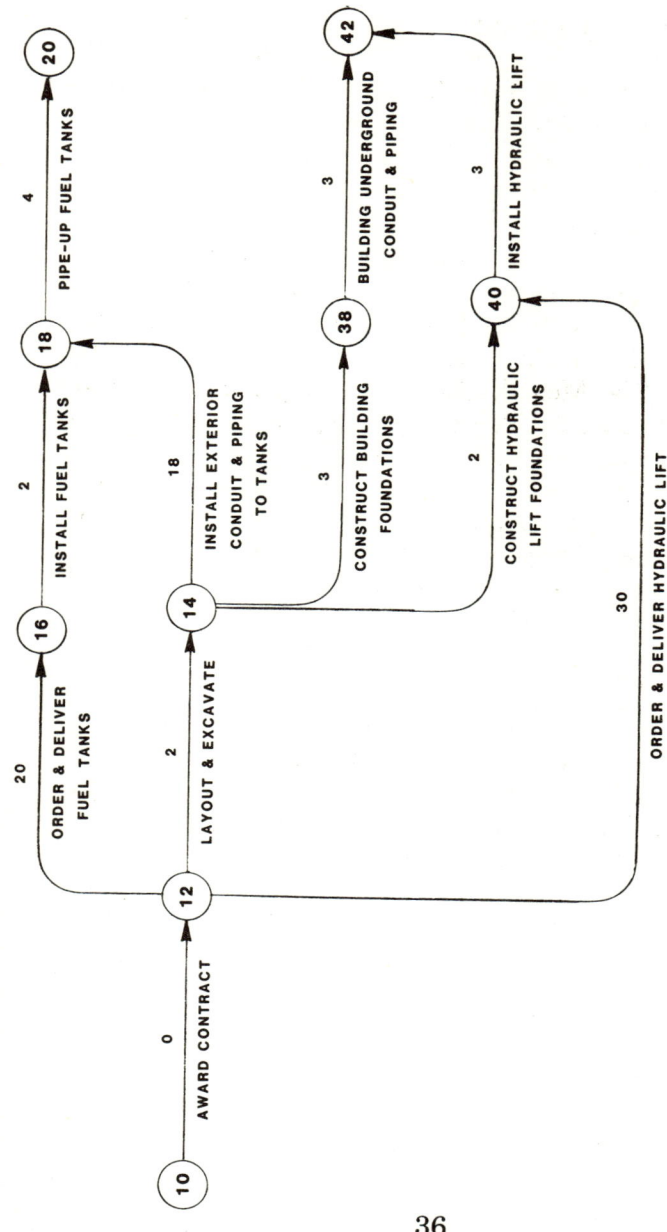

EXHIBIT 5   PARTIAL SUCCEEDENCE DIAGRAM

It is far easier and quicker to draw a precedence diagram than an I-J diagram. Lap techniques are used universally. The diagram can be time scaled with the same alerts as CPM, but it is more difficult to update the precedence method since overlap, as well as duration, must be changed. Because of the variety of lap and lag that the scheduler may draw, the computer must have a variety of instructions to permit it to make the subsequent calculations. The necessity for more computer instructions than I-J makes the programmer much more of an artist. Programmers seem to prefer precedence. It lends an exotic ring to the programmer's life. Most high-powered logic programs are written for precedence. Precedence logic diagrams can be produced in 70% of the time required for production of I-J diagrams, but this 30% time savings is not attractive enough for use of precedence as the standard operating procedure at many large scheduling companies. We do not use precedence (unless forced by a more "knowing" customer), preferring I-J.

§ 2-3. Bar Charts.

Bar charts, sometimes called "gantt charts" after the man who is recognized as the inventor, are the traditional method for scheduling construction projects. A typical bar chart is shown on the following page as Exhibit 6.[19]

§ 2-3   CONSTRUCTION SCHEDULES

AREA	1968 F M A M J J A S O N D	1969 J F M A M J J A S O N D	1970 J F
FOUNDATION	▭		
STRUCTURAL STEEL	▭		
CONCRETE	▭		
ENCLOSURE STONE		▭	
MASONRY		▭	
WINDOW FRAMES		▭	
JAIL EQUIPMENT		▭	
FINISH WORK			▭

EXHIBIT 6 BAR CHART PROGRESS SCHEDULE

38

On uncomplicated jobs involving a minimum of tasks, bar charts do a reasonably good job. However, on larger projects, the bar charts have a fundamental weakness: they do not show dependencies among activities. Each activity may receive the same consideration with no indication of where management attention should be focused. However, it is possible to develop a critical path from a bar chart as illustrated in Exhibit 7.[20]

Bar charts contain a list of the major activities of a project which usually correspond to the specification headings. It is also possible to break activities down by floor, system, or area. A bar for each activity reflects start and end dates; however, the duration of each activity, as reflected by the bar does not necessarily indicate that work in the activity is being continually performed. A bar indicating plumbing work does not mean mechanics are working on the project on each work day included in the bar length. Rather, it represents the period from the first day the mechanic has work to be performed until the plumbing is completed. The number of days to be actually worked during this duration is not specified. No matter how detailed the bar chart, the interdependency of the activities is not made clear. The manner in which one activity follows another is not specified.[21]

§ 2-3   CONSTRUCTION SCHEDULES

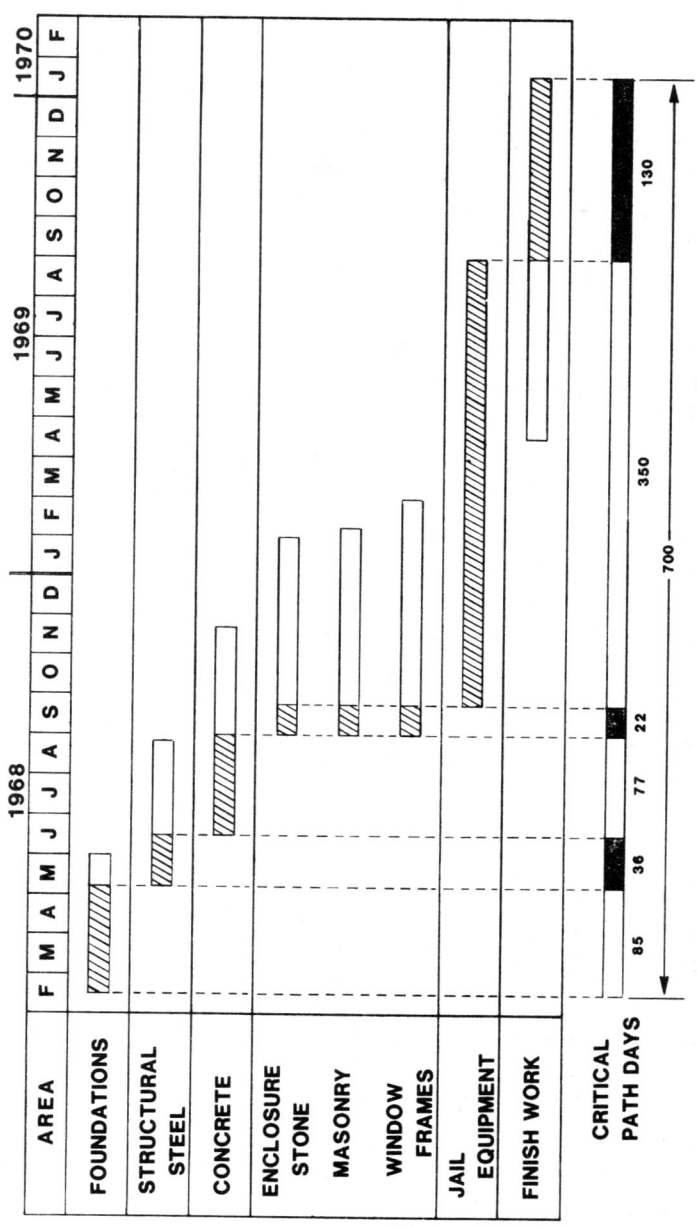

EXHIBIT 7 BAR CHART PROGRESS SCHEDULE WITH CRITICAL PATH

There is usually no rational basis for the development of the bar chart. It usually does not portray a detailed, integrated plan of operations. Bar charts are largely ineffective for project shortening and resource or equipment management. Normally, a bar chart is made by adjusting the individual work items to fit within an overall time frame. Usually, it is a seat-of-the-pants, off-the-wall method, easily juggled; it can be composed in a jiffy, with or without the plans and in many cases is totally useless and ignored, but bar charts are a favorite scheduling tool.

In fairness to the serious user, the visual clarity of the bar chart makes it a very valuable medium for displaying job schedule information. It is immediately intelligible to people who have no knowledge of CPM or network diagrams. Its familiarity breeds confidence. It affords an easy and convenient way in which to present information developed from a CPM study. It is far less expensive than CPM. For these reasons, bar charts undoubtedly will continue to be widely used in the construction industry.[22]

§ 2-4. PERT Charts.

PERT was intended to assist in evaluation of the Polaris Missile Program's progress where no historical or cost data was available as a guide. Lack of adequate project planning and control for previous Navy projects had resulted in actual costs which increased two or three times over estimated costs and project durations which averaged forty to fifty percent over estimated time.[23] In an attempt to recognize these deficiencies, as they were occurring instead of after they had occurred, the Navy assembled a research team which consisted of Lockheed Aircraft Corporation — the prime contractor on the Polaris program, the Navy Special Projects Office, and the consulting firm of Booze, Allen and Hamilton. The research project was designated PERT, or Program Evaluation and Review Technique.[24]

PERT is a statistical treatment of uncertain performance time. It estimates the probability of meeting specified completion dates. Thus, PERT was not originated to plan a project, but rather to evaluate the progress of an existing program. PERT is now more widely accepted and utilized in the area of systems and supply procurement. It maintains, however all the benefits and drawbacks of the network techniques discussed earlier.

CPM utilizes a single time estimate for each network activity because in construction each activity is "deterministic," similar construction work has been performed many times before. Such prior experience enables the contractor to estimate with reasonable accuracy the time required to carry out the scheduled activity. PERT, on the other hand, utilizes three time estimates for each event: (1) an optimistic or minimum time, (2) a most likely or model time, and (3) a pessimistic or maximum time. A formula reduces the three time estimates to one time estimate for each event. This "probablistic" approach lends itself to activities for which there is no historical record or experience, activities that in all likelihood are being done for the very first time. PERT charts are usually scheduled in weeks divided into tenths (half day of a five-day work week) rather than days as are CPM charts, and portions of a week are not uncommon.

The PERT system focuses on events that must occur prior to successful conclusion of a project. This emphasis has made PERT event-oriented, while CPM has been activity-oriented,[25] concentrating on the manner of completion as each activity is accomplished. PERT analyzes the event times in a manner similar to the calculation of critical path for a CPM schedule. Exhibit 8 [26] presents an example of a PERT network.

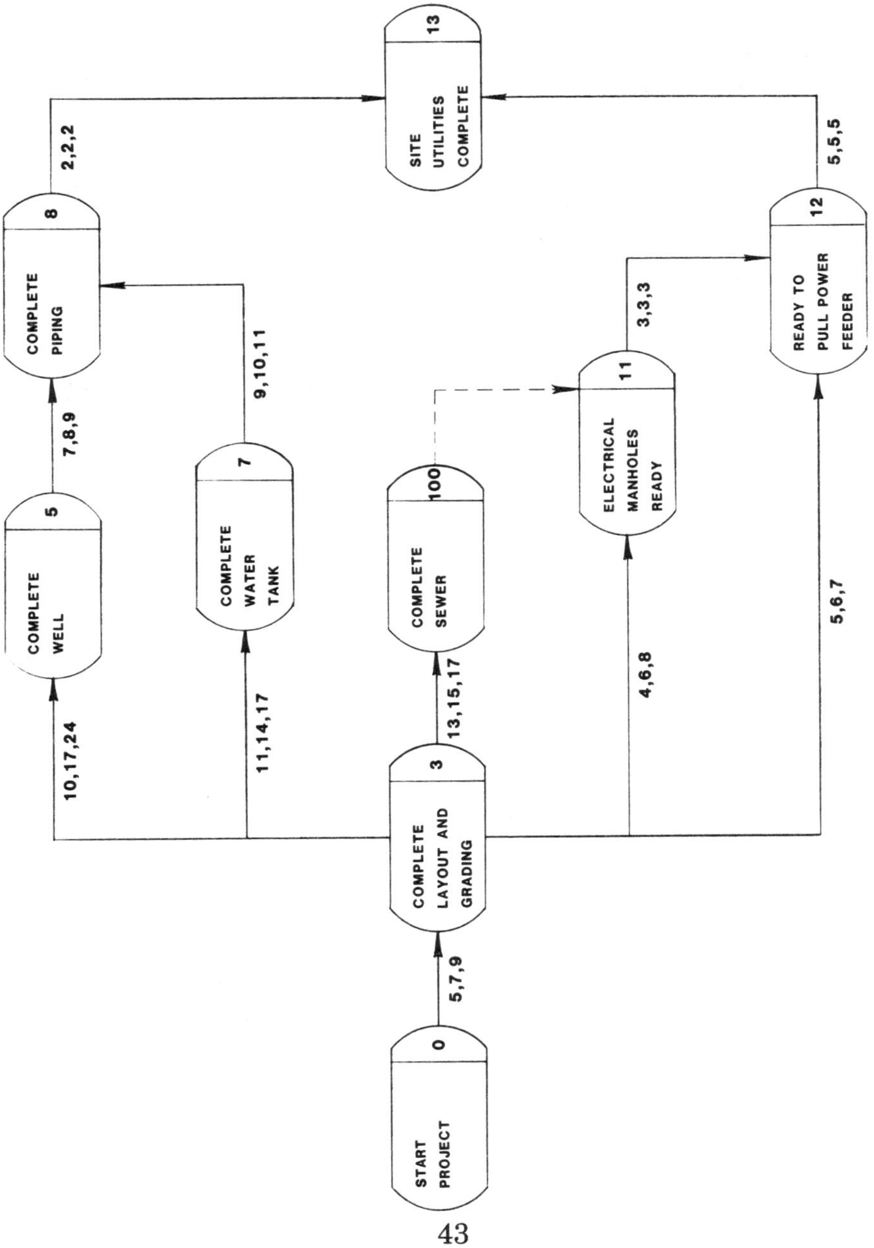

PROJECT SCHEDULING TECHNIQUES § 2-4

EXHIBIT 8 SAMPLE PERT NETWORK

The authors are unaware of any case law which discusses PERT. This brief description of the PERT technique has been provided as a basis for comparison to the critical path method. The techniques have some similarity which may permit subsequently discussed cases to be applied.

§ 2-5. Updating.

No schedule can be perfect. The scheduler cannot anticipate every future job circumstance and eventuality. Unforeseen problems, choices, good things, bad things, better knowledge, mistakes, corrections, and surprises arise every day. Also, more attention is given to the scheduling process as construction advances; indeed, as portions of the project are completed, better ideas arise. At times, job managers do not, and will not, plan specific work methods until the work is at hand. Adverse weather, delivery delays, labor disputes, change orders, and differing site conditions may also disrupt the original plan and schedule. It is not unusual that activities additional to those included in the original plan prove to be necessary. As a result, it is normal that construction projects deviate from their developed schedules.

Considerable time and effort are required during the construction period to check the progress of the job and to take whatever action is appropriate and necessary to bring the work back on schedule or report and adjust to the effects of irrecoverable delay. These actions constitute the monitoring and rescheduling phases of the job schedule known as "updating."

A single activity is generally so limited in scope that any loss of time on that activity is irrecoverable. Corrective action, if required and possible, is based on making up lost time through rescheduling of subsequent activities. Indispensable to the assessment of project delays and the devising of corrective rescheduling is an updated schedule

PROJECT SCHEDULING TECHNIQUES § 2-5

of those activities yet to occur. These updatings often reveal shifts in critical path and substantial change in the float of activities. To maintain a schedule as a realistic tool, updatings *must* occur with regularity.

How often field progress should be measured and reported depends upon the degree of time control that is considered desirable. Depending on size, complexity, and characteristic of the work, progress reporting may occur anywhere from daily to monthly or even longer; monthly is the normal guideline. Turn-around time to do an update is important. Schedules need to be current to be respected.

The degree of detail of the updating can also vary. Usually, each update attempts to identify actual start and finish dates for each activity, or if these "as-built" dates are unknown, records a date by when the subject activities had been started or completed. The update also usually includes an estimate of completion expressed as a percentage of each activity currently in progress. For instance, if "place rebar basement slab" is half complete, that activity would be designated 50 percent complete during the update. If the schedule is cost or "dollar" loaded, the estimate of completion when totalled for all activities will form the contractor's progress payment estimate. Durations of activities are adjusted according to actual conditions: completed activities are reduced to zero, partially completed activities are reduced to reflect only that time necessary for completion, and remaining activities are adjusted to reflect any now-known conditions which will affect performance. Revised logic is inserted to show change orders or to reflect new or different methods of construction.

This revised information is given to the computer, a new set of calculations is made, and an "updated" printout is produced. The "updated" printout predicts a new completion date based now on a larger amount of known facts.

Very often a "narrative" report will accompany the revised computer printout. This report describes in a narrative fashion the information reflected in the numbers and dates of the computer printout; hence the name "narrative" report. A narrative report will vary according to every author but will usually contain a description of progress since the last update, discussion of problem areas, for instance, material delivery or activity delays, identification of alternate critical paths, predict future problems, describe revisions to logic, and request action. The narrative report is easier to read than the computer printout and thus enjoys a wide circulation on the project site.

Because the degree of detail of the updating can vary, construction agencies will often mandate a procedure which must be followed on all their projects. One agency which specifies a detailed update procedure is the Veterans Administration. The Veterans Administration requires the update to be done monthly on a date mutually agreeable to the contractor and the VA.

One day prior to the update the VA is given a copy of the last update, marked-up by the contractor to reflect progress since the last update. The VA verifies the information on the marked-up printout. The update meeting is devoted to discussing and resolving areas where the VA and contractor disagree on information which the contractor has put on the marked-up update.

The VA requires progress on material procurement to be updated by changing the duration to the workday difference between the anticipated completion date and the as-of date. Work-in-progress activities are updated for both time and money. Completed work activities durations are changed to zero, the percentage is changed to 100, and the actual date of completion is written on the report. Activities representing the value of material stored on site are created and valued. Logic and activity data necessary to represent changed work are added. Finally, revisions necessary to permit the schedule to continue to monitor the progress of the project are made.

The VA itself produces part of the update information by summarizing important contract information such as the number of manhours worked, total value of change orders, and duration of all time extensions previously approved. The VA also updates those activities which are their responsibility such as approvals and government-furnished equipment. The VA also includes its opinion of actual job status and progress, and specific problem areas in their portion of the update. Most jobs, however, do not require as careful an updating process as the Veterans Administration demands.

---

7. P. Walstead, "Using CPM in Contract Disputes," in *Construction Claims and Disputes* 173, 181-82 (1978).

8. *Ecclesiastes* 9:11 (Revised Standard).

9. R. Clough, *Construction Project Management* 58 (1st ed. 1972).

10. *Id.,* at 60.

11. M. Callahan, "The Law Behind Construction Schedules," at 55, from *Deskbook of Construction Contract Law — With Forms,* H. Murray Hohns, editor, 1981.

12. H. Hohns, *Preventing and Solving Construction Contracts Disputes* 34 (1st ed. 1979).

13. R. Clough, *supra* note 9, at 64.

14. R. Clough, *supra* note 9, at 95.

15. R. Clough, *supra* note 9, at 97.

16. R. Clough, *supra* note 9, at 115.

17. Associated General Contractors of America, *CPM in Construction — A Manual for General Contractors* 7 (1975).

18. J. Moder and C. Phillips, *Project Management With CPM and PERT,* 123 (2d ed. 1970). (Hereinafter cited as J. Moder.)

19. Hohns, *supra* note 12, at 57.

20. *Id.,* at 58.

21. P. Walstead, *supra* note 7, at 179.

22. R. Clough, *supra* note 9, at 118.

23. J. Moder, *supra* note 18, at 5.

24. *Id.,* at 6.
25. O'Brien, *CPM in Construction Management, supra* note 2, at 90-91.
26. O'Brien, *CPM in Construction Management, supra* note 2, at 94.

CHAPTER 3
CONTRACT SCHEDULING REQUIREMENTS

Since the development of the critical path method, construction scheduling has occupied a more significant position in the building process. Contractors give more attention to the development of initial schedules and place more reliance on the evolving schedule as revised through updates. Owners recognize the value of construction schedules and often require their contractors to utilize some form of advance planning.

Owner's specification requirements vary in the complexity of the schedules mandated. The American Institute of Architects Form A201,[27] one of the most widely used contract forms for private Owners, requires merely that:

> The Contractor, immediately after being awarded the Contract, shall prepare and submit for the Owner's and Architect's information an estimated progress schedule for the Work. The progress schedule shall be related to the entire Project to the extent required by the Contract Documents, and shall provide for expeditious and practicable execution of the Work.[28]

In federal construction procurement governed by the Armed Services Procurement Regulations, (ASPR)[29] Contractors are required:

> (a) ... within five days or within such time as determined by the Contracting Officer, after date of commencement of work, prepare and submit to the Contractor Officer for approval a practicable schedule, showing the order in which the Contractor proposes to carry on the work, the date on which he will start the several salient features (including procurement of materials, plant and equipment) and the contemplated dates for completing the same. The schedule shall be in the form of a progress chart of suitable scale to indicate appropriately the percentage of work scheduled for completion at any time. The Contractor shall enter on

the chart the actual progress at such intervals as directed by the Contracting Officer, and shall immediately deliver to the Contracting Officer three copies thereof. If the Contractor fails to submit a progress schedule within the time herein prescribed, the Contracting Officer may withhold approval of progress payment estimates until such time as the Contractor submits the required progress schedule.[30]

Although not mandatory, ASPR permits a more detailed scheduling requirement for Contractors at the Government's option:

7-604.7(c) Contractor-Prepared Network Analysis System.

A progress chart shall be prepared by the Contractor pursuant to the General Provisions entitled "Progress Charts and Requirements for Overtime Work" which will consist of a network analysis system as described below. In preparing this system the scheduling of construction is the responsibility of the Contractor. The requirement for the system is included to assure adequate planning and execution of the work and to assist the Contracting Officer in appraising the reasonableness of the proposed schedule and evaluating progress of the work, and to serve as a basis for periodic progress payments.

(a) An example of one of the numerous acceptable types of network analysis systems is shown in Appendix 1 of Corps of Engineers Regulation ER 1-1-11 entitled "Network Analysis System," single copies of which are available to bona fide bidders on request. Other systems which are designed to serve the same purpose and employ the same basic principles as are illustrated in Appendix 1 will be accepted subject to the approval of the Contracting Officer.

(b) The system shall consist of diagrams and accompanying mathematical analyses. The diagrams shall show elements of the project in detail and the entire project in summary.

CONTRACT SCHEDULING REQUIREMENTS

(1) Diagrams shall show the order and interdependence of activities and the sequence in which the work is to be accomplished as planned by the Contractor. The basic concept of a network analysis diagram will be followed to show how the start of a given activity is dependent on the completion of preceding activities and its completion restricts the start of following activities.

(2) Detailed network activities shown on a detailed or sub-network diagram shall include, in addition to construction activities, the procurement of critical materials and equipment, the submittal and approval of samples of materials and shop drawings, fabrication of special material and equipment and their installation and testing. The network shall clearly show all MILESTONES (if any) specified in the special provisions, and all activities of the government that affect progress. The detail of information shall be such that duration times of activities will range from three (3) to thirty (30) days with not over two percent (2%) of the activities exceeding these limits. The activities which comprise the different areas of construction or building shall be separately identifiable by coding or use of sub-networks or both:

Building locations or features . . . .

Activity numbering system . . . .

The selection and number of activities shall be subject to the Contracting Officer's approval. A minimum number of activities, excluding restraints, is normally specified to ensure an acceptable level of detail in which to monitor progress. Detailed networks, when summary networks are also furnished, need not be time scaled but shall be drafted to show a continuous flow from left to right with no arrows from right to left. The following information shall be shown on the diagrams for each activity: preceding and following event numbers, description of the activity, cost, and activity duration in calendar days.

(3) Summary Network. If the project is of such size that the entire network cannot be readily shown on a

CONSTRUCTION SCHEDULES

single sheet, a summary network diagram shall be provided. The summary network diagram shall consist of a minimum of fifty activities and a maximum of one hundred and fifty activities, and shall be based on and supported by detailed diagrams. Related activities shall be grouped on the network. The critical path shall be plotted generally along the center of the sheet with channels with increasing float placed towards the top or bottom. The summary network shall be time scaled using units of approximately one-half inch equals one week or other suitable scale approved by the Contracting Officer. Where slack exists, the activities shall be plotted on an early start and early finish basis with the slack being indicated as a dashed line restraining the start of the following activity.

(4) The mathematical analysis of the network diagram shall include a tabulation of each activity shown on the detailed network diagrams. The following information will be furnished as a minimum for each activity on the initial schedule submittal or during the course of schedule updates:

(i) preceding and following event numbers (numbers shall be selected and assigned so as to permit identification of the activities with bid items);

(ii) activity description;

(iii) estimated duration of activities in calendar days (the best estimate available at time of computation;

(iv) earliest start date (by calendar date);

(v) earliest finish date (by calendar date);

(vi) scheduled or actual start date (by calendar date);

(vii) scheduled or actual finish date (by calendar date);

(viii) latest start date (by calendar date);

(ix) latest finish date (by calendar date);

(x) slack or float;

(xi) monetary value of activity;

(xii) responsibility for activity (Prime contractor, subcontractors, suppliers, Government, etc.);

(xiii) manpower required;

(xiv) percentage of activity completed;

(xv) contractor's earnings based on portion of activity completed; and

CONTRACT SCHEDULING REQUIREMENTS

(xvi) bid item of which activity is part.

(5) The program or means used in making the mathematical computation shall be capable of compiling the total value of completed and partially completed activities and subtotals from separate buildings or features listed in paragraph (b) (2).

(6) In addition to the tabulation of activities, the computation will include the following data:

(i) identification of activities which are planned to be expedited by use of overtime or double shifts to be worked including Saturdays, Sundays and holidays;

(ii) on-site manpower loading schedule;

(iii) a description of the major items of construction equipment planned for operations of the project. (The description shall include the type, number of units and unit capacities. A schedule showing proposed time equipment will be on the job keyed to activities on which equipment will be used shall be provided); and

(iv) where portions of the work are to be paid by unit costs, the estimated number of units in an activity which was used in developing the total activity cost.

(7) The analysis shall list the activities in sorts or groups as follows:

(i) by the preceding event number from lowest to highest and then in the order of the following event number;

(ii) by the amount of slack, then in order of preceding event number;

(iii) by responsibility in order of earliest allowable start dates;

(iv) in order of latest allowable start dates, then in order of preceding event numbers, and then in order of succeeding event numbers; and

(v) in order of latest allowable finish date, then in order of preceding event number.

(c) Submission and approval of the system shall be as follows:

(1) A preliminary network defining the Contractor's planned operations during the first sixty (60) calendar days after notice to proceed will be submitted within ten (10) days. The Contractor's general approach for the balance of the project shall be indicated. Cost of

CONSTRUCTION SCHEDULES

activities expected to be completed or partially completed before submission and approval of the whole schedule should be included.

(2) The complete network analysis consisting of the detailed network mathematical analysis (on-site manpower loading schedule, equipment schedule) and network diagrams shall be submitted within forty (40) calendar days after receipt of notice to proceed.

(d) The Contractor shall participate in a review and evaluation of the proposed network diagrams and analysis by the Contracting Officer. Any revisions necessary as a result of this review shall be resubmitted for approval of the Contracting Officer within ten (10) calendar days after the conference. The approved schedule shall then be the schedule to be used by the Contractor for planning, organizing and directing the work and for reporting progress. If the Contractor thereafter desires to make changes in his method of operating and scheduling he shall notify the Contracting Officer in writing stating the reasons for the change. If the Contracting Officer considers these changes to be of a major nature he may require the Contractor to revise and submit detailed diagrams and mathematical analysis and the summary diagram to show the effect on the entire project. A change may be considered of a major nature if the time estimated to be required or actually used for an activity or the logic of sequence of activities is varied from the original plan to a degree that there is a reasonable doubt as to the effect on the contract completion date or dates. Changes which affect activities with adequate slack time shall be considered as minor changes, except that an accumulation of minor changes may be considered a major change when their cumulative effect might affect the contract completion date.

(e) The Contractor shall submit monthly a report of the actual construction progress by updating the mathematical analyses. Revisions causing changes in the detailed network shall be noted on the summary network, or a revised issue of affected portions of the detailed network furnished. The summary network shall be revised as necessary for the sake of clarity.

CONTRACT SCHEDULING REQUIREMENTS

However, only the initial submission or complete revisions need be time scaled. Subsequent minor revisions need not be time scaled.

(f) The report shall show the activities or portions of activities completed during the reporting period and their total value as basis for the Contractor's periodic request for payment. Payment made pursuant to the General Provision entitled "Payments to Contractor" will be based on the total value of such activities completed or partially completed after verification by the Contracting Officer. The report will state the percentage of the work actually completed and scheduled as of the report date and the progress along the critical path in terms of days ahead or behind the allowable dates. If the project is behind schedule, progress along other paths with negative slack shall also be reported. The Contractor shall also submit a narrative report with the updated analysis which shall include but not be limited to a description of the problem areas, current and anticipated, delaying factors and their impact, and an explanation of corrective actions taken or proposed.

(g) Sheet size of diagrams shall be 30 by 42 inches. Each updated copy shall show a date of the latest revision.

(h) Initial submittal and complete revisions shall be submitted in six (6) copies.

(i) Periodic reports shall be submitted in four (4) copies.[31]

The Armed Services Procurement Regulations also provide for Government preparation of the construction schedule if the Owner wishes to utilize a more detailed schedule than that required from the Contractor under the "Progress Charts and Requirements for Overtime Work" clause.[32] The Government prepared schedule is not, however, a substitute for the Contractor schedule, but is rather intended as a supplement. Given a chance, one can build an empire producing useless data containing impressive looking schedule information all of which is highly regarded and more often than not totally in error and useless.

CONSTRUCTION SCHEDULES

The Veterans Administration requires CPM schedules on all its projects over $1 million.

Federal construction procurement under other federal agencies may have no mandatory scheduling requirements. Similarly, private, municipal, and state construction have no standard forms; the Owner's designer through its specification writer who has never done a CPM schedule usually prepares the scheduling clause. As the reader can imagine, this is the major cause of scheduling clauses that require useless or inappropriate information. Consequently, scheduling clauses in private construction contracts take many forms. Both private Owners and other federal agencies, however, may utilize the ASPR standard forms as guides.

As an example, Holiday Inns, on its major building projects, uses the following scheduling clause:

SECTION 01310 CONSTRUCTION SCHEDULES

1.0 General

1.1 Purchase of Materials and Equipment:

A. Within 50 days after the execution of the Contract covering the Work, the Contractor shall furnish the Owner a written statement that required orders have been placed for all major items of materials, products, and equipment and that all necessary sub-contracts have been executed, as required, so as not to delay the Work.

1.2 Monthly Construction Progress Schedule:

A. As soon as possible and in any case not later than 21 days after receipt of Notice to Proceed, the Contractor shall attend a meeting at which he shall submit to the Owner a CPM Arrow Diagram/Schedule ("CPM Diagram/Schedule") in Level 3 activity detail covering all phases of the Work. Following agreement between the Owner and Contractor as to the exact format of the schedule, the Contractor shall thereafter submit monthly

CONTRACT SCHEDULING REQUIREMENTS

updated progress schedules in accordance with other provisions herein.

1.3 CPM Schedules and Reports:
A. To assure adequate planning and execution of the work so that the Work is completed within the number of calendar days allowed in the Contract, and to assist the Owner in evaluating the progress of the Work, the Contractor shall prepare and maintain the schedules and reports described in this Section.
B. "Day" used throughout the Contract, unless otherwise stated, means "calendar day." "Day" used for CPM network durations will be the work days, and reported as calendar dates in Construction Schedules.

1.4 Quality Assurance:
A. The Contractor shall designate a scheduler who is thoroughly trained and experienced in compiling construction scheduling data, in analyzing by use of critical path method, and in preparation and issuance of periodic reports as required herein. The name and contract information of that scheduler shall be delivered to the Owner at the meeting referenced in 1.2 hereof and the Contractor shall not reassign a replacement without at least fourteen (14) days written notice to the Owner; sickness of the assigned scheduler excepted.

1.5 Reliance Upon Approved Schedule:
A. The CPM Diagram/Schedule as approved by the Owner will be an integral part of the Contract, and will establish interim contract completion dates for the various activities.
B. Should any activity fall 15 days or more job work days behind the CPM Diagram/Schedule approved by the Owner, the Owner shall have the right to order the Contractor to expedite completion of such activity by whatever means the Owner deems appropriate and necessary, without additional compensation to the Contractor.
C. Should any activity fall 20 or more job work days behind the CPM Diagram/Schedule approved by the

CONSTRUCTION SCHEDULES

Owner, the Owner shall have the right to perform the activity or have the activity performed by whatever method the Owner deems appropriate. All costs incurred by the Owner in connection with expediting such activity under this sub-paragraph shall be reimbursed promptly to the Owner by the Contractor.

D. It is expressly understood and agreed that failure by the Owner to either order the Contractor to expedite an activity or to expedite the activity by other means, pursuant to B or C above, shall not be considered precedent-setting with respect to any other activities which may fall behind the CPM Diagram/Schedule approved by the Owner.

1.6 Submittals:

A. All submittals shall comply with the provisions of this Section.

B. The bidder shall submit a CPM Diagram/Schedule, in major activities detail only, manually computed, along with his bid. Such diagram/schedule shall outline his general plan, methods, sequence of erection and proposed major equipment and the Arrow Diagram format shall be an outlined version of the construction schedules the Contractor will be required to submit pursuant to 1.2A above.

2.0 Materials

2.1 Not Applicable

3.0 Execution

3.1 Construction Schedules:

A. The Contractor shall, within 30 days after receipt of notice to proceed, submit one reproducible and three prints of the CPM Diagram/Schedule prepared in Level 3 activity detail, as previously approved by the Owner, in accordance with 1.2. He shall submit three sets of the four computer processed CPM Schedule reports (See 3.4 C1-4 below) and one copy of the job calendar.

CONTRACT SCHEDULING REQUIREMENTS

3.2 Periodic Reports:

A. The Contractor shall submit three prints of the CPM Diagram/Schedule updated, three copies of a progress narrative report and three sets of the four computer processed CPM Schedule reports, with each monthly Application for Payment. Such periodic reports shall reflect the progress of the Work through the period for which payment is requested. Accompanying each periodic report submittal, the Contractor shall submit three prints of the Materials and Equipment Status Reports updated.

B. All required schedules or reports shall be airmailed to the Owner, addressed to the Owner's designated Project Manager.

C. The Contractor shall inform and coordinate the schedule requirements with all subcontractors, suppliers, test and inspection agencies, and all other responsible participants on the project. This schedule coordination shall be performed through the Owner's Project Manager for those participants who are not under the Contractor's responsibility for control.

D. If it is discovered by or reported to the Contractor that a delay causing problem exists or is foreseen, the Contractor will forward an Exception Report to the Owner as quickly as possible. The Report shall include the problem identification, cause, impact analysis, and the Contractor's plan for corrective action.

E. The Contractor shall submit the Superintendent's Daily Report ("S.D.R.") daily to Owner (one copy), along with the S.D.R. Schedule attachment.

3.3 Construction Analysis:

A. The CPM Diagram/Schedule shall graphically show the order and interdependence of all activities necessary to complete the Work, and the sequence in which each activity is to be accomplished, as planned by the Contractor in cooperation with all Subcontractors and others whose work will be shown on the Diagram/Schedule. Activities shown

CONSTRUCTION SCHEDULES

on the Diagram/Schedule shall include, but are not necessarily limited to:
1. Project mobilization.
2. Submittals and approvals of Shop Drawings and Samples. Allocate sufficient time for proper review by Architects and Engineers.
3. Major milestone events and scheduled dates.
4. Procurement of equipment and materials.
5. Site work, structural erection/construction, closure, systems, tests, and finish plans; include small orientation sketch to key buildings, areas, to the Project site and North.
6. Fabrication of special material and equipment and their installation and testing, FF&E and installation; including schedule for all "N.I.C." and "O.S.C.I." activities, and grand opening startup.
7. Final cleanup.
8. Final inspection and testing and issuance of "Certificate of Occupancy."
9. All activities by the Owner, and other participants that affect progress, required dates for completion, or both for all and for each part of the Work, and
10. Title blocks which should include title, drawing number, approval spaces, revision record, dates, names, etc.

B. The detail of information shall be such that duration times of work activities shall normally range from 1 to 20 job work days, to facilitate the monthly reporting cycles. The work breakdown structure and level of activities shall be subject to the Owner's approval. See Activity Detailing Levels Sheet, attached. Activity Descriptions shall be uniquely understandable at the working level. Networks should be "Banded" re: logical layouts.

C. The CPM Diagram/Schedule must show, as a minimum for each activity, preceding and following event numbers, description of each activity and activity duration in job work days. The Contractor shall submit Diagram/Schedules on a sheet (32 inches) high by the width/length required. Sub-nets must be interfaced and matchlined to allow assembly as one total project, graphically portrayed. The networks may be reduced in size, but read-out clarity must be retained.

3.4. Mathematical Analysis:

A. The Contractor shall furnish a mathematical analysis of the of the CPM Diagram/Schedule by computer-aided means, including a tabulation of each activity and must show the following information as a minimum for each activity:

1. Preceding and following event numbers.
2. Activity description.
3. Estimated duration of activities.
4. Earliest start date (by calendar date).
5. Latest start date (by calendar date).
6. Earliest finish date (by calendar date).
7. Latest finish date (by calendar date).
8. Float (in job calendar days).
9. Percentage of activity completed or status.

B. The program used in making the mathematical analysis shall be capable of compiling the total value of completed and partially completed activities, and be capable of accepting modifications approved for time and logic sequence.

C. The computer processed CPM Schedule reports shall list the activities in computer print-out sorts as follows:

1. By succeeding event number from lowest to highest, and then in order of the preceding event number or, equivalent numerical listing of all network activities and known as the Numerical Listing Report.
2. By the amount of float, then in order of early start, and then in order of succeeding event numbers and known as the Float/Criticality Report.
3. In order of early start and succeeding event numbers; and then in order of preceding event numbers and known as the Chronological/Early Start Report.
4. Other sorts requested by the Owner, such as 60-90-day Bar Charts sorted by responsibility

CONSTRUCTION SCHEDULES

codes, early start, and succeeding event number and known as the Bar Chart.

3.5. Materials and Equipment Status Report:

A. Format: The Contractor's standard Materials and Equipment Status Report form will be acceptable if, in the Owner's judgment, it provides sufficient pertinent data to determine the materials procurement flow is adequate for all needs of the Work.

B. Content: The Materials and Equipment Status Report must show, at least, the following information:

1. Item description, listed in accordance with Specifications Section number in which the item is called for.
2. Purchase order number and date of issue.
3. Vendor name.
4. Date shipped, and shipping means utilized.
5. Estimated date of arrival at Project site.
6. Actual date of arrival at Project site, and receiving report number.
7. Expediting action and dates.

Holiday Inn scheduling specification continues:

THREE LEVELS OF CPM NETWORKS

MAJOR TASK NETWORK

A Level One network contains only the major items which summarize the project. It expresses in broad terms the plan of arriving at the objective. If CPM was described by the terms "what," "who/when," and "how," the level one network would be the "what." It is used for planning and management monitoring.

EXAMPLE LEVEL ONE

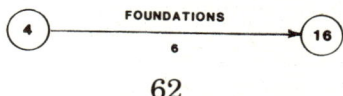

CONTRACT SCHEDULING REQUIREMENTS

INTERMEDIATE NETWORK

A Level Two network is an expansion of the Level One network by adding responsibility assignments. This network would be described by the terms "what," "who/when." It would be used for preliminary negotiations with Sub-Contractors and assigning work responsibilities.

EXAMPLE LEVEL TWO

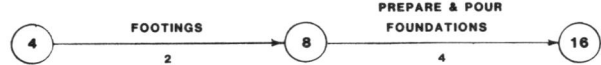

INITIAL DETAIL NETWORK

A Level Three network is an expansion of the Level Two network to a detailed working plan. It contains the "what," "who/when," and "how." It is used in managing the project for planning, monitoring, and carrying out the work.

EXAMPLE LEVEL THREE

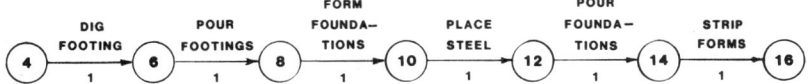

Our reaction is that the Holiday Inn specification is more than needed or really wanted and what is required will simply not be delivered. Contractors have a way of ignoring things to death.

Whether general or detailed, the purpose of all scheduling clauses is to impose a requirement to schedule the project: that is, to assure the owner that the contractor has a reasonable plan for accomplishing the work within the specified time and for providing a common basis for evaluating the actual rate of progress of work proceeding. Detailed clauses attempt to impose a particular scheduling technique or regulate the complexity of the schedule. General clauses permit Contractor flexibility in selection of technique and complexity. The AIA philosophy to take hands off and run away bespeaks the problems its members and its insurers have had in the recent past with construction delays. There is thus some justification for a scheduling clause with greater detail than the AIA's. Regardless of the form, however, the purpose of the clause remains unchanged: the project must be scheduled.

It is nonetheless implied in the scheduling requirement that the schedule be drawn and updated according to good industry practice. Whatever the technique adopted, the schedule is thus intended to establish the sequential order in which construction is to be completed; to provide direction and control of work; to anticipate the need for material, equipment, and labor; and to encourage good project coordination. Industry practice does not require the scheduled start and finish dates of individual activities to be inflexible. Schedules created and implemented according to industry practice facilitate the purpose of scheduling clauses.

Scheduling clauses may be improved by reducing the implied requirements by stating the goals the schedule is intended to achieve. Reducing implied requirements will lessen the possibility of errors in interpretation of scheduling clauses in the event the clause must be enforced. As will be seen, courts responsible for enforcing the clause often do not understand either the concept of scheduling or its goals. Stating the goals of a scheduling requirement imposed on a contractor may help courts interpret and

CONTRACT SCHEDULING REQUIREMENTS

enforce scheduling clauses in the same manner as the construction industry uses schedules.

---

27. American Institute of Architects, "Document A201, General Conditions of the Contract for Construction" (13th ed. 1976).
28. *Id.,* at 4.10.1.
29. 32 C.F.R. Parts 1-30 (1976).
30. 32 C.F.R. 7-603.48, "Progress Charts and Requirements for Overtime Work" (1976).
31. 32 C.F.R. 7-604.7(c), "Contractor-Prepared Network Analysis System" (1976).
32. 32 C.F.R. 7-604.8, "Government-Prepared Network Analysis System" (1976).

CHAPTER 4

THE LAW AND CONSTRUCTION SCHEDULES

§ 4-1. The Law's View of Schedules.
§ 4-2. The Schedule Must Be Complete.
§ 4-3. The Schedule Must Be Substantiated.
§ 4-4. The CPM Consultant.
§ 4-5. The Dates in the Schedule: A Commitment or Guide?
§ 4-6. The Benefit of Float.
§ 4-7. Mistakes in the Schedule.
§ 4-8. Pre-Bid Schedules.
§ 4-9. Mutual Responsibilities Under the Schedule.
§ 4-10. Updating the Schedule.
§ 4-11. Changes in Scheduled Sequence.
§ 4-12. The Schedule as Notice.
§ 4-13. Improvements in Contract Scheduling Requirements.

§ 4-1. The Law's View of Schedules.

Courts, administrative boards and arbitration panels throughout the United States have dealt with schedules and scheduling techniques. The latter group does not publish their observations or findings but as to the courts and boards most have recognized the superior ability of the critical path method to coordinate and schedule. The United States District Court for the Western District of Missouri in *Natkin & Co. v. George A. Fuller Co.*,[33] observed that, "The Critical Path Method is a valuable tool on a complex job, saving time and money for owners and contractors."

Generally, the courts have accepted the construction industry definition of the critical path method. As will be seen later, however, courts have not consistently applied the technique to construction disputes in the same manner as it is applied as a planning and scheduling tool in the industry. The authors have learned that courts, boards and arbitors are slow to learn and often cannot or will not understand the basic foundations of scheduling. The trier of the facts too often assumes a level of competence and accom-

§ 4-1   CONSTRUCTION SCHEDULES

panying effort in the industry that does not always exist. Construction is an art, not a science and even worse, people are the artists, the scientists and the judges. We would not have it any other way, but one should be prepared for the simple truth that some ears do not work and that people and judges make errors.

The Corps of Engineers Board of Contract Appeals in *Continental Consolidated Corp.*,[34] viewed the critical path method of scheduling as follows:

> The CPM scheduling technique is one which requires a breakdown of the entire work into individual tasks and an analysis of the number of days required to perform each task. The analysis is then programmed into a computer which produces a chart showing the tasks and a line which controls the completion of the overall work. The line through the nodes, the junction points for completion of these essential tasks, is known as the Critical Path. In addition, there are numerous side paths for subordinate tasks which normally can be performed without affecting the critical paths. However, these subordinate tasks, if improperly scheduled or unduly delayed in performance, can on occasion become critical and thus change the critical path of the entire work.
>
> The critical path method of scheduling requires the logical analysis of all the individual tasks entering into the complete job and the periodic review and reanalysis of progress during performance. It is essential that any changes in the work and time extensions due to the Contractor be incorporated into the progress analysis concurrently with the performance of the changes or immediately after the delay and thus integrated into the periodic computer runs to reflect the effect on the critical path. Otherwise the critical path chart produced by the computer will not reflect the current status of work performed or the actual progress being obtained.[35]

The New Jersey Superior Court in *Dobson v. Rutgers*,[36] utilized a definition of CPM from *Critical Path Methods in Construction Practice* by Antill Woodhead (2d ed. 1970):

The Critical Path Method is a new and powerful tool for planning and management of all types of projects. Essentially, it is the representation of a project plan by a schematic diagram or network that depicts the sequence and interrelation of all of the component parts of the project, and the logical analysis and manipulation of this network in determining the best overall program of operation. It is a method admirably suited to the construction industry, and it provides a far more useful and precise approach from the conventional bar graphs and progress charts that previously formed the basis of construction planning and control. Furthermore, it permits the ready evaluation and comparison of alternative works programs, construction methods, and types of equipment. When the best plan has been prepared in this way, the critical path diagram clearly indicates the site operations that control the smooth execution of the works. Finally, as construction proceeds, the diagram provides the project manager with precise information on the effects of each variation or delay in the adopted plan, thus enabling him to identify the operations that require remedial action.[37]

In *Peter Kiewit Sons' Co. v. Iowa Southern Utilities Co.*,[38] the U.S. District Court for the Southern District of Iowa showed a slightly different view of the method:

... the Critical Path Method (CPM), a method of planning, which, as the name suggests, is designed to assure that the most critical construction work is done in the most expeditious manner, while at the same time assuring that all contractors on the site can proceed with their work in a coordinated manner.[39]

Blackhawk Heating & Plumbing Co.,[40] recognized that "activities not regarded as critical in the planning stage can become so if actual delay is excessive."[41]

Courts have accepted these and similar brief industry definitions of the critical path method whenever called upon to review a problem which concerned schedules. Such general definitions, however, have not provided a sufficient background in network scheduling techniques to permit a court to apply the detailed analysis necessary to resolve a complicated construction scheduling dispute. Thought should be given to presenting a source as a standard guide to the application of scheduling techniques to scheduling disputes early in the trial or hearing so that continued and detailed reference when necessary could be made. Alternately, the education given the court concerning schedules and scheduling methods should be expanded to permit accurate court use of the technique. Regardless, as will be seen in the analysis of court decisions later in this text, these general definitions are insufficient instruction.

Courts have consistently held bar charts to be less effective as a project schedule recognizing the inherent limitations of the bar chart: "[B]ar charts ... were (not) ... designed to afford an over-all coordinated schedule of the total work covered by the contract." [42]

The General Services Board of Contract Appeals in *Minmar Builders, Inc.*[43] refused to find a delay to project completion where the contractor's proof was limited to two bar-chart schedules and testimony by the contractor's president that the ceiling work was the "pacing" work element affecting project completion. The contractor alleged that Government delay in issuing ceiling change instructions delayed the project. The Board found the bar-chart schedules failed to show whether the ceiling work was indeed the "pacing" element or that the delay affected project completion:

> Since no interrelationship was shown as between the tasks the charts cannot show what project activities were dependent on the prior performance of the plaster and ceiling work, much less whether overall project completion was thereby affected. In short, the schedules were not prepared by the Critical Path

Method (CPM) and hence are not probative as to whether any particular activity or group of activities was on the critical path or constituted the pacing element for the project.[44]

The *Minmar* Board found the tasks affecting completion of the project had no relationship to the ceiling work. The Board concluded that project completion was not affected by Government delay in ordering ceiling changes.

In its publication "Modification Impact Evaluation Guide," the Corps of Engineers recommends breaking the large units of work shown in the bar chart into networks of individual activities to evaluate the effect of changes on the schedule even when a network schedule has not been required. Corps of Engineers construction contracts require either a network analysis system (for example, a critical path method schedule) or a bar chart. For identification of impact, the Corps states the network analysis system is more detailed than the bar chart and suggests changing the bar chart to a network system to permit a CPM analysis despite no contract requirement for a CPM schedule.[45]

Because of the high visibility of bar charts, however, they may be used to demonstrate a critical path analysis. For instance, in *Dawson Construction Co.*,[46] the CPM consultant illustrated an as-built CPM in bar chart form to reflect the effect of delay on the excavation and pouring of footings, grade beams, piers, and slabs. In these and similar situations, the bar chart is used to illustrate a detailed network analysis, not substitute for it.

Regardless of the network scheduling techniques utilized, they can be of considerable assistance in supporting claims for price adjustments and time extensions. Similarly they can aid in the defense of claims and in justifying assessments of liquidated damages for late contract performance.[47]

It is a well-settled proposition in the law that where both owner and contractor contribute to a delay, neither can recover damages unless clear proof of the apportionment of the delay is presented.[48] When sufficient evidence permitting an allocation of responsibility for delay is present, the court may allocate the delay among several parties. Bar chart schedules cannot show the interrelationship among multiple causes of delay and therefore have not been accepted as clear proof of the apportionment of delay. Critical path method schedules have, however. The court in *Pathman Construction Co. v. Hi-Way Electric Co.* noted:

> Where there is sufficient evidence to allow the court to make a reasonably certain division of responsibility for delay, the assessment ... may be allocated among several parties. Although the task is particularly difficult where, as here, the performance of the work is sequential and the delay is the result of multiple causes, it is not impossible ... technological advances and the use of computers to devise work schedules and chart progress on a particular project have facilitated the court's ability to allocate damages.[49]

In a delay analysis, the schedule is viewed as essentially neutral, almost as an independent expert. One's own schedule can even be used against it. For instance, the *Dobson* court used the schedule submitted by the contractors to prove owner's delay, to show some of the claimed inefficiency for lack of stairways could not have occurred because the schedule showed no stairways were planned to be available until well within the claimed inefficiency period.

The importance of schedules to support claims is illustrated in *American Sanitary Sales Co. v. New Jersey.*[50] Critical path method data had been prepared by a private consultant and supplied to the state for a youth correctional complex in Yardville, New Jersey, built by multiple prime contractors. The plaintiff held the prime contract for the plumbing and drainage work. The trial judge found that because of seven causes, a twenty-two month delay resulted that cost American Sanitary Sales damages of $455,250. The judge failed to award any part of the damages to the plaintiff, however, because plaintiff could not prove that the seven causes of delay were the state's fault.

The state had been unable to locate the scheduling data in answer to plaintiff's request for discovery. On appeal, both counsel agreed that if the critical path method data had been available, the contractor could have shown the state responsible for some of the seven causes of delay which damaged it. The appellate court then ordered the trial judge to extend the discovery period to permit depositions of the prime contractor for the general construction and the consultant who prepared the schedule, all of whom might be expected to have copies, anticipating that this scheduling information would show the owner's responsibility for at least some part of the contractor's delay. The scheduling information was deemed of sufficient importance to reopen discovery *after* the trial court had made its award.

Although courts uniformly recognize the value of scheduling, whether bar chart or CPM, they will not find a scheduling requirement if none was provided in the construction agreement. In *Drew Brown, Ltd. v. Joseph Rugo, Inc.*,[51] Rugo, the general contractor, and Brown, the structural steel subcontractor, executed a contract which required Brown to "carry to completion the work undertaken by the agreement as the progress of the work requires."[52] No other scheduling clauses were present. Brown alleged Rugo breached the contract by failing to coordinate and schedule Brown's work. The court found Rugo's responsibilities to Brown, as enumerated in the subcontract, did not include the *advance* scheduling of work for Brown's convenience. It is interesting to note that

§ 4-2   CONSTRUCTION SCHEDULES

Brown was unable to prove that scheduling was a custom of the trade. In refusing to find a breach of contract, the court opined that if Brown had felt scheduling was so important, he should have added a clause in the subcontract requiring it.

§ 4-2. The Schedule Must Be Complete.

No schedule will be accepted by a court to prove or refute an alleged construction delay until it is complete. Schedules without procurement can be considered incomplete. *Dobson v. Rutgers* illustrates the importance of complete information in a construction schedule. There, Rutgers, the State University of New Jersey, constructed the College of Medicine and Dentistry of New Jersey with multiple prime contractors. Edwin J. Dobson Jr., Inc., held the prime contract for plumbing and fire protection aggregating $998,413. Other prime contractors in the $14,188,636 project included Frank J. Briscoe Co., who held a $7,932,000 contract for general construction, and Broadway Maintenance Corp., who held a $2,508,650 contract for electrical construction. The project consisted of three components: a two-story teaching wing with a basement; an eight-story faculty wing with a basement; and the "link," a two-story structure with a basement which joined the teaching and faculty wing.

Rutgers employed a consultant to develop a critical path method schedule to illustrate a method of completing the project. The consultant's schedule was reviewed by an independent general contractor to determine whether the project could be completed within the estimated time of 700 days indicated in the contract documents and diagrammed by the CPM. Rutgers incorporated the schedule in the bid documents as an illustration of one feasible way of executing the project.

74

Project completion was delayed twenty-five months and Dobson sued Rutgers in 1971 alleging that Rutgers failed to take affirmative action to maintain the work schedule, disrupted Dobson's work by directing Dobson to perform out-of-sequence work, and that the delay was so inordinate that the parties could not have contemplated it at the time of contracting. Briscoe and Broadway also sued Rutgers, Briscoe alleging that it was impossible to complete the work in the originally scheduled 700 days.

One of the first issues to confront the *Dobson* court was what CPM schedule should be used to measure the parties' performance? All parties conceded at a supplemental hearing that despite the schedule included in the bid documents (prepared by a scheduling consultant and reviewed by an independent general contractor) there never was a schedule approved by Rutgers as envisioned by General Conditions G4-F.4(c) which required the CPM consultant to meet with the prime contractors and establish a working schedule. General Condition G4-F.4(c) stated:

> *G4-F.4(c) Project Planning and Scheduling:* After Contract Awards have been made to the Contractors, the CPM Consultant will meet the Contractors to establish a schedule for the development of a Working Plan and Schedule.
>
> The CPM Consultant will conduct an orientation conference for the successful Contractors in the Critical Path Method. The Contractors shall supply information necessary to work of the CPM Consultant. The Working Plan and Schedule will be developed in the form of a CPM arrow network diagram using the Contractors' logic and time estimates. Initially, the CPM Consultant will work with the General Contractor to detail his work, and then meet with each of the other Contractors to include all of their work in the Plan.
>
> The arrow network diagram will be drawn in a level of detail suitable for display of all salient features of the work of each Contractor, including the placing of orders

for materials, submission of shop drawings for approval, approval of shop drawings, delivery of material and all work activities to be performed by each Contractor. Each activity will be assigned a time estimate by the Contractors. With the exception of material deliveries, the time duration for any activity shall not exceed fifteen (15) days. One day shall be the smallest time unit used.

On completion of the arrow network diagram, the CPM Consultant will have computer input data prepared. A computer run will then be made to generate a schedule for the project based on the information supplied by all Contractors. In the event the completion date indicated by the schedule exceeds the contractual date, the logic and time estimates used to develop the Plan will be reviewed with all Contractors. After changes in logic and time estimates have been agreed upon, another computer run will be made to generate a new schedule. This procedure will be repeated, if necessary, to provide a Plan and Schedule meeting the Contract requirements. *When completed, the Working Plan and Schedule will be submitted to the Owner for approval.* The computer printout of the computed Working Plan will show job identification, job duration, job description; calendar dates for early start, early finish, late start, and late finish for each job; the total float and the jobs critical to completion of the project on schedule. *When approved by the Owner, this shall become the Plan and Schedule for the Project. Each Contractor and his sub-contractors shall recognize their target dates and work toward their fulfillment.* (Emphasis added.)

The Dobson Court found that it was not until the third update that sufficient data was available for a complete plan for the project to exist. At the time of the first update, the *Dobson* schedule reflected the scheduling consultant's manifestation of the Mechanical, Electrical, and General Contractors' intent to construct the building. The schedule was complete through the close-in or until the building was "tight," but omitted finishing activities such as installing toilets and laboratory equipment and hooking up equipment. The Mechanical and Electrical Contractors indicated that the schedule, as reflected at the time of the first update, was the basis for the planning of their activities. The schedule at the time of the second update had advanced to include information on Laboratory Equipment, Owner Furnished Equipment, Finishing Details, and Procurement Items for the Electrical Contractor. But it was not until the third update, when the schedule reflected the General Contractor's procurement schedule, that the Court found sufficient information included within the schedule to be considered a plan for the project.

The critical path method is intended to arrange all activities required to complete a project in a logical sequence. The importance of including all activities before a schedule can be considered complete is illustrated in *Dobson v. Rutgers.* Despite testimony that the schedule at the time of the first update reflected the manner in which two prime contractors intended to construct the project, the court did not accept the schedule as complete until the third update when the general contractor's procurement schedule was finally included.

Equipment procurement is a vital, although often overlooked and always disdained, part of the construction schedule. Contractors too often pay little, if any, attention to equipment procurement. *Dobson v. Rutgers* is not only a lesson in how important including all parts of the schedule can be, but also an illustration of how significant a court views the procurement schedule.

A court may even accept the most complete schedule even if it was not what the contractor used to construct the building. In *Blackhawk Heating & Plumbing Co.* the Board of Contract Appeals utilized an outside scheduling consultant's schedule prepared after project completion rather than Blackhawk's because Blackhawk's "did not . . . break certain activities down into components which would necessarily be helpful in analyzing subsequent project delays."[53] The scheduling consultant had broken down Blackhawk's CPM activities into more detail, permitting more meaningful analysis of project delays. In adding activities, the Board found the consultant was only making the contractor's schedule more useful while maintaining the basic construction plan. This was so even though the consultant changed logic from the "planned" floor to floor sequence to work being performed on several floors simultaneously because the project had actually been completed in that manner.

A schedule may be accepted by a court indicating the manner and method of completion despite lack of formal approval. The *Dobson* decision illustrates the significance a court places on the "formal approval" of a construction schedule. In *Dobson,* there was never a formally approved working plan as required by General Conditions. The court accepted the schedule as manifested by the third update as the working plan because it represented the most complete schedule and the one most frequently used throughout the job. But more importantly, *without* utilizing the *most* complete schedule, despite the absence of "formal" approval, there would be nothing upon which to measure any rights or damages and no complete plan for the work as called for under the contract. The absence of approval did not inhibit the court's use of the construction schedule actually used to build the project as *the* project schedule.

What is the liability for a schedule that is not complete? It can be argued that by failing to complete the schedule, the party responsible has failed to provide a schedule and breached its contract by failing to perform according to whatever scheduling clause is present. In *Dobson v. Rutgers* the plumbing contractor sued for a million dollars caused by twenty-five month's delay due to failure to schedule (among other reasons). The party in *Dobson* responsible for schedule failure may have exposed itself to liability to the extent Dobson prevailed and Rutgers decided to seek indemnity. Since delay claims on construction projects are frequently valued in the millions of dollars, liability for such failure may be quite large.

§ 4-3. The Schedule Must Be Substantiated.

Critical Path Schedules are not entitled to automatic acceptance. Courts require a CPM to satisfy certain fundamental tests before presented to illustrate the method and manner of construction. The authenticity or validity of the data used to prepare the schedule; the intended purpose of the schedule, whether to estimate or construct; and how the schedule was actually used must be established.

In *Chaney & James Construction Co.*[54] (perhaps the first case which ever evaluated a network diagram as proof of delay) the Federal Aviation Agency Contract Appeals Panel found a critical path schedule could not be accepted as establishing either the facts portrayed or the reasonableness of the contractor's assertions as to the influence of specific incidences of work progress. Chaney & James Construction Co. had submitted a bar chart as required by the contract which was approved by the contracting officer. Later, Chaney & James submitted a critical path schedule but failed to state why the CPM had been submitted. A CPM had not been required by the contract. At the hearing no satisfactory evidence as to the origin of the data that went into the preparation of the chart, the purpose that the chart was meant to serve, or what use was actually made of it was presented. In fact, the contractor's president and project manager testified that the CPM was not used either in preparing the bid or in managing the project.

During the hearing, Chaney & James Construction Co. submitted an updated version of the CPM and an additional critical path diagram purporting to show the relationship of the work elements and the impact on work progress of the specific instances of claimed Government caused delays. The Board, however, refused to consider the CPM schedules as evidence. It found the work sequence shown was not demonstrated to be the only possible sequence in which the work could have been accomplished, nor was it demonstrated that the sequence presented in the charts was necessarily the best one. Further, the CPM work sequence shown was not used in estimating and bidding the job; the sequence shown on the CPM chart was not followed in performing the contract work.

Although the *Chaney & James* decision refusing to consider the CPM can be accepted on the basis of the contractor's failure to substantiate the schedule by, for instance, demonstrating that the contractor utilized or relied on it during the construction process, the CPM should not have been rejected because it was not the "only possible" or "best" sequence in which the work could have been accomplished. By industry definition, a CPM schedule is developed to illustrate only one method of construction. Industry standards recognize many ways in which a project can be completed. In insisting upon an "only possible" or "best" sequence as conditions of acceptance, the Board failed to understand the critical path technique.

The *Chaney & James* decision illustrates the importance of substantiating the schedule. When studying the decision, one gets the impression that the network analysis (which was introduced) was not accompanied with any explanation of its post-completion development, or, more importantly, how the court was expected to use the CPM. When a schedule merely "drops from the sky," is it any wonder that the court refused to consider it? Post completion schedule analyses are important. They are an important part of delay claim analysis. They have been accepted in the past, and will continue in the future to be accepted as evidence of responsibility of delay. The Corps of Engineers in its "Modification Impact Evaluation Guide" recommends the use of such analysis to allocate and define delay even if a network system was not an original contract requirement and, presumably, was not used to guide the actual construction. The Corps-recommended schedule analysis, however, has a clear purpose: no substantiation is lacking. In using post-completion schedule analysis, remember that a reason, purpose, use, or significance must be established before a court will accept it. Lack of substantiation for a schedule analysis is further discussed by a court in *Lane-Verdugo.*

In *Lane-Verdugo,*[55] the Armed Services Board of Contract Appeals was asked to grant Lane-Verdugo, a joint-venture contractor, a $162,000 equitable adjustment for delays caused by the Government on two contracts for renovation and addition to existing buildings at an airforce base. Several critical path networks were the primary evidence submitted by Lane-Verdugo to establish the relationship of the claimed delays to the extended period of performance of the work and other delays subsequent to the completion of the contracts. These critical path networks were the documentation prepared in support of the claim.

However, the contractor presented no testimony or documentation to show what information was furnished, or the accuracy or validity of that information, for the purpose of preparing the critical path networks both during the period of construction or subsequent thereto. On cross-examination, the contractor's scheduling consultant testified:

Q. Well, a change consummated at the beginning of the job would appear immediately in the network, would it not?

A. Not unless I was told to put it on.

Q. Oh, not unless you were told to put it on?

A. Right.
Q. Well then, this entire network is based on information that you get —
A. — from the contractor.
Q. — from the contractor. And if that information is incorrect, then your chart is incorrect?
A. If that's true, you could assume that.[56]

Although the contractor made many allegations as to what the schedules establish, the Board found no evidence establishing the authenticity or validity of the data that was used in the preparation of the critical path schedules or accompanying printouts. Since the networks depict information only as furnished by the contractor, the Board found that the schedules cannot and do not directly depict responsibility. Under such circumstances, the Board concluded that Lane-Verdugo did not prove Government responsibility for the claimed delay.

§ 4-4. The CPM Consultant.

What is the responsibility of a CPM or scheduling consultant? The question may only be answered presently in commentator's books and articles. The 1978 case of *Dobson v. Rutgers* stated, "No counsel has referred the court to any decision where the role of a CPM consultant has been defined. The court has found none."[57] To this may be added that the authors have found none.

A CPM consultant may assist in the preparation or updating of a schedule. But what is the responsibility of the scheduling consultant for this assistance? The *Dobson* Court held that a CPM scheduling consultant was no more than a testing laboratory. The scheduling clause there gave the CPM consultant no power toward any contractor to do anything. The Court found that in respect to time, the CPM consultant's role was to perform a function similar to that of an independent testing laboratory responsible for material testing. It also found that all the parties involved treated the CPM consultant as an independent expert. The general conditions which defined the role of the scheduling consultant in *Dobson* are reproduced at page 75.

The Court's decision in *Dobson* can be criticized. The CPM consultant's responsibility should be in the nature of a *professional* responsibility rather than similar to a testing lab. Scheduling requires a reasonable understanding of all phases of construction, although many schedulers do not understand their trade well enough to do their work. Scheduling requires the ability to understand some mathematics, computers, data processing, and drafting. It requires sufficient construction background to recognize the limitations of labor and equipment. It requires sufficient design background to understand how the elements of a project should go together. The *Dobson* decision recognized the CPM consultant as an "independent expert," despite relegating it to the status of a testing laboratory. Scheduling consultants should be held to "expert" standards. A scheduling consultant should be held to the "expert" standards of care of similar schedulers.

The General Services Board of Contract Appeals in *Economy Mechanical Industries, Inc.*,[58] indicated that the nature of skills, if not the professional standards, required from those responsible for developing schedules is important. In this case, a construction manager said:

> We do not mean to imply that (the construction manager) could have established a final schedule which would have required (the contractor) to perform work in an absurd manner or completely contrary to established construction practices, nor could critical milestone dates be arbitrarily revised at will once a final schedule ... was established....[59]

The professional standards required to schedule a construction project were discussed in *Peter Kiewit Sons' Co. v.*

Iowa Southern Utilities Co.[60] Kiewit sued Black and Veatch, the designer of a fossil fuel steam generating plant for Iowa Southern Utilities, for negligence in failing to prepare schedules of performance (among other things) which would allow an orderly and efficient construction and in accordance with the good and accepted customs of the trade.

Black and Veatch prepared a construction schedule in the form of a modified bar chart known as G-1. The schedule was designed to establish the basic working periods, construction sequence, and completion dates for certain phases of the work for all prime contractors involved in this multi-prime project. Kiewit's construction contract, however, required it to submit a detailed construction schedule of its work based on Black and Veatch's modified bar chart but to be expanded to include a complete breakdown of all elements of the work. Kiewit did submit a detailed construction schedule which followed G-1 but also included some substantial deviations.

Despite Black and Veatch's modified bar chart and Kiewit's detailed construction schedule, Kiewit was unable to complete its work at the times anticipated by the schedules. Among the more significant reasons for this delay were the failures of the structural steel erection prime contractor, and the boiler, generator, and turbine suppliers to meet their schedules.

When the steel erection prime contractor began to fall behind its schedule, Black and Veatch suggested methods to speed up that prime contractor's preparation of its shop drawings and suggested longer day shifts at premium time to speed up the steel erection as much as possible. Delay by the boiler supplier was not to be overcome, however, since the delay was caused by a strike at supplier's plant, boiler installation could only be extended by the length of the strike since the plant would not make up any time for the convenience of remote construction sites. Despite Black and

Veatch's suggestions, it could not bring these prime contractors back on schedule and at the same time arrange conditions so that the remaining prime contractors coming onto the site would also be able to work.

At trial, Kiewit failed to present any evidence that Black and Veatch prepared faulty construction schedules. In fact, Kiewit conceded that the schedule prepared by Black and Veatch was workable. Further, Kiewit had carefully studied the modified bar chart before bidding, found it to be a reasonable and feasible schedule, and had relied on it to determine its bid. The court rejected Kiewit's allegations of negligence in preparing the performance schedule. The court found Black and Veatch prepared all construction documents and schedules "consistent with customs and usages in the trade."[61]

Schedulers see themselves as possessing a distinct organized knowledge, the very definition of "professional" in modern society. To the construction project, they are no longer an ornament or luxury, but rather a necessity. Industry must demand that schedulers think through their schedules and be held accountable for them. Schedulers must accept responsibility for their contributions to the construction industry. The contributions of a scheduler can be measured by other schedulers; the schedules can, and should be, judged. There are, of course, economies as well. One does not get a Cadillac for Ford prices in schedule-land.

§ 4-5. The Dates in the Schedule: A Commitment or Guide?

The law does not uniformly apply scheduling techniques to disputes in the same manner as the construction industry applies scheduling techniques to project management. Some courts see project schedules as being a definite commitment, rather than a flexible planning tool. Some courts adopt this position despite accepting "industry" definitions of the schedule as subject to change as time changes scheduling assumption to fact.

In *Dobson,* electrical, mechanical, and general prime contractors were to "input" into the construction schedule prepared by the scheduling consultant. The Court held that when the Contractors gave their input to the CPM consultant, they essentially agreed with one another that the work would be performed in that manner, sequence, and time. The Court adopted the view that the CPM schedule may not vary with time. This is contrary to the accepted understanding in the construction industry that the schedule is a *flexible* device based on the best known information at the time the schedule is drawn.

In *Natkin,* Western Electric Company negotiated, then assigned a subcontract for mechanical construction with Natkin and Company to George A. Fuller, the general contractor. The Fuller-Natkin contract required the critical path method of scheduling in accordance with a pre-bid schedule to be followed throughout the job. Although a CPM was prepared, it was not continually updated. A computer was not used for calculations. All work order changes were not incorporated into the schedule at schedule updatings. Completion dates for Natkin work were established without Natkin's consent. The CPM was subsequently abandoned when Western Electric demanded early occupancy of certain areas and would not accept the later completion dates which the CPM indicated.

Natkin and Western Electric Company had entered into a contract under which Natkin was to perform the mechanical work connected with the construction of Western Electric's Shreveport Manufacturing Plant. The mechanical contract was for a fixed price of $2,979,261.00 and was to be performed between July, 1966, and July, 1967. The contract included nine milestone dates for completion of certain designated areas of work. Under the various contract documents, it was provided that Fuller, the general contractor, would be responsible for preparing and maintaining the original logic diagram. The first update was prepared by Fuller on July 15, 1966, but not delivered for twenty-five days and already outdated when finally received. Another update was prepared on December 2, 1966, but improperly completed resulting in an erroneous final completion date. The critical path method of scheduling was abandoned for the project on January 6, 1967, because Fuller could not keep up with it, among other reasons.

The *Natkin* court found that no accurate or reasonable completion date was established in accordance with contract scheduling methods; and that the failure to schedule and control the work in accordance with the CPM sequence caused Natkin manpower shortages, congestion, material shortages, and loss of efficiency, the value of which Natkin was entitled to recover from Fuller *and* Western Electric.

The Tenth Circuit Court of Appeals in *Steenberg Construction Co. v. Prepakt Concrete Co.*[62] stated when a subcontractor agrees to perform in accordance with a specific schedule, the contractor must meet that schedule as a constructive condition precedent to the duty of the subcontractor to perform its part of the bargain. In *Steenberg*, the subcontractor was permitted to abandon the project when the contractor's performance fell behind the agreed-upon schedule, forcing the subcontractor's work into difficult winter conditions.

The *Dobson* Court adopted the principle that where Contractors among themselves agree that segments of the work shall be done by certain dates, then the Contractor who fails to perform on time is liable in damages for breach of contract, whether the Contractor has overall supervision or is responsible only for a portion of the work. The *Natkin* court adopted a similar position. It stated that failure to schedule and control work "in accordance with the sequence set by the Critical Path Plan" [63] permitted recovery of additional costs. *Steenberg* required contractor conformance to agreed-upon schedules before subcontractors were obligated to perform their work.

The Court, in *Dobson*, stated that Contractors have the ability to enforce this contract right by lawsuit: "Fortunately, most Contractors honor their commitment or the Courts would be overwhelmed." [64]

The authors submit that courts escape being overwhelmed not because most contractors maintain schedules, but rather that most contractors recognize the CPM schedule as a *flexible* identification of sequence, start, and finish; a general tool to coordinate a complicated construction project, not an agreement that work must start and finish as indicated.

Experienced users have also recognized the flexible nature of the schedule. The Corps of Engineers views the schedule as

> a realistic sequencing and timing of the remaining work, but is only a working tool for the estimator's use, with no other contractual implications. It represents one method, but not necessarily the only method, for completing the remaining work.[65]

One court to recognize the flexibility of the schedule was the U.S. District Court for the Southern District of Iowa in *Peter Kiewit Sons' Co. v. Iowa Southern Utilities.*

In *Iowa Southern,* the utility's engineers, Black and Veatch, prepared a prebid construction schedule in the form of a modified bar chart, known as G-1, to assist the multiple prime contractors in completing the work within the period required by Iowa Southern Utilities Company. G-1 set out estimated dates for delivery of major components and the schedule and sequence for constructing the plant. Black and

Veatch intended the schedule to coordinate the work under the various prime contracts and to establish the basic working periods, construction sequence, and completion dates for certain phases of the work. G-1 was made a part of the general, mechanical, and electrical contracts but not made a part of the other prime contracts because they had been awarded prior to the issuance of G-1.[66]

In addition to G-1, the prime contracts required the contractors to submit "a detailed construction schedule showing the time schedule for completion of each element of the work"[67] after construction contracts were let. The detailed schedule was to be based on G-1 but expanded to include a complete breakdown of all elements of work. The contract clauses which defined the scheduling requirements are reproduced below:

> Article III of the Contract Agreement provided that:
>
> Time of completion is of the essence of the Contract Agreement, and that the Contractor shall proceed with the work in accordance with the specified schedule.
>
> *GC-34. Beginning, Progress, and Time of Completion of Work.* Unless otherwise specified the Contractor shall begin work under this contract within ten (10) days after the date designated in a written order from the Owner to begin work. The rate of progress shall be such that the work will be completed in accordance with the terms of the contract on or before termination of the construction period named in the Contract Agreement. The Contractor shall furnish the Engineer a detailed schedule setting forth the procedure he proposes to follow and giving the dates he expects to start and to complete portions of the work. If in the opinion of the Engineer proper progress is not being maintained, changes shall be made in the Contractor's operations to ensure proper progress.
>
> *Special Conditions. Construction Schedule.* The time of completion and commercial operation of the new station is of the essence of this contract. The work shall be vigorously and systematically prosecuted to the end

that all systems will be ready for start-up and initial operation as a complete electric power generating unit not later than March 1, 1968, and that the unit will be in firm commercial operation not later than May 1, 1968. The installation of the equipment, systems and subsystems shall be completed so that they can be given trial operation and necessary adjustments can be made before the plant start-up and initial operation specified above.

In addition to compliance with the above dates, the Contractor shall comply with the intermediate dates set forth in the Construction Schedule and shall complete all work and remove all of his construction plant facilities from the site before July 1, 1968. . . .

The Construction Schedule, Sheet G-1 of the construction drawings, shows in graphical form all construction to be performed concurrently at the site. The purpose of this construction schedule is to coordinate related work under the various construction and erection contracts and to establish the basic working periods, construction sequence, and completion dates for certain phases of the work.

Starting dates graphically shown on the schedule are intended to designate the latest starting date permissible for compliance with the overall schedule. Earlier starting dates shall be adopted whenever possible.

The Contractor shall cooperate with the Engineer as set forth herein under "PROJECT MANAGEMENT" to ensure maximum coordination and efficiency in the construction progress.

Failure of the Engineer to inform the Contractor that he is behind schedule or to direct and enforce procedures for complying with the schedule shall not relieve the Contractor of his responsibility for completing his work in accordance with the Construction Schedule and shall not be cause for an extension of time.

Contractor's Detailed Schedule. Within thirty (30) days after award of contract, the Contractor shall submit a detailed construction schedule showing the time schedule for completion of each element of the work. The detailed schedule shall be based on the Construction Schedule but shall be expanded to include a complete breakdown of all elements of work. The schedule shall be presented in graphical form using the bar graph method, the critical path method (CPM), or the time-sequence method similar to the Construction Schedule.

The Contractor's detailed schedule shall be periodically revised to reflect the actual progress of the work, and shall be modified as necessary for coordination of his operations with those of other contractors.

In addition to the above detailed schedule covering the entire life of the project, the Contractor shall prepare and submit at the beginning of each month during the construction period a schedule covering his operations for the coming thirty (30) day period. Included with this schedule shall be an estimate of the total manpower required and the necessary equipment for the anticipated construction operations. This information shall be submitted to the Engineer's Project Manager at the site and shall be used to coordinate all contractor's operations at the weekly meetings as set forth under "Project Management."

Special Conditions. Project Management. The coordination of all field construction shall be under the direction of the Engineer acting through its Project Manager at the site.

A meeting of the Engineer and all contractors at the site will be held each week at the time and place designated by the Engineer. The Contractor's superintendent shall attend each weekly meeting. The purpose of the weekly meeting will be for the scheduling and coordination of each Contractor's work within the requirements of the overall project. In the event conflicts arise between Contractors concerning scheduling or coordination, the Engineer will make the final decision resolving the conflict. The Engineer's decision shall not be cause for extra compensation or for extensions of time.

If at any time the Contractor's work is behind schedule (as set forth herein under "Construction Schedule"), the Engineer may direct him to increase his forces or otherwise accelerate his operations to comply with the schedule and the Contractor shall put into effect immediately definite procedures approved by the Engineer for getting back on schedule. The Contractor will not be allowed extra compensation for costs incurred by him because of additional regular or premium time required to keep his work on schedule.

Work fell behind the G-1 schedule. In an attempt to bring the project back on schedule, Black and Veatch began making modifications in the construction schedule to adjust to existing conditions. At monthly intervals they devised a modified overall schedule using the critical path method. They attempted to assure that the critical construction work was done while at the same time permitting all contractors on the site to proceed with their work in a coordinated manner. Because new problems continually arose on the site, the CPM's became obsolete almost as soon as they were issued. Black and Veatch attempted to make modifications as often as new problems arose.

Black and Veatch used as criteria for the monthly schedules: the project completion date necessary, its previous experience in supervising construction of power plants, and the economic impact of the scheduling decisions on all contractors. The engineer's scheduling decisions did not continuously favor one contractor over another but rather were attempts to get critical construction work completed first. However, the general contractor, Peter Kiewit, encountered interference because the delays forced Black and Veatch to schedule simultaneous work of more contractors than was originally contemplated by G-1.

Kiewit alleged that Iowa Southern had breached the contract by deviating from the construction dates in G-1. The court found no breach by Iowa Southern for failure to meet the G-1 Schedule. The court stated that the purpose of G-1, as indicated in the Special Conditions under "Construction Schedule" *supra*, was to give a *basic* idea of when the various phases of Kiewit's, and other contractor's work should start and how rapidly it should be prosecuted in order for all contractors to make the May 1, 1968, completion date.[68] The presence of a Suspension of Work Clause, Delay Clause, and Extensions of Time Clause in the General Conditions further indicated that G-1 was only a basic idea of when the phases must start and how rapidly they should be prosecuted. The court concluded that there was no express agreement that G-1 was binding on Iowa Southern Utilities Co., but rather many items in the documents suggested the construction schedule could change as circumstances dictated. The court refused to find breach of contract by Iowa Southern stating that Kiewit had no right to rely upon the dates contained in G-1 as being absolute time periods for construction. This view corresponded closely with the construction industry acceptance of CPM as a flexible scheduling tool rather than a firm commitment.

Another court which recognized schedules as only a flexible tool to coordinate a complicated construction project is the Eighth Circuit Court of Appeals in *Southern Fireproofing Co. v. R.F. Ball Construction Co.*[69] Southern Fireproofing and Ball executed a subcontract in which Southern, as subcontractor, agreed to perform interior and exterior masonry for two high schools near Cedar Rapids, Iowa, for Ball, the general contractor. Significant portions of the subcontract are reproduced below:

> ARTICLE I. This Contract Agreement is subject to and shall be governed by all ... General Conditions and Special Conditions of the Specifications and those contained in Contract between Owners and R.F. Ball Construction Company (A Joint Venture), where applicable.
>
> ARTICLE IX. The Contractor shall prosecute the work rapidly, continuously and uninterruptedly and shall complete the entire work within *as required* so as not to interfere or delay R.F. Ball — Southwest Ball Con-

§ 4-5   CONSTRUCTION SCHEDULES

> struction Company in completing contract on the entire building *as required by Owner.*
>
> The Contractor in agreeing to complete the work within the time mentioned, has taken into consideration and made allowance for the ordinary delays and hindrances incident to such work, whether growing out of delays of Common Carriers, delays in securing materials or workmen, changes, omissions, alterations, or otherwise, and is cognizant of the fact that R.F. Ball — Southwest Ball Construction Company in their contract with the Owner, is required to finish the entire work within a certain time, and failure on their part to do so renders them liable to heavy damages.
>
> For the convenience of the Contractor, R.F. Ball — Southwest Ball Construction Company estimates that the building or buildings will be ready for the commencement of the work or its installation about *when notified,* 195. . . .
>
> But R.F. Ball — Southwest Ball Construction Company is not to be held responsible for any loss or damage incurred by the Contractor in the event the Contractor is unable to start or complete its work as herein contemplated.
>
> Delays by the Contractor occasioned by failure on the part of Contractor to co-ordinate his work with that of other contractors on the job or failure on the part of other contractors to coordinate their work with that of Contractor, shall be at and for the Contractor's responsibility; and such delays, when so occasioned, shall not relieve Contractor from any of its liabilities hereunder.

Southern Fireproofing sued Ball to recover damages allegedly due to Ball's delay. Among other reasons for recovery, Southern alleged that Ball's progress schedules "required enclosure by December 1, 1956, so as to relieve Southern of the greater expenses which would be occasioned by exterior" masonry work in the winter.[70] Ball replied that the subcontract contained no warranty as to dates for Southern's work; that the subcontract, in fact, indicated the possibility of delay; that the progress schedules were not warranties; and that Southern had not seen the schedules until after the subcontract was executed.

Ball had prepared schedules both before and during construction and revised them from time to time in accordance to Article 3 of the General Conditions which stated the schedules "were subject to change from time to time in accordance with the progress of the work." [71]

In finding that Ball was not responsible for Southern's additional costs due to delay, the court found the progress schedules to be "nothing more than serious estimates and calendars, revised from time to time, for work coordination purposes and perhaps as a disciplinary and incentive measure for all concerned." [72] The court found nothing in the schedules which indicated guaranty, warranty, or positive representation. Like the court in *Drew Brown Ltd. v. Joseph Rugo, Inc.*,[73] the *Southern Fireproofing* court opined that if completion of exterior masonry were vital, language to that effect should have appeared in the subcontract. The *Southern Fireproofing* court further found that there had been no reliance on the schedule by Southern.

Examination of the subcontract clauses in *Southern Fireproofing, supra,* shows the subcontract itself denied specificity in Southern's work dates. Although the printed form possessed blanks for the statement of any desired definiteness as to the completion of Southern's work, Ball's overall work, and Ball's estimate of the time when Southern's work might begin, these three blanks were filled in, respectively, with "as required," "as required by owners," and "when notified." These are terms of indefiniteness. They fall far short of any date assurance to Southern. They fit instead into a concept of reasonable flexibility and into the practical necessities of the overall progress of the work. They give, as seems proper, the prime contractor some right as to the placement of Southern's work into its appropriate niche in the project's development. Scheduling "within the bounds of reason" is the most Southern could expect.

Cases holding schedules to be commitments incorrectly interpret the purpose of schedules. The misinterpretation most often occurs when a particular schedule has been presented for use on the project. In these situations, courts have incorrectly perceived something akin to detrimental reliance on a particular schedule by the aggrieved party. In *Dobson,* the contract required one schedule to be prepared for all prime contractors by an outside expert. The court perceived that each prime contractor relied on the schedule to determine when other prime contractors' work was to be completed to permit its work to proceed. In *Natkin,* the court perceived that a subcontractor relied on both a pre-bid schedule and the use of a particular scheduling method, both of which were denied to it. In *Steenberg,* the court perceived that a subcontractor undertook the performance of a subcontract in reliance on a particular schedule. In the industry, however, there is no reliance on a schedule in the same manner as the law perceives detrimental reliance. Construction schedules are without doubt a guide and a management tool to plan, but they are not intended to result in absolute commitments.

In contrast to *Dobson, Natkin,* and *Steenberg, Iowa Southern's* pre-bid schedule was clearly identified as only "general" and its construction schedules were submitted individually by the multiple primes. *Southern Fireproofing's* schedules were identified in the contract documents as subject to change from time to time as the work progressed. Neither permitted any detrimental reliance on the schedules by the various contractors.

The Illinois Appellate Court in *Pathman Construction Co. v. Hi-Way Electric Co.*[74] expressed a view of schedules similar to the "flexible" standard adopted by *Peter Kiewit Sons' Co. v. Iowa Southern Utilities* and *Southern Fireproofing Co. v. R.F. Ball Construction Co.* In *Pathman,* Hi-Way Electric was required by subcontract to "work in accordance with the critical path schedule and as directed by the contractor." [75] The CPM organized the various construction phases in sequence and assigned a certain period of time to each phase in an effort to ensure completion of the project by the finish date required by Pathman's prime contract. The CPM was revised periodically to reflect time extensions granted to Pathman from the Owner.

Hi-Way Electric was accused of delaying concrete floor pours and completion of final lighting. In order to determine whether such delay had occurred, the trial court compared the planned performance for Hi-Way under the CPM with Hi-Way's actual performance. Although a period of delay could be precisely identified in this manner, since planned and actual completion dates were known, the trial court chose to reduce the resultant calculation and hold Hi-Way responsible for a reduced amount of delay. The Appellate Court upheld the trial court allocation of delay as being in accordance with the weight of the evidence. The Appellate Court determined that the trial court employed the schedule "as a *general* guide to determine when Hi-Way's performance was due under the subcontract" [76] (emphasis added). The court was able to correctly perceive schedules as "guides" despite the presence of a particular schedule.

The General Services Board of Contract Appeals recently expressed another view that schedules are not rigid commitments. In a contract which provided a construction manager with the general authority to prepare a comprehensive construction schedule and adjust it as long as the total time allowed to perform the work was not changed, and required the multiple-prime contractors to cooperate with the construction manager in the schedule preparation and to furnish information in reevaluating and updating it, the Board held "changes in work sequence, CPM logic, and duration of activities . . . were to be expected in this method of contracting." [77] The General Services Board in *Economy*

Mechanical Industries, Inc.[78] characterized the schedule development process as "proposing certain schedules and *changes in schedule* and mutually discussing these revisions"[79] (emphasis added). The Board found the contractor's contention that changes in the initial schedule resulting from the required interchange among the construction manager and several prime contractors constituting a constructive change order under the Changes Clause had no merit.[80]

The trial court in *E.C. Ernst, Inc. v. Koppers Co.*[81] was required to evaluate the performance of Ernst when judged by the critical path method schedule prepared and imposed by Koppers. Despite the presence of a particular schedule, the *Ernst* court was also able to balance the nature of a schedule as a guide and the actual reliance Ernst had placed upon it to guide Ernst's bid preparation and performance in reaching its decision.

Ernst was the electrical subcontractor for Jones and Laughlin Steel Corporation's innovative coke oven battery A-5 being constructed to provide a unique method for preheating and delivering coal to furnaces for the production of steel at Aliquippa, Pennsylvania. Koppers was the design-build contractor. Kopper's Engineering Department prepared plans and specifications and issued an electrical bid package which included, among other things, a current schedule of electrical activities so that electrical bidders could plan labor and equipment requirements. Koppers developed the schedules to coordinate the engineering, procurement, and construction of the project. "There were more than 100 CPM network logic diagrams ... containing approximately 10,000 activities, some 340 of which were electrical."[82] Ernst submitted estimated manpower requirements based on its analysis of the CPM schedule. The Koppers-Ernst contract contained a clause which required Ernst to "follow the plan as currently shown and to perform the work in the allotted time designated as activity durations." The scheduling clause was:

PERT/CPM Requirement:

Seller acknowledges that Koppers is planning and scheduling this work by the PERT/CPM Method.

Seller is cognizant of this PERT/CPM requirement to provide qualified personnel to maintain correct networks for his portion of the work and to report progress monthly/bi-monthly, by submitting a "marked-up" copy of the electrical construction network.

Seller agrees to follow the plan as currently shown and to perform the work in the allotted time designated as activity duration. Seller agrees to suggest revisions to the network plan that in his judgment would be mutually beneficial; time being of the essence.

Koppers' schedules called for major construction activity to begin in the early Fall, 1974. Ernst, a "follow on" contractor, was dependent upon the availability of work areas created by preceding contractors. Preceding work, however, was not completed as scheduled:

On August 22, 1974, Koppers' CPM analysis showed that of 339 "total activities" for the electrical contractor, 332 were not available. As of October 17, 1974, 329 activities could not start, on November 14, 1974, 317 could not start, and by January 9, 1975, 282 activities could not be started, far less than the original CPM schedule contemplated.[83]

Ernst submitted a claim for additional compensation caused by the project's delay due to constant design changes necessary to permit the innovative method to preheat and deliver coal to the furnaces to work. Ernst received 289 drawings in its original bid package. It received over 1,300 revisions, twenty percent of which arrived after the originally scheduled completion date. "Many drawings were revisions of revisions, and some were revised as many as seven times."[84] The massive amount of revisions affected Ernst's ability to perform work according to the initial (and periodically updated) schedule. Some revisions affected completed work, requiring Ernst to remove and replace work already done.

The court repeated the testimony of Koppers' scheduling engineer in its decision. The testimony stated the flexible nature of schedules, a tool to manage projects:

> Q. ... would you explain ... what the CPM ... system is ...?
>
> A. ... the CPM network is a management tool. It is a guide on how to build your job ...
>
> Q. Would you state whether the CPM is a static thing or an ongoing thing?
>
> A. ... the network, it is just a guide, it is just a management tool to help us build the job. It is flexible, it can be changed.... Duration changes, and if it is taking us longer to do a job than I originally anticipated, I extend that duration to show it is going to take a little while longer. I change the logic sometimes if something pops up to where it is a piece of material a manufacturer originally said was going to take ten weeks and it is now going to take him 20 weeks to fabricate and we get into a negative critical path that is really running bad and I can't get that piece of equipment there any sooner, I then go back and I take a look at my logic. Maybe I can go ahead and work on the work I said would follow that. I might have to break that tie and put it downstream of the activities a little. When all that information is put down on the paper, I again send it to our planning and scheduling experts. Engineering and procurement does the same thing with theirs every three weeks, so we get all the current information, they assemble it, run it through the computer and we get a new printout.[85]

The court accepted the Koppers' scheduling engineer's testimony in finding that Ernst had cooperated with the CPM program: a program that required flexibility and change sufficiently to indicate Ernst had not contributed to the project delay and caused some part of its own damages.

To be balanced against the court's conclusion that schedules are flexible and subject to change was Koppers' claim that Ernst did not start its work promptly as it became available (as distinguished from as scheduled) and this caused the project's delay. The court reviewed the testimony of Koppers' Assistant Resident Superintendent who believed, "Ernst created the problem themselves by not doing (work) months ahead of time when the areas were open to them." [86] However, the court noted that the superintendent did not testify that Ernst did not perform the work *as scheduled* in the CPM and found this did not delay the project.

In finding that Ernst did not delay the project by failing to start its work when available, the court recognized an important distinction between the sequence in which activities may be scheduled and the activities proposed start and end dates. Ernst had planned its manpower on its analysis of the CPM schedule. Crew size was anticipated to increase and decrease as the activities were ordered in the schedule. Ernst sent its proposed manloading to Koppers. Ernst was required by its contract to "follow the plan as currently shown." To change the manloading by changing the activity sequence would have changed *the plan,* a violation of the Ernst-Koppers contract. Ernst had relied on the order of activities as shown in the Kopper schedule. The court properly refused Koppers' claim that Ernst should have done the electrical work contrary to that order. The court observed:

> Furthermore, it may be true that changes in sequence of work frequently occur in major construction

contracts, and that this Project was no different. But these are not bases for a denial of claims for extras.[87]

Although schedules are to be interpreted as guides, they are certainly not to be ignored. Just as the court in *E.C. Ernst v. Koppers* was required to balance the flexible nature of a schedule against the reliance placed by the contractor, the Court in *J.A. Jones Construction Co. v. Dover*[88] was called upon to make the same balance.

Jones was a prime contractor on Dover's expansion of its electric generating plant. The progress of Jones' work was dependent upon the work of other prime contractors on the job and upon proper deliveries by various suppliers of equipment. Jones' contract provided for completion within fifteen months. However, because of several delays, Jones was required to spend an additional fifteen months in completing his work. Jones sued Dover for $925,285.92 additional expense incurred because of the delays. Dover defended on the basis that Jones' claim was barred by the terms of the contract. Among other provisions to which Dover pointed to defeat the claim was: "(B) Dates are based on the present job schedule and are not guaranteed. No extra compensation will be due this contractor if those dates are not met."

The Court found that while Jones clearly accepted the risk of delay in performance, Jones only assumed the risk of reasonable delays. The Court reasoned the clause language neither addressed damages for breaches nor addressed itself to results of unreasonable actions causing delay. The Court therefore refused to permit Dover to escape liability for unreasonable delays because of the clause. Presumably, reasonable delays to Jones' performance would be tolerated without additional cost to Dover. The Court thus refused to ignore the schedule while still respecting its flexible nature.

In other words, the dates in a schedule, while certainly not commitments, should not be ignored. The dates in a schedule should be a flexible guide; flexible, but not to be broken. What is sufficient delay to warrant ignoring the schedule? How much flexibility should be present? Look at each situation separately. The *J.A. Jones* court found in that situation a fifteen-month delay to a fifteen-month performance period was too flexible.

Perhaps the most affirmative statement of the flexibility of the dates in a schedule comes from the Tenth Circuit Court of Appeals in *Burgess Construction Co. v. M. Morrin & Son Co.*[89] There, Morrin, the concrete subcontractor to Burgess on a Bureau of Reclamation Dam, submitted a schedule to Burgess which showed its planned sequence of construction and dates necessary for preceding work (by Burgess) to be completed so that Morrin's work could be completed within the time desired by Burgess for the entire project's completion. The start dates for Morrin's activities had been previously incorporated in the subcontract between Burgess and Morrin as follows:

> *Section 4. Time of Performance:* The Subcontractor agrees to keep himself informed as to the progress of the project and to faithfully prosecute his work, and the several parts thereof, *at such times in such order as the Contractor considers necessary* to keep the same sufficiently in advance of the other parts of the project and to avoid any delay in the completion of the construction as a whole. The scheduled *Time of Performance* of the work forming a part of this Subcontract is in Exhibit B.

The text of Exhibit B read:

> Time for completion of this work shall be as follows:
>
> 1. Concrete in lower tunnel, stilling basins and lower trash rack shall be complete to allow diversion of river through tunnel on or before 1 August 1971 *subject* to:
>
> a. Lower tunnel excavation *must be* complete to allow access from both ends by 1 April 1971.

b. Excavation for lower tunnel chute and the stilling basins for both chutes *must be* completed by 1 April 1971.

c. Gates and steel liners for lower gate chamber *must be* delivered on or before 15 May 1971 and installed not later than 1 June 1971.

The subcontractor will be entitled to a time extension equal to any delay created by a, b or c above. (Emphasis added.) [90]

Preceding Burgess work was, in fact, not completed as indicated in either the Morrin schedule or Burgess-Morrin subcontract. Morrin was unable to begin its work in the lower outlet tunnel until May 18 instead of the scheduled April 1; in the lower inlet tunnel until July 18 instead of the scheduled April 1; and the gate liners for lower gate chamber were not delivered until September 18 instead of the scheduled May 15. Even when available, however, Morrin's work was neither promptly initiated nor continuously prosecuted. Morrin claimed against Burgess for failure to make work sites available in sequence as specified by dates and changes in the schedules. Burgess terminated Morrin for failure to prosecute the work.

The court found against Morrin. Apparently ignoring the subsequently submitted schedule, the court looked to the subcontract clause and interpreted the words, "The subcontractor agrees ... to prosecute its work ... at such times in such order as the Contractor considers necessary" to mean Burgess "retained the right to direct the order of Morrin's performance in the manner necessary to the completion of the project as a whole." [91] Further, the court found Burgess had not guaranteed that Morrin would be allowed to work in the sequence its schedule proposed. It found the words "subject to" in Exhibit B which stated the dates in which Burgess' preceding work was to be completed to be merely a condition of Morrin's performance and not a promise by Burgess.

The court's apparently harsh decision ignoring Morrin's subcontract and schedule dates may be attributed to Morrin's failure to prosecute the work even after preceding work became available. Morrin's subsequent failure was so aggravated that Burgess terminated Morrin. The dates in a schedule must be recognized as flexible management tools. But they should not be ignored. The Tenth Circuit's decision should be treated as a precedent for interpreting the dates in a schedule as guides not promises, but guides to be considered in evaluating performance.

§ 4-6. **The Benefit of Float.**

A key issue in project scheduling is the question of whether the Contractor or Owner would receive the benefit of float time. Some construction contracts expressly state who has the control or benefit of float. Some state no extension of time will be granted unless the delay directly affects the critical path thus requiring the delay to consume any float present, transforming a noncritical activity to a critical one before a time extension will be granted.[92] Most construction contracts, however, make no reference to the issue.

Ownership of float affects the method and manner of calculation of delay. If the Contractor owns float, the beginning of a delay should start at the early finish date of any activity whether critical or not. This maintains the Contractor's control over the difference between the early finish and late finish times of all activities. If the owner has the benefit of float, delay calculations should begin at late finish dates of critical activities only. If Contractors own float, noncritical activities which are delayed should receive time extensions. If the Owner has the benefit of float, only delayed critical activities should be granted extensions of time.

One should recognize that late finish times are less meaningful than early finish times. This is so because of the difference between the forward and backward pass — the method used to calculate critical activities and float. A forward pass begins on the project's start date and follows the logic diagram in the sequence developed by adding durations of each succeeding activity to the total of durations of all preceding activities. The early finish times more accurately reflect the contractor's thinking at the time of the forward pass since the forward pass begins at the project's start (as the contractor intends) and continues through the planned construction sequence (as the contractor intends to perform the work) by adding each activity's duration (the period in which the contractor intends to complete the activity) to the total duration of all preceding activities (completed as intended by the contractor).

In contrast, the backward pass starts at the end of the project and works backward, through the sequence in reverse, by subtracting durations from the total duration which the forward pass provided. The late finish dates which the backward pass calculates are thus less meaningful to the contractor due to their artificial nature.

In its advice to contracting officers who are negotiating change orders, the Corps of Engineers suggests calculating the effect of schedule changes by taking advantage of any float time. In fact, the Corps urges contract modifications to be issued early in the job "before float time is depleted." [93] According to the Corps, if a modification affects only activities off the critical path and sufficient float time is available to absorb the modified work, the completion date will not change, thus, no extension of time will be due. However, not all agree with the Corps' position.

Courts and Boards that have considered the ownership of float have not reached similar conclusions. Contributing to the inconsistent decisions is the conflict between two common provisions in construction contracts. First, that the risk of construction lies with the contractor, tends to support owner claims to float. The provision generally states that the unknowns of construction which cause risk are the contractor's responsibility. Delays which reduce float cannot always be anticipated and are part of the unknowns of construction, therefore, delays which reduce float are the contractor's risk. Second, that the contractor is responsible for the means, methods, and techniques of construction, tends to support the contractor's claims to float.

If the contractor is responsible for the means and techniques should he not also be permitted to change them? To reduce or extend the time necessary to accomplish any particular activity which may result from a change in method or technique?

The Board in *Blackhawk Heating & Plumbing Co.* would not permit extensions of time to be granted unless the affected activities were on the critical path. The Board stated, "the real question is whether the ... delay caused delay in project completion." [94] The Board in *Chaney & James Construction Co.* refused to permit the contractor's recovery for the Government caused delays not affecting the project's completion date. These decisions conform to the general principle accepted by administrative boards and are best stated in *Montgomery-Marci Co. & Western Line Construction Co.:* "The duration of a time extension is calculated as the amount of time a delay increases the period of contract work as a whole." [95] Similarly, the Tenth Circuit Court of Appeals in *Brooks Tower Corp. v. Hunkin-Conkey Construction Co.*[96] refused to consider non-critical requests of the contractor for time extensions in determining when a building should have been completed. These cases all support the position that float belongs to the Owner.

Dobson v. Rutgers accepted the parties' proposition that "late" finish dates are the dates from which delay is measured, rather than early finish dates similarly giving the owner the benefit of float. *Dobson,* however, made no attempt to determine if delayed late finish dates must be on the critical path.

In contrast, *Natkin v. Fuller* stated that total float (the period in which delay may occur without affecting the project's completion date) may be used by all contractors, but that free float (the period in which delay may occur without affecting any other activity) belongs to the particular contractor for scheduling that activity. *Natkin* additionally stated that neither total nor free float is to be used for changes requiring additional performance time.[97] *Natkin* gave the contractor the benefit of the float.

The Armed Services Board of Contract Appeals in *Heat Exchangers, Inc.*[98] held that a contractor's original "cushion" of extra time, not necessary for performance maintained in an earlier time extension for design defects by the Government, should be retained in a subsequent time extension for other design defects. The first extension was calculated on the basis of the time between the contractor's request for clarification and the Government's mailing of the requested information. The Board held that the second extension should be calculated in the same manner. Thus the second time extension maintained the contractor's right to a "cushion" of extra time and gave the contractor the benefit of the float.

Owners and designers are frequently advised to grant all contractor's requests for extensions of time as a technique to reduce, if not eliminate, the contractor's delay claims. It is argued that granting extensions of time as they are requested by the contractor will deny the contractor the opportunity to connect a denied extension of time to a cost overrun or make a legitimate delay claim longer. Further, it is argued that since the schedule is intended to measure and plan the contractor's work, the schedule must list all requested time extensions in order to continue the goal. Without the inclusion of extensions of time, the schedule's ability to measure and plan is reduced.

These arguments in support of granting the contractor's requests for time extensions are in many ways merely rephrasing the contractor's claims to float. Granting time extension requests maintains the contractor's "cushions" of extra time as argued successfully in *Heat Exchangers, Inc.* Granting time extension requests to maintain the contractor's ability to measure and plan with an updated, current schedule also serves to maintain the contractor's float. Thus, there is industry support for the contractor's ownership of float.

In *E.C. Ernst, Inc. v. Manhattan Construction Co.*[99] the owner was given the benefit of float. In 1967, Providence Hospital of Mobile decided to substantially expand its facilities and to renovate and remodel its existing buildings. Providence contracted with Charles H. McCauley Associates to prepare plans and specifications. In 1968, Providence let a $6,117,500.00 general construction contract to Manhattan Construction Company. Manhattan subsequently entered into a subcontract with E.C. Ernst to perform all electrical work for $982,215.00.

The plans called for an electric sewage ejection pump to be installed to lift sewage to the level at which it could be discharged into the municipal sewer lines. The building engineer for Providence, however, realized that by running the sewage line through the basement rather than under the floor the sewage could be made to flow out of the hospital by gravity and thus eliminate the need for an ejection pump. Unfortunately, this relevation came after Manhattan had completed the excavation, pilings, pile caps, walls, and underground piping as originally designed.

On November 14, 1968, Manhattan was requested to submit a change in the contract price to eliminate the ejection pump and change the sewage line to a gravity flow system. The work had progressed so far, however, that at the time the change was proposed, it would have cost more to change the design than to proceed with the original design although it would certainly have been less expensive to have installed a gravity flow system initially. Manhattan submitted a proposal for the change on December 11, 1968. It was disapproved by the designer, McCauley. The proposal was resubmitted on February 21, 1969. Manhattan was notified on March 25, 1969, that the proposal was rejected. Manhattan thereupon resumed its work to install the pump as originally designed. As a result of the belated effort to reduce costs, there was a delay of 131 days in the installation of the sewage system. Manhattan requested an extension of time of 131 days but it was denied by the architect.

In its decision, the United States District Court indeed found a 131-day delay in the installation of the sewage system. The Court further found that Providence and McCauley caused the delay by failing to decide promptly what sewage system would be used. The Court did not find, however, that Manhattan was entitled to a 131-day extension of the project completion date. Instead, the Court found that with proper supervision and coordination by Manhattan and McCauley, the entire 131 days could have been absorbed within the original contract time limit for the job. Because the entire 131 days were not actually absorbed, however, the Court granted Manhattan a 65-day extension.

Other incidents which caused delay were also studied by the Court. Extensions of time were not granted unless the project's completion date had been extended. In *E.C. Ernst v. Manhattan,* the owner was given the benefit of float.

Author Hohns, in a previously published book, suggested that float belongs to the project rather than exclusively to either party.[100] This is the better view. Some "use of a portion of the float by the owner will not affect the contractor nor will some use of float by the contractor affect its work for the owner."[101] Using early start and finish dates to measure the liability for some part of extended performance time, but not all, fits well the more meaningful nature of early start dates. The contractor's early start and finish dates are the real dates in the schedule.

Determining at what point one's use of float begins to cause the other damage is not easy. When "the line" is crossed, an adjustment is due. But who, and how, should decide this? The Contracting Officer, subject to review by the Board of Contract Appeals, and the Architect in their positions as defined by standard form contracts have the power, if not the ability, to make such decisions. If the decision maker recognizes its responsibility to the project rather than to any individual or party, the decision will be made correctly.

Support for this position can be seen in *Continental Consolidated Corp.* where the Corps of Engineers Board of Contract Appeals, in determining the responsibility for concurrent delays, permitted the contractor to use float to eliminate the effect of delays it had caused, "although cable installation under this scheduling would be started 18 days later than planned, appellant could probably have met the original completion date ... by using float time ..."[102] and at the same time refused to permit contractor reimbursement for Government caused delays unless the delays affected activities critical to project completion. Float in *Continental Consolidated Corp.* was treated as belonging to the project.

§ 4-7. Mistakes in the Schedule.

The critical path method of scheduling requires the logical analysis of all the individual tasks that enter into the complete job. To be logical, a CPM schedule must accurately reflect both the contractor's intent to construct the job and the practical field restraints that apply to the job activities. Failing this, the CPM is not a proper scheduling tool. The schedule may fail for any number of reasons.

Joseph E. Bennett Co.[103] illustrates one type of failure: ignorance of practical field conditions. In *Bennett,* a New England general contractor attempted to show the effect of Government delays by utilizing its CPM. The General Services Board of Contract Appeals refused to permit the contractor to use the CPM because of errors in the schedule. First, the schedule ignored foreseeable New England winter weather conditions. The schedule showed compact fill to be installed in December, January, February, and March. During the trial, the contractor conceded the folly of attempting to place compact fill on frozen ground. Further, six mathematical errors were found, one of which generated six additional errors. Finally, fundamental changes were made to the original schedule when the contractor began its computerized study of the effect of Government delays. Float time was reduced causing a change in the critical path. Because of these deficiencies, the Board rejected the CPM as a "fully reliable standard for performance under the contract." [104]

E.C. Ernst, Inc. v. Manhattan Construction Co.[105] illustrates another way the schedule may fail: intentional deviation from the manner in which the contractor intends to complete the job. In this case, Manhattan Construction Company, the general contractor, had prepared a bar chart schedule which showed anticipated commencement and completion dates for the job but abandoned the bar chart early in the project. Further, the initial bar chart schedule was not prepared until six months after the project's start date. During trial, Manhattan presented a bar chart which had been especially adapted to demonstrate delays to the performance of a number of activities. This bar chart compared the delayed activities intended period for completion with the period in which the work was actually performed.

Unknown to its subcontractors, Manhattan had contemplated there would be an additional period of one year beyond the contract's specified completion date within which the work could be performed without penalty. Despite this, Manhattan prepared the initial bar chart schedule which showed completion within the original performance time. The bar chart did not indicate any additional time for performance of the work. Manhattan personnel testified at trial that they believed they were to have received an additional one year for performance of the work. Manhattan personnel also testified that they were never aware that the owner would have contemplated a liquidated damages claim without allowing at least a one year extension. Due to these inconsistencies, the Court found Manhattan failed to schedule the work properly, and thereby caused additional delays which the Court concluded to be a total of sixty days.

Not only may the initial schedule fail because of mistakes, but a subsequently prepared scheduling analysis of the project's delays may also fail because of the same types of errors. *E.C. Ernst, Inc. v. Koppers Co.*[106] illustrates how failure to properly evaluate and consider scheduling restraints can invalidate a schedule analysis as failure to consider practical restraints invalidated an initial schedule in *Joseph E. Bennett Co.*

In defense of Ernst's claim for additional costs caused by project delay (among other problems) Koppers attempted to show that Ernst failed to perform work as it became available by comparing the first CPM schedule, dated May 30, 1975, to the last schedule, dated September 18, 1975. The court refused to accept this comparison because no consideration of changes in restraints was made as the work had progressed.

The authors' partner, William B. Wagner, compared Koppers' initial schedule with the subsequent updated schedules, noting that the original restraints (as determined by Koppers) had been, in many cases, changed at Ernst's suggestion. Wagner concluded that any comparison of the first schedule with the last which did not consider changed restraints during the eighteen-month period in which work was performed was not valid. For example, Koppers' comparison indicated a certain activity was available on December 30, 1974, when in fact, its restraint had not been released until February 5, 1975, although Ernst actually began work on the particular activity on January 29, 1975, a week ahead of what could have been expected. The court noted that Koppers attempted to make it appear as if Ernst was responsible for the delay. When restraints were considered, Wagner concluded that Ernst had done all that could have been expected under the circumstances indicated by the CPM schedules.

Rejecting the Koppers' analysis for failure to consider restraints, the court stated: "We find the Wagner testimony to carry more weight than the testimony of Koppers' expert, who has not reviewed the CPM updates." [107]

Lane-Verdugo [108] illustrates how a subsequently prepared scheduling analysis may fail due to mistakes in updating the original logic to show delays. Lane-Verdugo was a joint venture contractor which had won two contracts for renovation and expansion of facilities on an air force base. Lane-Verdugo made a claim against the Department of Defense for $162,000 which the contractor claimed was due to government delay. The contractor's primary evidence was the critical path schedules which the contractor alleged indicated the government's delay.

In rejecting the contractor's scheduling analysis, the Board found the contractor's schedules to contain "some duplication in the work, or 'event' sequences shown." [109] The contractor had developed one sequence of events to demonstrate a delay for clarification of the plastic rebar requirements. However, that sequence was apparently duplicated by another series of activities which had appeared on the original logic. Both sequences appeared to pertain to the same structure and included submission, approval, fabrication, and delivery of plastic rebar. No explanation was given why the original sequence was retained on the revised network or why two separate sequences were necessary to show the same work.

Further, the Board found that the contractor had initially estimated thirty days to place siding on a structure. Due to a problem with the anchor bolts, a period of forty-one days was shown as being required to resolve the matter, followed by an additional eight days for the installation of the siding, all of which represented a claimed forty-nine day delay. Lane-Verdugo failed to consider, however, the fact that the claimed forty-nine days delay ran concurrently with the initial estimate of thirty days. The contractor claimed that this delay was responsible for the delayed completion of the entire project although the critical path ran through an entirely different segment of the work.

Finally, the schedules conflicted with the testimony of the witnesses. The contractor testified that the items which extended final completion were: delay on the utility line, blocking of trenching, flooding of trenches, problems with the gas line, problems with suspended ceilings, problems with cement asbestos board, pier redesign, and problems with the suspension system. The critical path charts, however, indicated that the critical path ran through the cement asbestos board from the start of the work until near completion. The court reasoned that since the critical path is defined as representing those items of work which if delayed would extend the completion date of the project, none of the other claimed delays could have resulted in a delay to the completion of the work (apparently ignoring the contractor's potential claim to the work). For these and other reasons, the Board concluded that Lane-Verdugo had not proven the government's responsibility for the total claimed job delay.

The contractor in *William Passalacqua Builders, Inc.*[110] attempted to support its claim before the General Services Board of Contract Appeals by utilizing a "Change Study Analysis" which showed a series of small critical path networks representing the sequence and effect of the different change orders and change requests issued for the project. The Analysis contained the change order completion dates and the late start date of the next sequential activity on the original CPM. If the change order work was completed subsequent to the claimed late start of the next activity a delay was shown in the critical path of the original schedule. The Change Analysis also contained change request dates, Passalacqua proposal dates, and the Government's review times. The study did not, however, apportion responsibilities for delays.

The board found the Change Study Analysis of no value because it was: "replete with inaccuracies and draws some questionable conclusions. As a result the most complimentary word that we could use to describe it is 'suspect.'"[111]

As in *E.C. Ernst Inc. v. Koppers Co.*, the Court in *William Passalacqua Builders* determined that the scheduling analysis failed because of mistakes. Some examples of the mistakes made in the Change Study Analysis are:

1. The Change Analysis showed a 223-day delay as a result of Change Order 1. The Analysis erroneously showed only 10 days taken for submission of Passalacqua's proposal and 179 days taken by the Government for review and approval of the proposal. Actually, Passalacqua took 131 days for the proposal submission, and the Government's review took 58 days.

2. Change Analysis incorrectly showed a period of two days taken for Passalacqua's submission of a price for Change Request 16, and 41 days taken for the Government's approval of the price.

3. A clerical error existed in the Change Analysis study of Change Request 118. The 77-day delay indicated should have been 42 days.

4. Change Request 116 involved replacing an installed manhole with a larger one. The Board found the 65-day duration for the change excessive, but Passalacqua could offer no explanation.

5. Change Requests 158, 163 and 165 involved adding small sidewalk areas and lowering an isolated manhole that took one or two days. Their direct cost totalled less than $500.00. All changes were issued after the Government's acceptance of the project. The Board could not understand how those small changes could have delayed the project from 129 to 164 days as indicated in the Change Study Analysis merely because they were issued after the originally scheduled completion date.

6. The Change Study Analysis contained a "39-day" clerical error in Change Request 165.

7. Although Change Request 149 was rescinded 15 days after issuance, the Analysis showed a 60-day project delay. Passalacqua could not explain the reason for such a significant impact.

8. Change Study Analysis indicated a 276-day delay for Change Request 10 although the work was completed

February 21 and the late start date for the same activity on the original schedule was June 13. The Board characterized this as "grossly erroneous." [112]

9. The Government's review of Change Request 145 was shown as taking 139 days when it actually took 80 days.

10. Change Request 152, which was alleged to have delayed the project 102 days, merely provided for the furnishing of tile in boxes for storage on the work site for future use.

11. Change Request 157, which was alleged to have caused 167 days' delay, provided for the installation of sixteen feet of railing and was performed within 19 days after Passalacqua issued the Change Order to its subcontractor.

12. Change Request 159, which was alleged to have caused 157 days' delay, covered relocated partitions in some areas of the third floor and was performed nine days after the Change Order was issued to subcontractors.

13. Change Request 167, which was alleged to have caused 166 days' delay, covered installation of pipe railing on a retaining wall. The work was completed thirty days prior to the issuance of a formal change order.

14. Change Request 169 required reworking some doors, installation of aluminum angles at the bottom of some matrix panels, and raising some carpeting. It cost only $4,098.00 to perform, yet a 228-day delay was claimed.

Passalacqua's method of calculating delay via the Change Study Analysis was rejected due to these and other errors.

Errors in the schedule which do not concern logic or durations may not, however, require rejection. *Dobson v. Rutgers* points out that CPM activity descriptions are one kind of minor mistakes which will not cause the schedule to fail. In *Dobson*, the specifications required the General Contractor to embed plumbing inserts in the concrete. However, the CPM listed these activities as being performed by

Plumbing and Mechanical Contractors. The Plumbing and Mechanical Contractors actually did the work. The *Dobson* Court permitted the Plumbing and Mechanical Contractor's recovery of the value of the labor performed despite the general contractor's defense that the CPM schedule had erroneously listed the activities as the Mechanical and Plumbing Contractor's responsibilities and that the specifications required it to do the work.

The General Services Board of Contract Appeals in *Blackhawk Heating & Plumbing Co.*,[113] agreed that activity descriptions are not absolute. The Board looked behind incorrect descriptions to determine the intent of the identifications. In *Blackhawk*, a CPM schedule had been developed after the project's completion by an outside scheduling consultant to illustrate the effect of project delays. The schedule had defined and inserted certain "delays" into the schedule in an attempt to determine the effect on the critical path and the project's completion date. The outside scheduling consultant had *in error* identified these several delays as "dummies," although the delays were intended to carry time durations and define an activity. Dummies, according to standard definitions, are *not* activities. Dummies carry no description or *time;* dummies are utilized only to maintain correct construction logic in the network.

The Board in *Blackhawk* recognized the labeling error as failing to conform to "standard CPM diagramming practice" [114] but refused to find any effect to the validity of the scheduling analysis. The Board found the intended meaning of the "dummies" in *Blackhawk* to be clear: an identifiable delay lasting a definable amount of time which affected certain following activities.

Schedules may also be attacked for errors in activity durations or activity detail. In *C.H. Leavell & Co.*[115] the Government alleged that the contractor's schedule, submitted *and approved* according to contract requirements, unrealistically provided excess durations to eliminate float and contained insufficient detail to accurately schedule some activities. A portion of the scheduling clause was:

> 2-34 Progress Charts and Construction Schedules
> 2-34(d): In addition to the aforementioned requirements for a progress schedule, the Contractor shall, within 30 days after receipt of notice to proceed, prepare and submit for approval a network schedule of the project. This network shall be of the type generally referred to as the critical path method (CPM), critical path schedule (CPS), and critical path analysis (CPA), and other similar designations. The network analysis shall include as a minimum a graphic representation of all activities and events included in the construction of the project. The network shall show the major subdivisions of the work, the activities involved in each part, the relations of activities to each other as to dependency, concurrency, etc., the duration of each activity, and the critical path of activities for the overall job showing a total job duration equal to the contract time. A written statement of explanation is to be submitted with the network designation.

Despite its earlier approval, the Government maintained the errors in the CPM schedule prevented proper analysis of alleged delay. The Contractor argued that the Contractor is the one required to develop the schedule and that no specifications were available which defined the time limit of the various activities.

In *Leavell,* the Contractor had allocated 285 days for "mechanical electrical rough-in." The Government contended that 120 days was a more reasonable duration and alleged a lack of detail existed in the broad category "mechanical-electrical rough-in." What the duration of "mechanical-electrical rough-in" should reasonably be was important because the activity was delayed. At 120 days, however, the activity maintained sufficient float to be *unaffected;* at 285 days the activity delayed the project's completion.

The Government's attack in *Leavell* had limited success. The Board found neither the Government nor the Contractor had demonstrated conclusively what the duration should have been. The Board did find, however, that analysis of the schedule was made difficult by the lack of breakdown of the broad mechanical-electrical category. The Board concluded the extent of the project's delay lay somewhere between the two positions and rendered a "jury verdict" decision.

The preceding cases confirm the proposition that to be accurate a schedule must accurately reflect both the contractor's intent to construct the project and the practical field restraints that apply to the activities. The schedule must be a logical analysis of the individual tasks which make up the project. It has been seen that this applies equally to job schedules prepared to complete the project and schedules prepared subsequently to prove delay. Each case reviewed has illustrated one type of failure. There are many, many more ways in which the schedule may fail. It would be of little benefit to list the mistakes to be avoided. Rather, the schedule user should keep the general rules in mind. Following them should ensure an acceptable schedule (in theory).

§ 4-8. Pre-Bid Schedules.

Dobson, Iowa Southern and *Natkin* presented an interesting contrast in the treatment of pre-bid schedules. *Dobson* held that the pre-bid schedule was not enforceable as a working plan, that it constituted merely an illustration for bid purposes, and that it was not based on the contractor's logic for the project. *Iowa Southern* found the prebid schedule, G-1, was only intended to give a basic idea of when the contractor's work would start and how rapidly it should be prosecuted in order for all contractors to make the required completion date. The *Natkin* court found, however, that the failure to meet the pre-bid schedule "delayed the entire job."[116]

Dobson and *Iowa Southern* presented the superior view. A pre-bid schedule available with other bid documents should be treated as only one method to coordinate the work. The contractor may choose other methods as the contractor controls the means, methods, and manner of construction. A pre-bid schedule should be considered an identification of time for purposes of wage rates, material prices, or interest rates much like soils information is provided as assistance to preparation of contractor bids. Remember, the Critical Path Method acknowledges there are many, many ways to build a building.

The primary distinction among the three cases is: The presence of an independent contractor's scheduling requirement in *Dobson* and *Iowa Southern*, was absent in *Natkin*. A detailed contractor's schedule shows the manner in which the contractor will complete the project as compared to the manner someone else suggests for the completion in the pre-bid schedule. No independent scheduling requirement was present in *Natkin* where the contractor adopted and relied on the pre-bid schedule. Thus, schedulers from whatever source — architect, engineer, contractor, or consultant may escape responsibility for errors in the pre-bid schedule by requiring the contractor's schedules once contracts have been awarded.

This conforms generally to the distinction between contractor performance responsibility under design or under performance specifications. Contractors under design specifications are required to merely follow the design — the designer is responsible for the success or failure of the design. Under performance specifications, however, the contractor is responsible for the construction and design. It is the authors' opinion that contracts which contain an independent scheduling requirement will clearly shift the scheduling responsibility to the contractor, despite the presence of a pre-bid schedule.

§ 4-9. Mutual Responsibilities Under the Schedule.

Most scheduling clauses in construction contracts attempt to make the contractor solely responsible for the planning and scheduling of work. By approving contractor schedules, however, the owner or designer assumes certain obligations. For example, the owner or designer agrees that it will fulfill its own performance responsibilities in a timely manner according to the approved project schedule. These may include approval of shop drawings, delivery of owner-furnished equipment, or rendering prompt decisions.[117]

Thus, when the Government in *Fullerton Construction Co.* failed to review critical shop drawings within the time period permitted by the Contractor's schedule, it was held to have unreasonably delayed the Contractor.[118] This finding was made even though the Government had advised the Contractor it would require a greater period of time for shop drawing review than provided in the schedule [119] and the Government never approved the Contractor's schedule.

Failure to approve may not release the owner from an obligation to perform within the time required by the schedule. In *Fullerton,* lack of approval did not prevent the Contractor from holding the Government to the submitted schedule. In *Dobson,* similarly, Owner-furnished equipment was delayed. Although the owner had not approved the construction schedule, it was found liable for the cost of the delays it had caused.[120]

In contrast, the NASA Board of Contract Appeals in *Carney General Constructors, Inc.,*[121] refused to require Government conformance to scheduled durations for shop drawing review when the approved cycle was unreasonably short, the Resident Engineer had objected to it, and the Contractor had acquiesced to a larger period.

Similarly, general contractors may be required to perform within schedules imposed on subcontractors. In *E.C. Ernst, Inc., v. Koppers Co.*, Koppers, the design-build contractor, included a CPM schedule in the initial bid package which required Ernst, the successful electrical subcontractor, "to follow the plan as currently shown ..."[122] and to use the schedule to coordinate the engineering, procurement, and construction. When Ernst subsequently brought a claim for additional costs due to delayed project completion, Koppers counter-claimed for Ernst's failure to perform activities when they became available regardless of when the activities were scheduled to be performed. The court rejected Koppers' arguments that Ernst should have performed work as-available rather than as-scheduled, awarded Ernst additional costs, and noted that Ernst "performed the work as expected by the CPM schedules."[123] The court found Koppers bound by the schedule it had required Ernst to follow.

The Tenth Circuit Court of Appeals in *Steenberg Construction Co. v. Prepakt Concrete Co.*[124] also held that a general contractor must conform to the schedule it imposes on subcontractors. In June, 1963, Steenberg contracted with the Bureau of Reclamation for the construction of an earthen dam on Lost Creek in Utah. Prepakt, a subcontractor, agreed to drill into the bedrock and render it impervious by pressure-pumping grouting material through the drillholes into the cracks and crevices of the bedrock. The progress schedule prepared by Steenberg and submitted to the Bureau indicated half of Prepakt's work would be completed between September 1 and November 15, 1963, shutdown for winter, then resume in the spring.

Steenberg's progress schedule was based on the Bureau engineer's estimate that the maximum depth of the excavation to bedrock would be approximately twenty-eight feet. However, once excavation had started, it was discovered that the estimates of the depth to bedrock were erroneous; instead it would be necessary to excavate to sixty-eight feet to reach bedrock in some areas of the trench. Because of the specified slope for side to the core trench the additional excavation increased the width of the core trench at surface from one-hundred-twenty feet to two-hundred-forty feet. Because of the additional excavation, the completion of the core trench was delayed and a revision of the progress schedule was necessary. A revised progress schedule which reflected the delay caused by the additional excavation was submitted to the Bureau of Reclamation on November 15, 1963.

Steenberg and Prepakt met to discuss the problems caused by the delay. Although revision of the work schedule was discussed, Steenberg did not inform Prepakt that a winter shutdown would be abandoned and that a revised schedule was to be submitted to the Bureau. Prepakt reminded Steenberg that it had nothing in its estimate for winter work and requested an adjustment in the contract sum if required to work through winter. Steenberg agreed to help with winter protection, but did not agree to a revised contract amount.

Because of the delay resulting from engineering errors, Steenberg was unable to make enough area in the core trench ready to permit Prepakt to operate two drills at once as had been planned. Preparation of the core trench to permit operation of two drills was a condition for winter work. Prepakt discontinued operations on the project on December 12, 1963, due to insurmountable and economically unfeasible difficulties. Between December 12, 1963, and February, 1964, Prepakt and Steenberg attempted to negotiate additional compensation. These negotiations failed and Prepakt abandoned the project and removed its supplies and equipment on February 12, 1964.

The Court found the evidence to indicate that Steenberg's original bar chart had indicated that Prepakt's work was to be commenced in September and finished before the mid-November winter shutdown. Implicit in this agreement was the understanding that all conditions precedent to the performance of Prepakt's work would be fully met. Prepakt would be provided a suitable place to commence and complete work within the time contemplated by Steenberg's bar chart. Having undertaken to perform its work according to the job schedule, Prepakt is entitled to receive performance from Steenberg that would similarly meet the job schedule. The Court stated that in situations like this, performance by the contractor of his end of the bargain is a constructive condition precedent to the duty of the subcontractor to perform his part of the bargain. This was found to be so even though the performance of Steenberg's work was frustrated through no fault of its own.

The Court concluded that when Steenberg and Prepakt met at the jobsite in November to discuss the delay, Prepakt was under no obligation to do anything. By asking for more money, Prepakt was merely asking for its original contract to be respected. Steenberg refused to provide additional money but agreed to winterize the project which it subsequently failed to do. Steenberg's failure to perform justified Prepakt's discontinuance of operations in December and the ultimate abandonment of the contract in February. The contractor in *Steenberg v. Prepakt* was required to meet the schedule which it imposed on its subcontractor before it could demand performance by the subcontractor.

Suppliers may not escape the mutual obligations which a schedule imposes. In *J.A. Jones Construction Co. v.*

Dover,[125] Jones contracted to install certain equipment and render services in connection with the expansion of Dover's electric generating plant for a contract price of $5,500,000. Jones' progress was dependent upon work of other contractors on the job and upon proper deliveries by various suppliers of equipment.

Dover did not have a general contractor in the traditional sense, but contracted directly with various suppliers and contractors for different portions of the project. Under its prime contract with Dover, General Electric undertook to provide a 100,000 kilowatt steam turbine generator and other equipment. Under its prime contract with Dover, Westinghouse agreed to provide motor control centers and drawings and technical data. Dover claimed delays which extended Jones' performance were caused by failure of General Electric and Westinghouse to perform on time. General Electric and Westinghouse denied liability for delay based on their standard disclaimer provisions in the contract.

The Jones' contract provided for completion of its portion of the work within fifteen months. Because of what it claimed to be delays which were beyond its control, Jones was required to spend an additional fifteen months in completing its contract. Jones sought $925,285.92 as additional expenses incurred because of delays. Dover sought to charge Jones' claims against it to General Electric and Westinghouse and in addition seek $3,320,297.68 in damages.

The Court found the supplier's standard disclaimers not to apply to a situation in which the performance of various contractors and suppliers are interdependent. The Court rather concluded that the disclaimers were intended to protect suppliers during a period in which replacement of defective goods was made. The Court concluded that delay by General Electric and Westinghouse may not be protected by standard disclaimers and held the suppliers to their obligations under the contract. Thus, when a schedule defines the mutual time responsibilities necessary to complete a project, suppliers, as well as owners and contractors, must meet the obligations on which others depend.

§ 4-10. Updating the Schedule.

Most courts have recognized that unanticipated changes and problems occur on a construction project which in turn require changes in the contractor's performance and schedule. The District of Columbia Court of Appeals in recognizing the difficulties of planning a project compared a construction job to a battlefield in *Blake Construction Co. v. C.J. Coakley Co.:*

> We note parenthetically and at the outset that, except in the middle of a battlefield, nowhere must men coordinate the movement of other men and all materials in the midst of such chaos and with such limited certainty of present facts and future occurrences as in a huge construction project such as the building of this 100 million dollar hospital. Even the most painstaking planning frequently turns out to be mere conjecture and accommodation to changes must necessarily be of the rough, quick and *ad hoc* sort, analogous to ever changing commands on the battlefield.[126]

Natkin v. Fuller restated the general scheduling proposition that the "critical path plan may become obsolete unless it is kept current."[127] *Continental Consolidated Corp.*[128] recognized that failure to incorporate changes in the work and time extensions will not permit the CPM to reflect the current status of work performed. An inaccurate schedule cannot control the progress of the ongoing work, it cannot show the effects of delay on the project's completion, or represent the actual manner in which the project was constructed.

The *Lane-Verdugo* Board found that the critical path schedule submitted was not accurate because of a failure to update the entire schedule. When updated no change was made in the initial estimates of time required to accomplish the work or the amount of time it actually took to accomplish the work. Further, logic changes made to reflect field conditions were made without changing the initial estimates of activity durations. The Board felt these inaccuracies prevented the contractor from relying on the schedule as an accurate measurement of construction progress.[129]

In contrast, the General Services Board of Contract Appeals in *Dawson Construction Co.*[130] permitted use of a CPM schedule to analyze delay that had been updated monthly but did not reflect all actual start and finish dates. Only about twenty-five percent of the activities, primarily the critical ones, were updated with actual start and finish dates. Progress on the remaining activities was not identified beyond the month in which a given activity was started or finished.

Similarly, the Illinois Appellate Court in *Pathman Construction Co. v. Hi-Way Electric Co.*,[131] despite protests from a subcontractor, permitted the use of a CPM schedule to measure delay which had not been updated to reflect all time extensions. The Court stated that time extensions do not automatically inure to the benefit of a subcontractor and held that the subcontractor's time of performance under a CPM schedule will be increased only if the time extension affects the subcontractor's work.[132] Although in both *Dawson* and *Pathman* the defects in the updating process probably did not effect the validity of the schedule, a schedule which has not been correctly or completely updated should not generally be considered a satisfactory representation of the construction sequence or duration.

The CPM schedule identifies many paths through the schedule. Not all are critical. Those paths that are not critical because they contain float may become critical if the float is eliminated. Likewise, those paths that originally are critical may develop float if a larger, delayed path develops. As the schedule is updated the critical paths are thus likely to change. Legal commentators have recognized this.[133] At least one Board, the General Services Board of Contract Appeals in *Blackhawk Heating & Plumbing Co.*,[134] has also recognized the proposition.

In *Blackhawk*, the Board considered the contractor's argument that certain ductwork delays affected the critical path of the *original* schedule and that the contractor should be entitled to extensions of time. The Board refused to grant extensions based on the *original* schedule because subsequent occurrences *changed* the critical path. The Board had before it an undated schedule which showed how the project was actually built and indicated ductwork delays were not critical. The Board concluded that time extensions should be granted on the best available evidence. The best available evidence is, of course, an updated schedule.

The United States District Court for the Western District of Pennsylvania in *E.C. Ernst, Inc. v. Koppers Co.* found that to validly measure delay durations and restraints, schedules must be updated. To refute Ernst's claim of additional costs caused by delayed project completion, Koppers compared its first schedule, dated May 30, 1974, with its last schedule, dated September 18, 1975. The comparison was intended to prove Ernst's failure to commence activities when they were available. The court rejected the Koppers' analysis because neither restraints nor durations were updated. Expert testimony established that in many cases original restraints and durations as assigned by Koppers were changed by Koppers at Ernst's suggestion. Ernst's performance was initiated and completed within the period required by *updated* durations and restraints. The Kopper's analysis of schedules without updated durations and restraints was rejected.

§ 4-11. Changes in Scheduled Sequence.

Perhaps the most important part of any schedule is the order or sequence of its activities. Much more than the dates in a schedule, the activitiy sequence is relied on to order material and arrange for equipment and labor. The anticipated sequence also represents the contractor's bid intent: defining the amount, and thus cost, of material and equipment estimated to complete the work and more importantly, when the material and equipment is due. Changing the sequence of a schedule may change the entire management plan forcing succeeding work to begin without all necessary material or equipment and imposing an unanticipated inefficiency on it or requiring additional material or labor thereby increasing the contractor's costs. For example, a contractor may release formwork and carpenters to Job B if Job A's sequence calls for completion of mass excavation before formwork. Changing the sequence to pre-build forms concurrent or prior to excavation will find the contractor short of necessary materials and labor. Without anticipated skilled labor or all needed materials, proceeding with pre-building forms may be inefficient and impose a penalty on construction costs not otherwise present if the work had proceeded as originally scheduled. Unlike the dates in a schedule which should be considered sufficiently flexible to permit variation, sequencing will invite reliance.

There are certain implicit duties between contracting parties, particularly the duty not to prevent performance by the other party.[135] Although with construction contracts these implicit duties must be interpreted with the uncertainties, vagaries, and necessity for change inherent

§ 4-11   CONSTRUCTION SCHEDULES

with construction projects, there can come a point when the necessary latitude of discretionary action has been exceeded.[136] Out-of-sequence work can indicate situations when the implicit duty not to prevent performance of another contracting party has been breached.

The importance of maintaining scheduled sequence was perhaps first recognized in *Henry Ericsson Co. v. United States*.[137] Ericsson entered into a contract with the United States Public Works Administration on September 3, 1936, to build the superstructures in the north sector of the Julia C. Lathrop Homes in Chicago for $2,097,600. The south sector, of comparable size, was to be built at the same time by other contractors. The project required the construction of seventeen buildings which were to contain 484 apartments, with a total of 1,690 rooms. Eleven buildings were to be three-story; five were to be two-story; and the administration building was to be one-story.

Ericsson's plan to complete the buildings was dictated largely by the nature of the structures. Except for interior supports, each floor slab supported the walls above it and each wall supported the concrete slab for the next floor, the walls of the highest floor supported the roof slab. The construction sequence for each building was:

1. Install interior column supports — form crew.
2. Pour first floor slab — concrete crew.
3. Cure first floor slab.
4. Erect first floor brick and tile walls — masonry crew.
5. Install interior column supports — form crew.
6. Pour second floor slab — concrete crew.
7. Cure second floor slab.
8. Erect second floor brick and tile walls — masonry crew.
9. Install interior support columns — form crew.
10. Pour third floor slab — Concrete crew.
11. Cure third floor slab.

12. Erect third floor brick and tile walls — masonry crew.
13. Install interior support columns — form crew.
14. Pour roof slab — concrete crew.
15. Cure roof slab.
16. Erect parapets and penthouse.
17. Install built-up roofing.

Ericsson planned to pour the floor slab of the first building and immediately thereafter to pour consecutively the first floor slab of six more buildings. By the time the first floor slab of the seventh building had been poured, the brick and tile first floor walls of the first building would have been completed and forms for the second floor slab would have been erected. The second floor slab in the first building would be ready to be poured. After the second floor slab of the first building had been poured, the second floor slab in the second building would be ready to be poured. Ericsson planned to move its labor crews, equipment, and forming materials from one building to the next, while waiting for the concrete of each floor to dry sufficiently to permit the placing of the next tier of walls on that floor. This process was intended to be completed for the first seven buildings. Thus, work on a number of buildings would progress simultaneously. A similar sequence was to have been followed in the remaining buildings.

A partial, hypothetical critical path method schedule for Ericsson's intended work is shown in Exhibit 9. Although certainly not in the critical path method shown in Exhibit 9, Ericsson submitted a progress schedule showing the proposed construction sequence and proposed dates of commencement and completion of the work. Subsequently Ericsson sent a written statement of the sequence, by building, in which it intended to work. Ericsson's work, unfortunately, did not follow the anticipated schedule.

Design details required stone trim for the front entrances. The stone had to be set into the walls as the brick was laid.

The masonry walls could not be completed until the stone was set. Ericsson was required to furnish shop drawings, approved by the government, for the manufacture of the stones. Before Ericsson could prepare the shop drawings, however, the government had to provide full-size detail drawings.

Ericsson's progress schedule showed Ericsson planned to complete the first floor walls of the first building on November 4. Usual shop drawing preparation and stone manufacture (in 1936) required the full size detail drawings for the stone to be received approximately five weeks before the stone was needed for setting the wall. The first full-size detail drawings for stone trim were received on October 30, less than a week before scheduled installation. Those received, however, were incomplete and did not include the first building. Only drawings for the fourth, sixth, and twelfth buildings were complete. Drawings for the first and second buildings in the planned construction sequence were not received until November 11. Those for the third building were not received until November 30 and those for the fifth building were received on December 12. The delay in receipt of the full-size drawings delayed the shop drawing preparation and approval, and the manufacture of the stone. The delay in receiving the stone delayed laying the brick first-story walls. This, in turn, delayed the next operation in the planned sequence, and the delay continued into each of the other planned work sequences.

LAW AND CONSTRUCTION SCHEDULES § 4-11

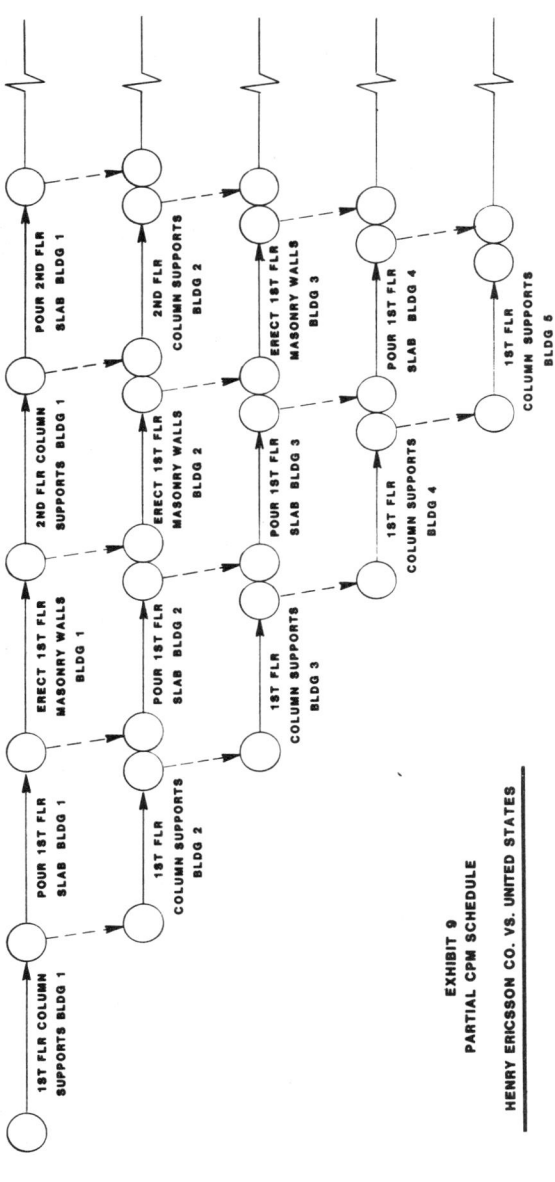

EXHIBIT 9
PARTIAL CPM SCHEDULE
HENRY ERICSSON CO. VS. UNITED STATES

The court found the entire job was delayed because of the disruption to Ericsson's planned operations and delay in the early part of the planned sequence due to the government delay in providing full-size drawings. Further, the court found the change in sequence cost Ericsson money.

Ericsson intended to sequence the first floor slab of the first seven buildings, but also planned to follow with second floor as soon as the first building permitted. The second floor slab was to be sequenced through the seven buildings as well. The other buildings were intended to be constructed in a similar manner. Because of delays to the stone drawings, Ericsson had to revise its intended construction sequence. Ericsson poured the first floor slabs of all the buildings before pouring the second story slabs of the first seven buildings in order to keep his losses as low as possible. Under its original sequence of operation, Ericsson would have reused form work from the first seven buildings, but under the revised sequence was obliged to purchase additional material and to build additional forms. The court awarded Ericsson the cost of the additional forming material required by the government's delay which caused the change in schedule sequence and delay-type damages.

Another early case which recognized the importance of maintaining schedule sequence is *Freeman Contractors, Inc. v. Central Surety & Insurance Corp.*[138] Freeman Contractors was a painting subcontractor to Peter Kiewit Sons' Co. and Morrison-Knudson, a general contract joint venture which provided temporary and permanent housing under a $7,000,000 contract in support of construction of a dam on the Missouri River in 1947. The Court's discussion of out-of-sequence work is interesting for two reasons. One, as in *Henry Ericsson Co. v. United States,* the dispute was considerably in advance of the development of the critical path method — the standard device for defining out-of-sequence work for present disputes. Two, no mention of the presence of *any* construction schedule was made by the Court.

In its complaint, Freeman alleged that Kiewit was indebted to it because Kiewit breached the subcontract by delaying and interfering with the subcontractor's work. Freeman Contractors pointed out that Kiewit was unable to provide sufficient carpenters to keep Kiewit's work ahead of the subcontractor's painters; that Freeman, although ordered to proceed, was never able to complete its painting in any one building or series of buildings before being ordered to move its crew to another location or building. Freeman presented evidence that it was required to paint exterior trim before the trim's erection in buildings, making it necessary that this work be done by hand instead of by spraying as originally bid, adding to Freeman's costs.

When Kiewit was finally able to provide an adequate number of carpenters to keep ahead of the painters and other subcontractors, it was threatened by the owner with the penalty for delay provision in the general contract. To avoid this loss, Freeman and other subcontractors, whose work interfered with each other's work, were ordered to work on the same buildings at the same time. On occasion, Freeman was required to paint before crafts which should have preceded it, had finished their work, with the result that the painting was damaged and Freeman had to return to the building and repair the damage done by other crafts. Interferences of one craft with the work of another prevented orderly and economical operations, causing unusual and costly delays.

From the beginning of the work, Freeman contractors complained of delays and interferences with the orderly progress of the painting. Kiewit's superintendent admitted in his testimony that Kiewit had failed to coordinate the work and caused Freeman unusual and costly delays for which Freeman was entitled to reimbursement. While the work was proceeding, Freeman, at Kiewit superintendent's suggestion, prepared an analysis of the work which showed the anticipated cost if the work had proceeded in an orderly manner and the actual cost of the out-of-sequence work done. The analysis was presented to the president of Kiewit who recognized the merit of Freeman's claim and promised just compensation. Kiewit subsequently refused to allow Freeman contractors any additional sums.

The United States District Court concluded that the delays and additional costs suffered by Freeman might reasonably be expected in a large government construction contract upon which a considerable number of subcontractors were working and which was at all times subject to change in plans and specifications. The Court refused to permit the case to go to the jury.

On appeal, the United States Court of Appeals concluded that on large government construction projects involving many subcontractors and different crafts, custom and necessity require that the work be planned and executed on a production basis; that the work of different crafts proceed in an orderly sequence. For example, the foundation must first be constructed, followed by erection of the exterior walls and roof, the installation of exterior trim, finishing the interior, and the exterior and interior painting, in the order mentioned. The Court of Appeals found that Kiewit planned the project on such a production basis, and that the bid of Freeman contractors was made with that understanding. The Court of Appeals overruled the District Court and required the District Court to submit Freeman's case to the jury.

Maintaining scheduled sequence was also recognized in *Turnbull, Inc. v. United States*,[139] a 1967 case which dealt with a 1954 construction contract. The reader will recognize the date of the dispute to be similarly in advance of the development of the critical path method, thus the out-of-sequence claim had to be based on another form of schedule, most likely a bar chart.

Turnbull, Inc. and A & H, Inc. as a joint venture, were awarded a $2,480,479.00 contract to construct several buildings at the Longhorn Ordinance Works, located in Harrison County, Texas, for the Corps of Engineers. Shortly after work began, a disagreement arose between Turnbull and the Corps' contracting officer concerning the proper sequence of construction operations. Turnbull believed the buildings should be built by completing the walls and roofs first, then by pouring concrete floor slabs. The contracting officer maintained that floor slabs should be poured first with walls and roofs following. The dispute was resolved by an administrative decision to build walls and roofs first as Turnbull had proposed.

Despite the administrative decision, the contracting officer orally directed Turnbull to pour concrete floor slabs before walls and roofs were constructed. Turnbull complied, working two shifts and overtime to overcome the delay which the dispute had imposed on the construction schedule. Because of the disruption to Turnbull's work schedule, it was necessary for Turnbull and its suppliers to reschedule operations. The out-of-sequence work changed the schedule

> from a smooth operation to one where it was necessary for the prime contractor to proceed on a makeshift basis and switch from one place to another, building as far as it could on one structure and then transferring the work force to another structure and a different type of work. Such factors, coupled with the geographical size of the project and the necessity of "hedgehopping" from area to area with no well established plan of operation, increased the cost of the job.[140]

Turnbull demanded a change order to compensate for the losses it experienced resulting from the reversal of the construction sequence. The Corps of Engineers Claims and

Appeals Board agreed, finding that the changes in slab placement from the contractor's original sequence constituted a change in the contract.

The Supreme Court of Nebraska in *Kroeger v. Franchise Equities, Inc.*[141] also recognized out-of-sequence work as a substantial penalty. Kroeger agreed to perform all carpentry work necessary to construct a service station and restaurant in Omaha, Nebraska, according to a CPM Schedule which provided that the carpentry would be performed between December 3, 1970, and January 28, 1971. Kroeger began work on November 20, 1970, but stopped in December when the defendant shut down the job. Kroeger heard nothing until April, 1971, when he worked an additional eight hours. Thereafter Kroeger refused to complete the contract because carpenters' wages were about to increase and the job originally had been estimated to be winter work.

Defendant Franchise Equities claimed it had a right to reschedule the work under the contract. The Court found, however, that a delay in construction from December to April was not a revision of the critical path schedule within the meaning of the contract and contemplation of the parties.

Kroeger had relied on the scheduled sequence to bid the job; labor rates had been defined by wage requirements prior to April, 1971, and performance was to be winter work, presumably meant as inside work permitting continuous work until more favorable weather for outside work returned in the spring. Requiring such a dramatic change in sequence into a period of higher wage rates and demanding inside work when outside work was presumably available permitted Kroeger to terminate and recover its incurred expenses and lost profit. Thus, the Supreme Court of Nebraska recognized that changes in sequence which result in additional expenses are not permitted without compensation.

In *Natkin & Co. v. George A. Fuller Co.*[142] the Federal District Court for the Western District of Missouri recognized the reliance one, who uses the schedule, may place on the sequence of planned construction activities. There, Natkin had planned its manpower and material requirements according to the CPM schedule. For work performed in the planned sequence, Natkin was able to provide appropriate labor to complete the work in a timely manner. However, when Western Electric Co., the owner, required work to be done out of its scheduled sequence and set completion dates earlier than those established by the CPM, Natkin encountered manpower shortages, congestion, and materials problems which caused Natkin to have additional costs. The *Natkin* court found Western Electric Co. and George A. Fuller Co., the general contractor, responsible for all of Natkin's additional costs caused by the failure to permit performance according to the sequence defined in the CPM.

There is no doubt that changes to scheduled sequence may impose considerable penalty on contractor's costs. It is the authors' opinion that all additional costs resulting from changed sequence should be recovered. However, not all sequence changes will cost more time and money. Judgment is required to identify those sequence changes which do result in additional cost and those which do not.

The Tenth Circuit Court of Appeals in *Burgess Construction Co. v. M. Morrin & Son Co.*,[143] believed one expert's judgement and concluded that deviation from sequencing shown in a subcontractor's schedule did not result in additional subcontractor cost. Although the court presented a contractual reason for its decision, the authors believe the no-additional-cost nature of the sequence change to be the correct reasoning.

In *Burgess*, Morrin, the concrete subcontractor, submitted a schedule to Burgess, the general contractor, *after* execution of a subcontract. The schedule showed Morrin's planned sequence of operation for work in a tunnel of a dam: first in the lower inlet tunnel beginning at the gate chamber and moving outward to the tunnel entrance; followed by the contemporaneous installation of the lower outlet tunnel and gate chamber. Morrin planned to use a railway system to transport concrete into the tunnel, laying track once into the lower inlet tunnel and once into the lower outlet tunnel.

Burgess was not able to complete preceding work in order to permit Morrin to work either in its originally planned sequence or time periods. Instead of installing the railroad twice, Morrin had to install it five times. Activities were performed out of sequence. However, once work was available, Morrin failed to adequately prosecute its work. Burgess terminated Morrin and Morrin counter-claimed for excess costs due to delayed and out-of-sequence work. The court refused Morrin's counter-claim and ruled in Burgess' favor.

Ignoring the subsequently submitted schedule (it probably should have been treated as an amendment to the contract), the court interpreted a clause in the subcontract to eliminate Morrin's out-of-sequence claim. The clause stated:

> Section 4. Time of Performance: The subcontractor agrees to keep himself informed as to the progress of the project and to faithfully prosecute his work, and the several parts thereof, *at such times in such order as the Contractor considers necessary* to keep the same sufficiently in advance of the other parts of the project and to avoid any delay in the completion of the construction as a whole ... (emphasis added).[144]

The court interpreted this clause as expressly reserving to Burgess the right to direct the time and order of Morrin's performance. The court recognized "the schedule of operations was for the convenience of Burgess and Morrin and other subcontractors in coordinating the work," [145] but was unable to find inconvenience and additional costs to Morrin when the schedule's sequence was changed.

During the trial, an expert in this type of construction testified that Morrin should have been able to complete work on time notwithstanding the schedule changes. The expert did not consider it necessary to work in the sequence Morrin planned. With this and perhaps other testimony, the court found substantial evidence that the extra work caused by the schedule changes was insignificant. Thus, the case can support the industry standard that out-of-sequence work should be compensated. In Morrin's situation, however, the out-of-sequence work may not have caused any additional, compensable costs.

There is no doubt that the most important part of a schedule is the order or sequence of its activities. Much more than the dates in a schedule, the activity sequence is relied on to order material and arrange for equipment and labor. Changing the sequence of a schedule may impose considerable economic penalty on a contractor. To the extent that the additional cost resulting from out-of-sequence work is not the fault of the contractor, the contractor should be reimbursed for the additional cost. No matter how just the contractor's claim is for out-of-sequence work, there is no assurance that the full amount of the out-of-sequence claim will be recovered. Therefore, contractors naturally resist changes in their work sequence. How far can a contractor's resistance go? Can a contractor refuse to perform out-of-sequence work? *Vermont Marble Co. v. Baltimore Contractors, Inc.*[146] examines the question.

The dispute concerned the construction of an extension to the Everett M. Dirksen Senate Office Building in Washington, D.C. Baltimore Contractors Inc. (BCI) was the prime contractor for the Architect of the Capitol (Architect) to perform "Phase IV" in the construction. Vermont Marble

Company was a subcontractor to BCI. The BCI-Vermont subcontract required Vermont to do the stonework facing on the building. Phase IV involved the construction of the superstructure of the building. Under earlier phases, foundation work and stone quarrying and delivery had been completed.

BCI was awarded the contract and on October 28, 1977, was given a Notice to Proceed. Under BCI's contract with the Architect, certain milestone dates for completion of specified major steps in the construction process were defined. Starting at the Notice to Proceed date of October 28, 1977, the milestone dates were:

1. Commencement of structural steel installation, 185 days (April 30, 1978).
2. All concrete and fireproofing through the first six floors, 440 days (January 10, 1979).
3. All remaining concrete, 550 days (April 30, 1979).
4. Stone installation and masonry work through the first six floors, 745 days (November 11, 1979).
5. Completion of all work, 900 days (April 14, 1980).

BCI used Vermont's bid in its bid for the prime contract.

Among the key elements of the BCI-Vermont contract was Article IV which stated:

> Subcontractor shall ... prosecute the work ... in a prompt and diligent manner, and ... where necessary to expedite the performance thereof, the authorized representative of subcontractor shall take orders directly from the Superintendent of Contractor. Subcontractor shall do the several parts of the work at such times and such order as Contractor shall direct and shall proceed with and wholly finish the work in such time as not to delay Contractor or other Subcontractors, and to ensure completion of the Prime Contract within the time fixed therein; ... it being understood that time is of the essence of this Agreement.[147]

A rider represented that BCI would prepare an anticipated construction schedule outlining the work to be accomplished by each subcontractor to ensure completion of the project as required by the contract, and that a disputes clause which permitted Vermont to submit claims for additional costs due to owner-caused obstructions or delays or contractor-caused unreasonable delays to the work would be present. The subcontract was executed on February 15, 1978.

A critical path method schedule was prepared which accommodated all trades sufficiently to permit completion of the project within the limits of the prime contract and milestones. Despite the schedule, performance under the contract lagged. The delays prevented Vermont from commencing the stone installation until sometime in the Fall of 1979, and from beginning the major portion of the work until the Spring of 1980 — too late to meet the completion date of Milestone 5.

There were many factors which contributed to the delay. One major cause was the mislocation of anchor bolts in the foundation with which the superstructure was attached. The previous prime contractor under Phase II, the foundation work, was responsible for the mislocations. Another cause of delay was the improper coordination of steel erection and installation of metal floor decking. Stone installation could not commence until structural steel erection, metal decking, and concrete had been completed sufficiently to permit erection of scaffolds for the masons. Further, the architect ordered changes in the work to preserve the Belmont House, a historic structure located at the Southeast corner of the jobsite. Despite the delays, throughout 1979, Vermont maintained a job presence and willingness to proceed with stone installation when the work was ready.

The major portion of the project, the extension building, was not sufficiently completed to allow commencement of stonework in the agreed-upon sequence until the Spring of 1980. BCI contended, however, that the lesser portion of the work, the central wing, was ready for stonework in the Fall of 1979. BCI claimed that the central wing, a relatively small and largely separate portion of the Dirksen project, could have accepted stone by Mid-November, 1979. Vermont disputed this and claimed that regardless, the stone installation was sequenced by the readiness of the extension building. Vermont claimed that the central wing stonework was to commence a bit earlier than the extension building stonework and argued that commencing stonework out of the originally intended sequence on the central wing in mid-November, 1979, would only have converted a 15-month job into a 20-month job.

On October 26, 1979, Vermont wrote to BCI stating its belief that there had been unreasonable delays in commencement of stonework. Vermont stated its intention to rescind the contract if the delays were the contractor's fault. On November 16, 1979, Vermont withdrew from the site. On December 12, 1979, Vermont notified BCI by letter that it would henceforth treat the subcontract as rescinded.

BCI, prior to Vermont's rescission, suggested alternate sequencing of the stonework, and prior and succeeding activities in order to partially overcome the previous delays. Vermont refused to consider methods or sequences which deviated from the original CPM schedule. Vermont reasoned that the delays amounted to a material breach of the subcontract and gave Vermont the alternate remedies to terminate the subcontract or perform and sue for breach damages.

The court concluded that Vermont wrongfully rescinded the contract. The court felt that the BCI-Vermont subcontract anticipated the uncertainties which face participants in large construction projects such as the Dirksen project. The parties in Article IV and the disputes clause provided for their respective rights and obligations under various circumstances which might arise during the performance of the work. Because the details of the circumstances were unknown, the parties used general language to guide them in as broad a range of situations as possible.

Vermont alleged that the phrase ". . . time is of the essence of this Agreement" which appeared in Article IV entitled Vermont to rescind the contract when any slippage from the agree-upon performance dates occurred. The court found other parts of the contract belied the assertion that any delay gave rise to a right to rescind. For instance, the disputes clause provided Vermont was to submit a *claim* if Vermont's work was obstructed or delayed by actions of the owner. At least, when delays were attributed to the owner, rescission was not an option available to Vermont. The court found rescission as a remedy became available only when the remedies provided by other subcontract clauses failed. Since the other remedies had not failed, rescission as a remedy was not available to Vermont. To permit rescission would have "grossly warped and [effectively] diluted" [148] the other remedies of the contract.

Perhaps more importantly, to permit rescission would have eliminated the contractor's opportunities to control the project. The disputes clause and other remedies provided in the contract gave Vermont fair compensation for out-of-sequence work while permitting the project to continue uninterrupted by recalcitrant subcontractors walking away from their subcontracts. To permit rescission would have denied the prime contractor the control necessary to move the work along. Thus, subcontractors should not (if *Vermont Marble Co. v. Baltimore Contractors, Inc.* is followed) refuse to perform out-of-sequence work as long as other adequate remedies are available under the contract.

What happens when the remedies provided under the contract fail to provide adequate compensation for subcontractors required to perform out-of-sequence work? *Blake Construction Co. v. C.J. Coakley Co.*[149] examines such a situation.

Blake Construction Co. and U.S. Industries, Inc., as joint venturers, bid on and were awarded a contract as the general contractor by the Baltimore District Corps of Engineers for the construction of the new Walter Reed Hospital in the District of Columbia. The contract for $102,321,000 was executed on July 28, 1972. Blake was the managing partner of the joint venture.

C.J. Coakley was a subcontractor who provided sprayed-on fireproofing on structural steel in buildings under construction. Coakley submitted a $638,500 bid to Blake prior to Blake's bid to the Baltimore Corps for the sprayed fireproofing work. After award, Blake informed Coakley that Coakley's initial bid was too high and that fireproofing of tubes around hangar rods in the interstitial floors had been added to the work. After a physical inspection of the work, Coakley negotiated and executed a subcontract with Blake-USI for the fireproofing on July 9, 1974, in the amount of $570,000. Coakley assumed that its workmen could stand on the interstitial floors while applying the fireproofing to certain surfaces.

Specification 9K/6.6 of the prime contract (included in Coakley's subcontract) provided that ducts, piping or conduit, or other suspended equipment that could interfere with the uniform application of the fireproofing material was to be positioned after the application of sprayed fireproofing. The subcontract also obligated Blake to provide all heat necessary to heat tarpaulin enclosures free of charge. Blake was further obligated to make partial payments to Coakley if satisfactory progress was made in performance of the work.

Article 2(a) required Coakley to prosecute its work "in accordance with progress schedules prepared and issued to the subcontractor by the contractor."[150] Article 2(b) provided that the progress schedules might be changed from time to time and gave Coakley a right to request in writing extensions of time in which to perform under the subcontract. The contract did not, however, specify the manner in which the construction schedule was to sequence Coakley's or any other subcontractor's work. Article 23(a) gave Blake the right to make changes in Coakley's work in exchange for appropriate adjustments in the contract price.

Fireproofing is a process of spraying a water-saturated mixture of gypsum, vermiculite, and other additives onto structural steel, rods, and tubes. The fireproofing drys into a soft material susceptible to damage by water and abrasion. The fireproofing should be applied with spray nozzles at a uniform distance from the structural steel. Interrupted application causes the fireproofing material to congeal inside the spray nozzle and makes the spray either less efficient or inoperable until it is cleaned. The fireproofing material that does not adhere falls to the ground and must be removed. Spraying at more or less than the optimum distance increases the amount of material that does not adhere and cleanup costs increase. Fireproofing drys at a rate determined by the temperature and humidity.

Blake prepared a critical path method schedule as required by the contract. Soon, however, the work sequence on the hospital was at considerable variance with that proposed on the initial schedule. Due to delays in ordering and receiving structural steel, the steel superstructure, roof, and interstitial floors were not in place at an early stage in the construction as intended by Blake's initial CPM. Other trades began their work at earlier stages in the construction process than had been planned on the floors for which the structural steel had been delivered and erected.

§ 4-11   CONSTRUCTION SCHEDULES

Among the work which was installed earlier than scheduled was the installation of pipes, ducts, and electrical conduits. Some of this work was attached to the structural steel. Simultaneous work mingled several trades and created crowded work areas. Because fireproofing had to be installed in free work areas, Coakley often had to shift his men from floor to floor rather than completing work on a systematic, scheduled, floor-by-floor basis. Because the interstitial floors were not in place, Coakley had to rent and erect scaffolding from which its workers could spray portions of the structural steel. Since the roof and windows were missing, water fell on completed fireproofing and damaged it. Various change orders further disrupted Coakley's performance. Other subcontractors' work and change order work damaged fireproofing that had already been applied. Blake did not provide heat on all requested occasions and when heat was provided, the heat sources were often taken by other subcontractors. The work deviated from Blake's initial scheduled sequence.

From the moment Coakley began work, it advised Blake orally and by letter that Coakley's work was unable to be performed as originally contemplated. Pipes, ducts, and piping were installed before fireproofing in violation of specification 9K/6.6. Coakley advised additional compensation for the impediments was required. Although Blake did not formally respond to Coakley's letters, Blake did advise the duct and piping subcontractors that their work was interfering with the fireproofing. No effective steps were taken, however, to stop those subcontractors from continuing to install duct and pipe in a manner which interfered with Coakley.

On February 14, 1975, Coakley temporarily suspended work, citing Blake's non-compliance with specification 9K. Blake ordered Coakley in May and June, 1976, to complete patchwork of the fireproofing that had become unattached from the steel due to change order work and other subcontractor damage, but provided no assurance of additional compensation for such patchwork. Coakley agreed to do only that patching required under its contract. Blake repeated its order to Coakley to perform all patching and threatened to do the work itself and withhold further payment from Coakley if Coakley refused.

On June 18, 1976, Coakley gave notice of its intent to suspend work on the project in 72 hours due to Blake's improper conduct under the subcontract. Coakley thereafter removed its material and equipment from the jobsite and Blake completed the fireproofing work. Coakley sued Blake for $717,072 representing past payment requisitions and extra work costs.

The trial court determined that Blake did not provide a reasonably clear and convenient work area to Coakley, thus impeding Coakley's work and increasing its performance costs. The trial court also found that Blake failed to sequence the work so as to permit Coakley to perform under the subcontract and also caused damage to Coakley's work by allowing other subcontractors to take space heaters. Blake's mechanical subcontractor had been authorized by letter to install duct, pipe, and electrical conduits in advance of the fireproofing work in violation of Specification 9K/6.6. The trial court concluded that Blake had breached implicit and explicit provisions of Coakley's subcontract.

Blake appealed. Blake alleged the trial court had erred in finding a breach of subcontract on the basis of an implied duty to schedule work reasonably, when the contract was silent in what work sequence the contract was to be completed. Since the subcontract had required Coakley to work "as directed," Blake argued that there was no implied duty to schedule work to suit Coakley's convenience. The Appellate Court upheld the trial court's findings. It found implicit a duty by Blake not to prevent performance by Coakley. Despite the necessary flexibility in the manner of completion which a construction project imposes on the several contractors, the Appellate Court found Blake had exceeded the necessary latitude of discretionary action in construction contracts. The Appellate Court found sufficient evidence to indicate that Blake hindered and prevented Coakley's performance and agreed with the trial court that Blake had breached the subcontract. The Appellate Court found Coakley had acted properly in discontinuing performance under the subcontract.

§ 4-12. The Schedule as Notice.

One of the most significant aspects of the project schedule is its potential use as notice of changed conditions and delay. Although courts considering the issue have not always accepted the schedule as implied (if not actual) notice of performance deviations, the prudent builder (whether designer, owner, or contractor), will not overlook this possible use of the project schedule.

In *Lane-Verdugo*[151] the Armed Forces Board of Contract Appeals considered the contractor suggestions that its CPM schedules, periodically updated and submitted to the Corps of Engineers, be considered sufficient notice to satisfy the notice requirements for the Suspension of Work clause in Standard Form 23A (April 1961 edition). Although the Board refused to find the updated schedules adequate notice, the Board's logic in refusing to consider the updated schedules as notice is enlightening.

Lane-Verdugo, a joint venture, was awarded two contracts by the Corps of Engineers. The first was a $650,325.00 contract to construct a masonry addition to an armament and electronics plant and a pre-engineered steel building addition to an aircraft engine inspection and repair shop. Six change orders were issued to the contract which increased the contract price by $82,187.45 and extended the contract completion date by thirty calendar days. The second contract required Lane-Verdugo to construct seven additions to various existing buildings plus a new squadron operations building and two new aircraft weapons calibration shelters for $565,732. Ten change orders were issued to the second contract which increased the contract price by $17,031.17 and extended the time for completion of the aircraft weapons calibration shelters.

In addition to the standard suspension of work clause (November 1961) the contract provided:

> GC-5. Progress Charts, and Requirements for Overtime Work.
> b. If, in the opinion of the Contracting Officer, the Contractor falls behind the progress schedule, the Contractor shall take such steps as shall be necessary to improve his progress and the Contracting Officer may require him to increase the number of shifts, and/or overtime operations, days of work, and/or the amount of construction plant, and to submit for approval such supplementary schedule or schedules in chart form as may be deemed necessary to demonstrate the manner in which the agreed rate of progress will be regained, all without additional cost to the Government.

Both contracts also required Lane-Verdugo to furnish and maintain a critical path schedule, updated and furnished to the government monthly.

For various reasons work fell behind schedule. The contractor wrote the government, in response to government directives to increase men and equipment according to GC-5, claimed entitlement to time extensions, and stated that a revised CPM which would show the impact of the claimed delays would be forwarded. Two years later the contractor submitted a revised CPM which showed the effect of the delays and requested an equitable adjustment of some $162,000.00.

In its pleadings and briefs, Lane-Verdugo claimed that the government was on actual notice of the various claimed delays as they occurred. In rebuttal, government engineers stated that the contractor did not request an extension of time in its change order proposals. Further, government engineers testified that the various delays claimed by the contractor did not extend the performance time. The reasons for late completion was late delivery of a contractor-furnished, pre-engineered metal building and contractor-furnished open web steel joists.

Lane-Verdugo's primary evidence to measure the claimed delay was several critical path networks. Some of the networks were prepared during performance and others subsequent to completion to support the contractor's claim. It was Lane-Verdugo's position that the networks that were prepared during the performance of the work and submitted to the government in accordance with contract requirements, constituted notice to the government that the contractor was being delayed because of government action. The contractor testified that critical path networks and print-outs were usually submitted to the government on a monthly basis. However, not all the updates were submitted as evidence. Only selected networks were presented and accompanying computer print-outs were not provided for most of those presented. The contractor also submitted two transmittal sheets of the CPM's. One included the note that "these schedules have been revised to show the effect of delays to date on contract completion dates." [152]

However, the contractor's proof included no testimony or documentation which established how the critical path networks indicated the specific claims. In fact, many of the logic diagrams which purported to show the effect of the delays contained errors. For instance, activity sequences in the form of a subnetwork to demonstrate a delay were added, but the same activities were not eliminated from the original logic, this presented an apparent duplication. No explanation of the apparent duplication was offered. Thus, claimed delays seemed to run concurrently with the initial estimate of time. Throughout the updates, notwithstanding changes in the status of the work, no change in the initial estimates of time required to accomplish the work was made. No change in the amount of time it actually took to accomplish the work was made, either. Thus, the updates which were intended to show the effects of delays indicated many items were performed exactly within the time initially estimated. The Board found that all the activities were not updated monthly and that the networks did not accurately show the status of the work at the end of each month.

The Board concluded that the errors in the schedules presented serious questions as to the adequacy of the purported notice. The networks were updated to show delays in the work but the contractor presented no evidence to indicate the responsibility for the delays. The Board observed that construction delays are not unusual, some are caused by the government, some by the designer, and some by the contractor. The contractor's updated schedules, however, failed to indicate by whose fault the delays were caused. The mere fact that the critical path networks and associated printouts showed an estimated completion date later than that called for in the contract cannot be construed as notice of government delay sufficient to comply with the suspension of work clause. For these reasons, the Board held the updated schedules to be insufficient notice of delay.

The Court in *Vanderlinde Electric Corp. v. Rochester* [153] permitted the contractor to use updated schedules submitted monthly to the owner as evidence of notice of alleged delay. Vanderlinde had two contracts to provide electrical and instrumentation work for the City of Rochester's expansion of its sewage treatment plant, one contract was for liquid processing facilities, another for sludge processing facilities. Neither project was completed on time. Vanderlinde brought a claim against the City. Rochester, in its defense, asserted that Vanderlinde failed to file timely, written notices of intention to make claims under the contract.

General Conditions 58(a) of both contracts provided:

> If the Contractor claims compensation for any damages sustained by reason of any act or omission of the City, its agent, or employees, or of any other person, or for any other reason whatsoever, he shall, within five days after such claim shall have arisen, file with the Commissioner written notice of his intention to make claim for such damages, stating in such notice the nature and amount of the damages sustained and the basis of the claim against the City . . . the filing by the Contractor of a notice of claim . . . shall be a condition precedent . . . to the right to resort to any other remedy, proceeding, or action. The failure of the Contractor to file a notice of claim . . . shall be deemed to be a conclusive and binding determination on his part that he has no claim against the City for . . . compensation for damages . . . and shall be deemed a waiver by the Contractor of all claims for additional compensation or for damages.

Included in Vanderlinde's proof was presentation of documentary and oral evidence of the critical path method schedules used throughout the project. The schedules had been updated monthly and submitted to the City. The schedules reflected the regular postponement of the project's completion date from 1972 to 1976.

The Court concluded it was "clear from the record" that Rochester had been "fully and continuously aware of delays which stalled" the projects. The Court found Rochester had a continuing duty to inquire into the causes of delay and to minimize potential damages despite the City's argument that notice was required so that the cause of delay could be investigated and avoidable damages limited. The Court further stated that the language of the notice clause which required the contractor to include the amount of the damages it sustained in the notice, a condition impossible to meet until the damages are ascertained; and that the delays during the original contract term might not have risen to a claim if Vanderlinde had met the scheduled completion date.

For updated schedules to constitute notice of delay, the updates must be shown to reasonably call attention to the delay. In *Vanderlinde,* all the updates were submitted along with documentary and oral evidence of critical path method schedules and the updates were accepted as notice of delay. In *Lane-Verdugo,* not all the updates were submitted and no testimony or explanation of how the updates showed delays was offered. In fact, since neither the initial time estimates nor actual start or finish dates were recorded the updates showed many activities were completed exactly as originally planned. The *Lane-Verdugo* court refused to find the updated schedules a notice of delay. The updated schedules in *Vanderlinde* reasonably called attention to the delay while the updates in *Lane-Verdugo* did not.

§ 4-13. Improvements in Contract Scheduling Requirements.

The most frequent and significant error made in the interpretation of scheduling clauses occurs when the dates in a schedule are made a commitment rather than a guide. Schedules are developed according to industry standards to establish the sequential order of the work activities; to provide direction and control of work; to anticipate the need for material, equipment, and labor; and to facilitate project coordination. Schedules are not developed to identify four hundred or two thousand (or whatever the number of construction activities contained in the schedule) completion dates. The only committed dates existing in a construction schedule are the project completion and intermittent milestone dates established by the general conditions or the contractor. Schedules are planning tools, not contract commitments.

The court in *Dobson v. Rutgers* erred when it adopted the position that schedules may not vary with time. The court in *Natkin & Co. v. George A. Fuller Co.* deviated from industry practice in finding that the failure to schedule and control the work in accordance with the CPM schedule permitted recovery. The Federal Aviation Agency Contract Appeals Panel in *Chaney & James Construction Co.* erred when it refused to accept a schedule until it was demonstrated that the work sequence shown was the only possible way in which the work could be accomplished. The court in *Steenberg Construction Co. v. Prepakt Concrete Co.* erred when it stated that a contractor must meet a schedule as a condition precedent to a subcontractor performing its part of a contract. Although all courts have not adopted such interpretations of construction schedules, of the courts that have considered the question enough have failed to recognize schedules as planning tools to suggest standard contract scheduling clauses should be changed to clearly identify the industry's use of schedules as guides.

Further, courts and boards have identified scheduling clauses' failure to assign the ownership of float. Standard scheduling clauses should be amended to provide to whom the benefit of float accrues: the Contractor, the Owner, or the Project.

Standard scheduling clauses should be amended to clarify the role of project scheduling. This may be accomplished by adding a recital at the beginning of the clause which states the function the schedule is intended to serve. For instance:

> The construction progress schedule as herein used is intended to assist both the Contractor and Owner in

timely completion of the Project and to assist the Owner in its administration of the Project by establishing a sequential order and duration of construction activities by which the Project may be completed. As construction progresses it is recognized that both the sequential order and duration of the schedule may be changed to reflect improved means, methods, and techniques or to compensate for unanticipated occurrences which act to extend the time of performance.

Compare the recital used in the scheduling clause interpreted in *Dobson v. Rutgers.* There, the schedule was identified as "an aid ... to bring the completion of the project within the time allocated." The General Contractor was to "incorporate and enforce (the) schedule." Each Contractor agreed to "coordinate his own operations in order to meet effectively all scheduled task deadlines." With words such as these, understanding how the court misinterpreted and applied such an inflexible standard is easy.

In addition, words in the standard scheduling clauses that imply definiteness in the sequence, duration, start, or finish of portions of the work should be eliminated and suitable words describing the flexibility inherent in these elements of the scheduling process substituted in their stead. For instance, ASPR Clause "Progress Charts and Requirements for Overtime Work" should eliminate the words "the date on which he will start the several salient features ... and the contemplated dates for completing the same." Substitution for them should be "the dates which the Contractor's proposed schedule indicates the several salient features ... may be started or finished."

Further, it is suggested that standard scheduling clauses should assign the ownership of float to the project with the contracting officer or owner's representative determining how and when float is used: "Float shall belong to the

Project. The Contracting Officer shall determine when the float shall be used, the amounts to be allocated, and whether the Government shall receive the benefits of float." Disputes concerning the contracting officer's allocation of float may be resolved through existing contractual procedures under the Disputes Clauses. Unfortunately, our experience is such that the contracting officer will never adequately perform this job. There will be disputes and disputes. It is, however, probably the better way (under the circumstances) rather than the best way (which may never be determined).

Scheduling clauses should also permit sufficient time to develop the schedule. Contractors should be permitted to plan and formulate the best method in which the work can be completed. Recent studies, among them one conducted by the Department of Energy in 1979,[154] indicate a substantial amount of craftsmen's time is lost at the project site due to the contractor's inability to plan and manage the work. It is in the owner's best interest to give the contractor adequate time to develop a plan to complete the work and communicate that plan, through a schedule, to those responsible for implementing it. The authors recommend that forty-five to sixty days be allowed the contractor from contract award to the required submission of a schedule to permit the oft neglected planning.

In private, municipal, and state construction, because of the myriad of scheduling clauses possible and the authority of the people drafting the contract, it may be easy to implement such suggestions. However, federal scheduling clauses may be more difficult to change, since changes to standard forms require amending the applicable procurement regulations. Changes in standard federal scheduling clauses may also serve to guide similar changes in non-federal construction due to the influence federal standards have on other construction contracts and therefore the effort may be worthwhile.

The authors suggest the mandatory scheduling clause required under ASPR contracts [155] should be modified as follows:

PROGRESS CHARTS AND REQUIREMENTS FOR OVERTIME WORK

(a) The construction progress schedule as herein used is intended to assist both the Contractor and Government in timely completion of the Project and to assist the Government in its administration of the Project by establishing a sequential order and duration of construction activities by which the Project may be completed. As construction progresses it is recognized that both the sequential order and duration of the schedule may be changed to reflect improved knowledge means, methods, and techniques or to compensate for unanticipated occurrences which act to extend the time of performance.

(b) The Contractor shall within 60 days or within such time as determined by the Contracting Officer, after date of notice to proceed, prepare, and submit to the Contracting Officer for approval a practical schedule, showing the order in which the Contractor proposes to carry on the work and the dates on which the several salient features (including procurement of materials, plant, and equipment) may be started or finished. The schedule shall include a chart of suitable scale to indicate appropriately the percentage of work scheduled for completion at any time. The Contractor shall enter on the chart the actual progress at such intervals as directed by the Contracting Officer, and shall immediately deliver to the Contracting Officer three copies thereof. If the Contractor fails to submit a progress schedule within the time herein prescribed, the Contracting Officer may withhold approval of progress payment estimates until such time as the Contractor submits the required progress schedule.

(c) Float shall belong to the Project. The Contracting Officer shall determine when the float shall be used, the amounts to be allocated, and whether the Government or Contractor shall receive the benefit of float. The contractor shall have the right to request additional monies if the use of float by the government adversely effects the cost to the contractor. No contract adjustment will accrue to the government as to use of float so long as the project is timely completed. (Remainder of clause remains unchanged.)

Federal Procurement Regulations [156] should also be amended to include such a clause.

Municipal and State governments which have adopted the Model Procurement Code [157] may utilize it to provide for scheduling clauses similar to the suggested ASPR clause. The Model Procurement Code provides a statutory framework for the fundamentals of sound procurement and follows the concept that those fundamentals should be implemented by regulations consistent with the statutory framework.[158] Section 5-401, Contract Clauses and Their Administration, states:

> (1) Contract Clauses. The Policy Office shall promulgate regulations requiring the inclusion in state construction contracts of clauses providing for adjustments in prices, time of performance, *or other contract provisions,* as appropriate. . . .[159] (Emphasis added.)

The phrase "or other contract provisions" is intended to enable the parties to deal with the effects of changes, variations in estimated quantities, suspensions of work, and differing site conditions which most certainly would affect the manner of performance as controlled by a construction schedule.[160]

Other scheduling clauses may be similarly modified. For instance, the AIA clause, A201 4.10.1, needs only the identification of float ownership since the existing clause is sufficiently indefinite to eliminate concern of activity completion dates being interpreted as a commitment. In modifying scheduling clauses, courts and administrative boards will be better able to interpret and enforce them in a manner consistent with the industry's practice.

However, even with a perfect scheduling clause, it is far better to settle a delay dispute than risk the court deciding what scheduling is about. The authors give this advice sincerely hoping it will not be lost on the reader because similar thoughts are regularly repeated by others. Repetition should not diminish the significance of the advice. Review carefully the words of Judge Holcombe Thomas in *E.C. Ernst, Inc. v. Manhattan Construction Co.*[161] describing that construction dispute:

> Gentlemen, this is a case which should be settled between the parties. In present day thinking, it seems to be the idea that any problem can be cured in a Federal District Court. This, I assure you, is an erroneous approach.... Lawyers in their zeal to represent their clients many times fail to see but one side of the litigation and that is the side of his client. This litigation is not a one-sided bit of litigation.... You litigants are in a fairly closely related field. Being trained in this field, you are in a far better position to adjust your differences than those untrained in these related fields. As an illustration, I, who have had no training whatsoever in engineering, had to determine whether or not the emergency generator system proposed to be furnished by Fairbanks-Morse, met the specifications, when experts couldn't agree. That is a strange bit of logic....
>
> The object of litigation is to do substantial justice between the parties litigant, but the parties litigant should realize that, in most situations, they are by their particular training better able to accomplish this among themselves....[162]

Despite Judge Thomas' warning to the parties, the decision reports:

> The case was not settled, and the trial was commenced on August 6, 1973. It entailed 40 days of court time, 41 witnesses (34 live and 7 by deposition) and 1,056 exhibits. Presentation of the evidence was finally concluded on November 27, 1973. Thereafter, the

litigants were given until the 28th day of January, 1974, within which to file Findings of Fact and Conclusions of Law. This time was extended to February 11, 1974. The Court after studying these Findings and Conclusions set the matter for final argument on May 22, 1974, each litigant being given one hour's time. The pre-trial order entered in this case on the 26th day of April, 1975, and amended on the 6th day of July, 1975.[163]

---

33. 347 F. Supp. 17 (W.D. Mo. 1972).
34. 67-2 BCA ¶ 6624 (1967).
35. *Id.,* at 30,715.
36. 157 N.J. Super. 357, 384 A.2d 1121 (1978).
37. *Id.,* at 1126.
38. 355 F. Supp. 376 (S.D. Iowa 1973).
39. *Id.,* at 388.
40. 75-1 BCA ¶ 11,261 (1975).
41. *Id.,* at 53-685.
42. Natkin & Co. v. George A. Fuller Co., *supra* note 33, at 21.
43. 72-2 BCA ¶ 9599 (1972).
44. *Id.,* at 44,857.
45. "Modification Impact Evaluation Guide," Department of the Army, Office of the Chief of Engineers, EP-415-1-3 at 3-2 (July, 1979). (Hereinafter cited as Modification Guide.)
46. 75-2 BCA ¶ 11,563 (1975).
47. J. Wickwire, P. Walstead, & T. Asselin, "Project Scheduling," in 3 *The Briefing Papers Collection,* 233, 237 (1975). (Hereinafter cited as J. Wickwire.)
48. *See generally* Lee Turzillo Contracting Co. v. Frank Messer & Sons, Inc., 23 Ohio App. 2d 179, 261 N.E.2d 675 (1969); and William Passalacqua Builders, Inc., 77-1 BCA ¶ 12,406 (1977).
49. 382 N.E.2d 453, at 460 (Ill. 1978).
50. 429 A.2d 403 (N.J. Super. 1981).
51. 436 F.2d 632 (1st Cir. 1971).
52. *Id.,* at 637.
53. Blackhawk Heating & Plumbing Co., *supra* note 40, at 53,676.
54. 66-2 BCA ¶ 6066 (1966).
55. 73-2 BCA ¶ 10,271 (1973).
56. *Id.,* at 48,512.

57. *Supra* note 36, at 1138.
58. 79-1 BCA ¶ 13,571 (1979).
59. *Id.,* at 66,479.
60. *Supra* note 38.
61. *Id.,* at 95.
62. 381 F.2d 768 (10th Cir. 1967).
63. Natkin & Co. v. George A. Fuller Co., *supra* note 33, at 30.
64. Dobson v. Rutgers, *supra* note 36, at 1146.
65. Modification Guide, *supra* note 45, at 3-8.
66. Peter Kiewit Sons' Co. v. Iowa Southern Utilities, *supra* note 38, at 380.
67. *Id.*
68. *Id.,* at 391.
69. 334 F.2d 122 (8th Cir. 1964).
70. *Id.,* at 125.
71. *Id.,* at 127.
72. *Id.,* at 126.
73. 436 F.2d 632 (1st Cir. 1971).
74. 382 N.E.2d 453 (Ill. 1978).
75. *Id.,* at 456.
76. *Id.*
77. Economy Mechanical Indus., Inc., *supra* note 58, at 66,479.
78. *Id.*
79. *Id.,* at 66,479.
80. *Id.,* at 66,478.
81. 476 F. Supp. 729 (W.D. Pa. 1979).
82. *Id.,* at 736.
83. *Id.*
84. *Id.,* at 740.
85. *Id.,* at 745-46.
86. *Id.,* at 748.
87. *Id.,* at 756.
88. 372 A.2d 540 (Del. 1977).
89. 526 F.2d 108 (10th Cir. 1975).
90. *Id.,* at 113.
91. *Id.,* at 116.
92. J. Wickwire, *supra* note 47, at 238.
93. Modification Guide, *supra* note 45, at 3-6.
94. *Supra* note 40, at 53,676.
95. 1963 BCA ¶ 3819 (1963).
96. 454 F.2d 1203 (10th Cir. 1972).

97. Natkin & Co. v. George A. Fuller Co., *supra* note 33, at 31.
98. 1963 BCA ¶ 3881 (1963).
99. 387 F. Supp. 1001 (S.D. Ala. 1974).
100. H. Hohns, *Preventing and Solving Construction Contracts Disputes* 73 (1st ed. 1979).
101. *Id.*
102. Continental Consolidated Corp., *supra* note 34 at 30,716.
103. 72-1 BCA ¶ 9364 (1972).
104. *Id.*, at 43,457.
105. *Supra* note 99.
106. *Supra* note 81.
107. *Id.*, at 748.
108. *Supra* note 55.
109. *Id.*, at 48,511.
110. 77-1 BCA ¶ 12-406 (1977).
111. *Id.*, at 60,090.
112. *Id.*, at 60,085.
113. *Supra* note 40.
114. *Id.*, at 53,677.
115. 70-2 BCA ¶ 8437 (1970).
116. Natkin & Co. v. George A. Fuller Co., *supra* note 33, at 31.
117. J. Wickwire, *supra* note 47, at 237.
118. *Id.*, citing Fullerton Constr. Co.
119. J. Wickwire, *supra* note 47, at 237.
120. Dobson v. Rutgers, *supra* note 36.
121. 79-1 BCA ¶ 13,855 (1979).
122. *Supra,* note 81, at 736.
123. *Id.*, at 737.
124. *Supra* note 62.
125. *Supra* note 88.
126. 431 A.2d 569, 575 (D.C. App. 1981).
127. *Supra* note 33, at 30.
128. 67-2 BCA ¶ 6624 (1967).
129. 73-2 BCA ¶ 10,271 (1973).
130. 75-2 BCA ¶ 11,563 (1975).
131. *Supra* note 49.
132. The *Pathman* court misunderstood the effect of time extensions on construction schedules. Each time extension will affect all subcontractor work, except of course completed work, by extending the date of project completion and providing additional float time.
133. Wickwire & Smith, "The Use of Critical Path Method Techniques in Contract Claims," 7 Pub. Cont. L.J. 1, 43-45 (1974).

134. 76-1 BCA ¶ 11,649 (1975).
135. A.L. Corbin, 3 Contracts § 570, at 346 (1960).
136. Blake Constr. Co. v. C.J. Coakley Co., *supra* note 126, at 576.
137. 62 F. Supp. 312 (Ct. Cl. 1945).
138. 205 F.2d 607 (8th Cir. 1953).
139. 389 F.2d 1007 (Ct. Cl. 1967).
140. *Id.,* at 1009.
141. 212 N.W.2d 348 (Neb. 1973).
142. Natkin & Co. v. George A. Fuller Co., *supra* note 33.
143. *Supra* note 89.
144. *Id.,* at 113.
145. *Id.,* at 116.
146. 520 F. Supp. 922 (D.C.D.C. 1981).
147. *Id.,* at 924.
148. *Id.,* at 928.
149. *Supra* note 126.
150. *Id.,* at 572.
151. *Supra* note 55.
152. *Id.,* at 48,510.
153. 54 A.D.2d 155 (N.Y. 1976).
154. Garner, Borcherding, & Samelson, "Factors Influencing the Motivation and Productivity of Craftsmen and Foremen on Large Construction Projects," United States Department of Energy, Contract EQ-78-G-01-6333 (1979); *see generally* Parker & Oglesby, *Methods Improvement For Construction Managers* (1972).
155. 32 C.F.R. 7-603.48, "Progress Charts and Requirements for Overtime Work" (1976).
156. 41 C.F.R. Subtitle A (1976).
157. A Model Procurement Code for State and Local Governments, Final Draft for House of Delegates Approved, ABA (Dec. 15, 1978).
158. *Id.,* at vii.
159. *Id.,* at 38.
160. *Id.*
161. *Supra* note 99.
162. *Id.,* at 1005-1006.
163. *Id.,* at 1006.

CHAPTER 5

USING THE SCHEDULE TO PROVE TIME EXTENSIONS

Part of the claim epidemic which has swept the industry includes using CPM schedules to prove or disprove one's right to time extensions and to additional payment or occasionally reduction of payment. Tens of thousands of dollars are spent in construction contract disputes setting up CPM schedules and impacting them with delays and changes in scope "to prove the effect" of such on the duration and economics of the work.

The mystique of an impressive stack of computer printouts containing lists of information about schedules has unusual appeal to the construction attorney. The same addage that poor quality schedules are useless to help construct a project applies to proving a lawsuit, though it is far more difficult to convince an attorney or judge that poor logic renders the entire stack of computer printout totally valueless. They seem incapable of dismissing all that information as plainly wrong. Be sure you know the many arguments that have been won with totally useless CPM work as a key reference in the claim. It is therefore necessary to consider some of the techniques and drawbacks in "proving" delay claims. It is hoped that by presenting the authors' suggestions to prove or disprove a delay claim using a CPM schedule, the amount of useless computer studies will be reduced.

One should be aware that most of the learned journal treatments on how one proves and "wins" cases with CPM schedules use very limited arrow diagrams to demonstrate the writer's successful approach. It is relatively easy to describe how to show the effect of a change on a ten activity arrow diagram example. It is far different and often impossible to show the effect of a change on a detailed 1000 arrow network. Unfortunately the authors of these treatises showing how to prove delays with CPM do not deal with the real world problems created in degree of detail needed and available. In fact, since techniques for evaluating the impact of changes on the schedule are still in the formative stages, an in-depth experienced CPM construction-oriented person is required.

Regardless of what one thinks one can do with a CPM schedule, the impact of change on a construction job is best defined by a person who is well versed in scheduling mechanics but more importantly, simultaneously possesses the ability to judge what really went wrong with the construction process, and why. As an example, the Department of the Army's Office of the Chief of Engineers in its publication "Modification Impact Evaluation Guide," [164] suggests the following procedure to measure the impact of a change. The reader should note how the critical evaluations depend upon an understanding of the construction process distinct from the mechanics of scheduling.

First, the Army requires the current status of the job to be determined. The Chief of Engineers states that data on current job status should be developed without influence from the contractor's formal progress schedule. It is suggested that the contractor's real plan for pursuing the work may not be the same as that indicated on the formal schedule or the schedule may not have been revised to reflect the effects of previous modifications. For instance, some activities may start without regard to the sequence or time shown in the formal schedule; quality control and quality assurance reports may reveal past production inefficiency or delaying factors not shown on the formal schedule; or anticipated late delivery of materials which will delay parts of the work may be found. All will influence the current status of the job.

PROVE TIME EXTENSIONS

Further, the current status of the job requires the schedule reflect all changes to the original schedule regardless of the reasons for them. If all prior changes are not reflected in the schedule, the effect of the subject change may not be accurately measured. The progress schedule cannot be a valid tool to evaluate impact unless it reflects the current status of the job.

According to the Corps of Engineers, the next step is to analyze the scope of the modification to determine which remaining activities will be directly affected, that is, those activities having less work, more work, or other revisions. Have any activities been moved to an unfavorable weather season? Are more activities in progress at a given time than originally anticipated? Once the affected activities are identified, revised durations to accommodate the change are assigned.

If all or part of the work to be performed under a modification does not fit an existing activity, new activities tied to existing nodes can be created. The challenge is to find where the new activities will fit into the existing schedule. Prior restraining activities, material procurement, and weather must all be considered. Logic should be revised if any errors are found. When creating new activities or revising the existing logic one can see how important it is for the scheduler to be able to understand and judge the construction process.

The revised progress schedule now reflects the remaining work and the modification. Using durations previously assigned, new early start, early finish, late start, and late finish dates are calculated. The new calculations will indicate the revised time schedule for completing the project.

The Army suggests that now time extensions may be granted. The Chief of Engineers suggests no time extension permitted unless the project's critical path has changed;

that if non-critical activities with enough float to absorb the modified work is affected, the completion date will not change. The Chief of Engineers further suggests that a modification issued early in the job, before float time is depleted will usually not require a time extension. The Department of the Army claims the ownership of float. As discussed earlier, however, all who have considered the proposition do not agree that the owner controls the float. There exists well-reasoned arguments supporting contractor claims for the float. As one can see, the length of a time extension will depend on who owns the float. The Corps in its "Modification Impact Evaluation Guide" takes the position that it owns the float and thus argues for limited contractor time extensions.

The Army suggests that the schedule should be revised after each, separate modification. A revised schedule should become the basis upon which the next separate modification should be valuated. Once the new critical path has been established, the schedule may be analyzed for impacted unchanged activities.

The method suggested by the Chief of Engineers sounds easy, but is it? Even the Chief of Engineers cautions:

> Developing this schedule is not merely a mechanical exercise. *Many judgments must be made, and the schedule's reliability depends largely on their quality.* Personnel making such judgments must have thorough knowledge of the job site conditions, the contractor's capabilities and methods of operation, the schedule applicable before the modification occurred, the CPM scheduling system, and the Corps of Engineers' contractual liabilities pertaining to impact on the unchanged work. (Emphasis added.)[165]

The mechanics of scheduling will not indicate which activities will be affected by the change. Definition of affected activities will depend upon accurate judgment of the evaluator founded upon a firm construction background.

PROVE TIME EXTENSIONS

The Veterans Administration is another construction agency which publishes guidelines describing the preferred method of impacting a CPM schedule to show the effect of changes and delays.[166] Although similar to the Corps of Engineers, the methods recommended by the two agencies differ in several key areas.

Under the Veterans Administration method, the scope of changed or affected work is first reviewed to determine where and how the revisions should be incorporated in the schedule. The activity revisions and additions are then sketched on the current network. Work activities that will be performed by additional work forces are shown as being parallel with existing activities on the network. Activities to be performed by existing work forces are shown as sequential and inserted in series with an existing chain of work activities. The VA requires logic revisions to include separate activities for each involved trade and, if the activity occurs in more than one work area, separate activities for each involved area. In addition to activities which relate directly to the delay, network revisions which require modifications and adjustments caused by the change or delay should be defined and made.

The effect that changes or delays have a CPM schedule is determined by a comparison of the schedules before and after the delaying activities are incorporated in the network. Under the VA method, the contractor is only entitled to a time extension if the scheduled completion is delayed beyond the extended contract completion date. Changes to predicted completion dates which were earlier than the extended contract completion date do not qualify for time extensions.[167] The VA reduces the additional time required for changes and delays by all available float.

The VA analysis of the change is a step-by-step procedure. First, the float for the existing activities is determined. The predicted and extended contract completion

CONSTRUCTION SCHEDULES

dates are then compared and the number of work days ahead or behind are determined. Two forward passes are made to see whether the project duration was changed. The first forward pass is made on the existing network without any consideration for the changed or delayed work activities. The second forward pass includes the changed or delayed activities in the calculation. The difference between the two forward passes are reduced by existing float. A new predicted project completion date is defined and compared to the extended contract completion date.[168] The difference is the workday delay to the contract which is converted to a calendar day justification for additional contract time.

The VA states that delays to the project due to strikes, weather, and other acts of God are the only scheduling problems that require an "after-the-fact" CPM analysis. The CPM information required for analysis of in-progress delays of this type cannot be known until the project resumes. All other delays and time extensions are inserted into the schedule as they occur.

One of the key areas where the VA and Corps differ in evaluating the effect of a change or delay to the schedule is the timing of the analysis. The Corps requires a step-by-step evaluation. The VA requires all CPM information for the alleged delays to be analyzed at one time rather than make separate calculations for each change.[169] The analysis must wait until all the contractor's requests for changes or delays have been submitted. The authors believe the step-by-step method of the Corps of Engineers to be superior.

A project is usually not built according to the strict I-J logic that assumes the preceding activity must be complete before the succeeding activity may start. As an example, masonry walls are usually built around metal doors and window frames. The door frames must be installed before the walls can be completed. This sequence is usually scheduled like this:

PROVE TIME EXTENSIONS

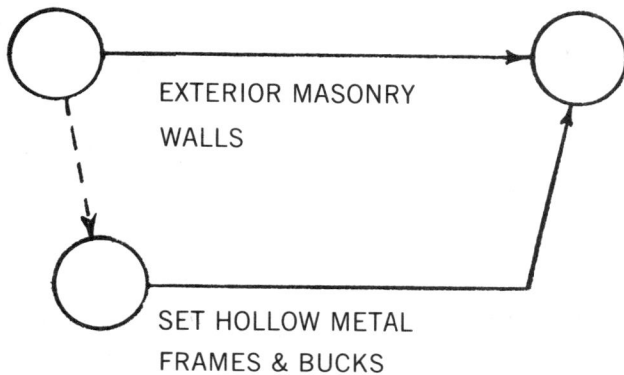

The schedule shows the work done at the same time, but not the required interaction. The door frames must be available shortly after the start of masonry work. Scheduling mechanics will indicate that a modification of the size of the door frames will affect the activity "Set Hollow Metal Frames and Bucks," but how will the "Exterior Masonry Walls" be affected? Only experience, judgment, and a knowledge of the status of the wall construction at the time of the modification can make that determination.

An error in judgment in impacting the schedule will not be immediately apparent on the revised schedule. Modification only to the "Hollow Metal Frame" activity will not indicate that "Exterior Masonry Walls" must also be affected. Only experience with the construction process will disclose the error. But the judgment error will be "supported" by impressive, revised logic diagrams and computer print-outs. Despite an error in judgment, an attack on it will be difficult because of the "back up." Would a computer lie?

The typical construction job is a place of constant crisis. All day long things go wrong. Equipment breaks down, people do not show up, everyone gets in everyone's way, delay and confusion abound. It is the ultimate environment filled with undetected error. The complexity of understanding the record to be able to decide what really went wrong requires more than an impacted CPM diagram.

Recall the analogy of a construction project to a battlefield in *Blake Construction Co. v. C.J. Coakley Co.* The District of Columbia Court of Appeals recognized the problem:

> ... except in the middle of a battlefield, nowhere must men coordinate the movement of other men and all materials in the midst of such chaos and with such limited certainty of present facts and future occurrences as in a huge construction project.... Even the most painstaking planning frequently turns out to be mere conjecture and accommodation to changes must necessarily be of the rough, quick and *ad hoc* sort, analogous to ever changing commands on the battlefield. Further, it is a difficult task for a court to be able to examine testimony and evidence in the quiet of a courtroom several years later concerning such confusion and then extract from them a determination of precisely when the disorder and constant readjustment, which is to be expected by any subcontractor on a job site, become so extreme, so debilitating and so unreasonable as to constitute a breach of contract between a contractor and a subcontractor.[170]

Take the case of a five-story apartment building. The initial CPM schedule along with all its logic shows the critical path in part to go through the sheet rock starting with the first floor, then through a planned crew shift or sequence to the second, third, fourth, fifth floors and then

PROVE TIME EXTENSIONS

through the fifth floor finish work to the end of the job. The critical path looks like this:

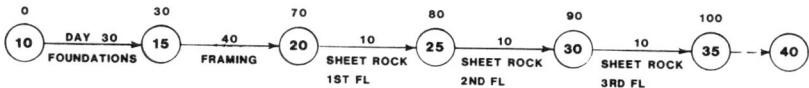

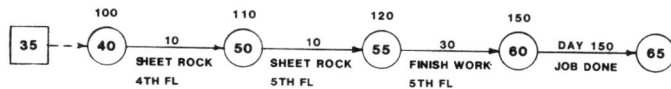

Now suppose the owner decided to totally change the first floor layout on day 65 and as a result 50 days go by before the sheet rock can start. A delay has occurred and its impact can be shown as follows.

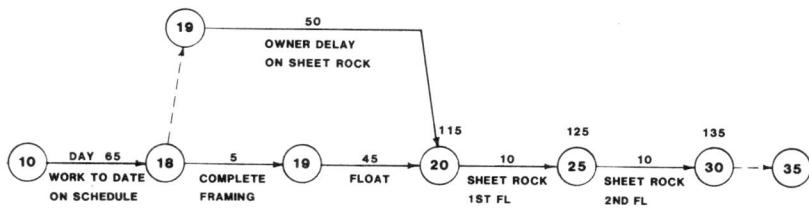

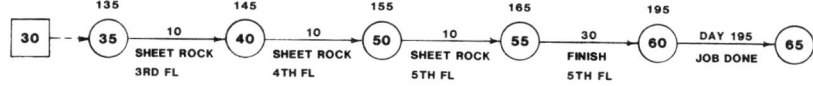

CONSTRUCTION SCHEDULES

Looks easy. Contractor is due a 45-day time increase and the added costs. However, suppose the contractor hearing about the owner's hold on the first floor, without telling anyone, started on the second floor at the same time it planned first to do the first floor, and finally suppose the contractor continued its work, finished the fifth floor and moved its crew down to floor one and finished the job on the same day 150. Now what's the contractor entitled to? The owner imposed a 45-day delay, the contractor worked out of sequence, the impacted CPM shows the contractor's due time and dollars. Real life reaction canceled the extra cost or most of it. Who pays for what? AIA 201 says the architect will decide. Good luck to the architect.

Suppose the contractor was behind schedule when the owner said a change was coming on the first floor and had only reached day 30 on the 70 days work it had planned before it could start sheet rocking the first floor. Now what? The impacted CPM says the contractor gets a reprieve; or is it due but a 10-day adjustment since it had already caused 35 days of delay on the project by itself? If the owner insists the latter is true and refuses to grant a longer time extension that ten days in spite of the contractor's demands, has acceleration been implied? Suppose the 70-day schedule logic was wrong? Suppose the contractor had already done some miraculous act to overcome its early stage lateness at high personal cost on day 61 and now can't be advantaged by that act? What if it rains while the sheet rock is going on? Suppose a carpenter strike occurs during the second floor sheet rocking? If the contractor had waited and kept its original sequence, the owner delay would have negated the strike effect. Who bears the risk of the strike? Suppose the work was late because it rained 35 days at the beginning? Suppose the contractor made more money by changing its sequence? Does the owner get a credit? Is a contractor really late until the job is done and the completion date missed?

Are you confused? Spread this type of question over a $50,000,000 project, four years, fifty entities, two to ten parties in the dispute and realize what the analyst faces as he works-up his as-built schedule.

Is a contractor entitled to recover the cost of owner changes on its bid concept of the work? Or are its economics actually existent at the moment of the change first being understood or directed? Or at the end of the job when all the errors have been experienced and all the economics have been recorded and mixed together so they cannot be separated?

Now add the vagueries of the court room or the intrinsic prejudices of the arbitration tribunal. Realize too there is no fixed answer. Each case, each dispute has to be regarded in its own parameters. What really happened? What does the contract language impose on what really happened? The federal government says that it will pay the contractor for the cost of a partial or full suspension of work starting twenty days before the contractor gives notice that cost is being increased but that no adjustment is due if concurrent delay exists because of contractor caused problems. The federal government won't permit any profit on suspension of work costs and will argue at times it has the right to suspend work to make time consuming changes since the contractor was behind anyway and thus no adjustment is due except the direct cost.

When does suspension of work become a constructive change? When does a constructive change become a cardinal change? When does a cardinal change become breach?

The potential of the meaning of the schedule becomes mind boggling.

How about another example? The logic below is a simple initial schedule. The schedule is perfect, free from errors in

CONSTRUCTION SCHEDULES

logic; all agree on it. The project is to be built in the desert and it never rains. Never, not one day, ever.

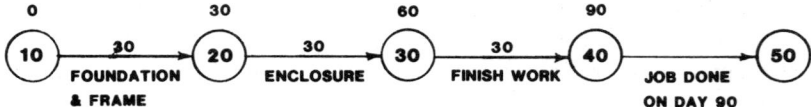

Guess what? It rains for 30 days starting the day the job is to start. Thus one can agree and impact the schedule.

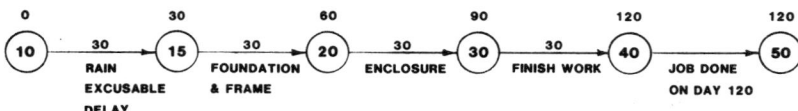

Suppose we did it this way.

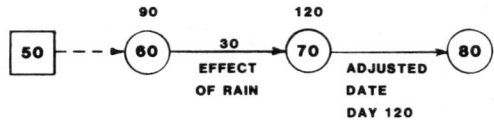

PROVE TIME EXTENSIONS

Is this correct? The answer is the same. The rain delay shown either way is probably all right. Rain is a mutual risk.

Suppose it rained 10 days during each work period. Now how do you show the delay? The second diagram can be correct. Why can't the first one be correct? Is this better?

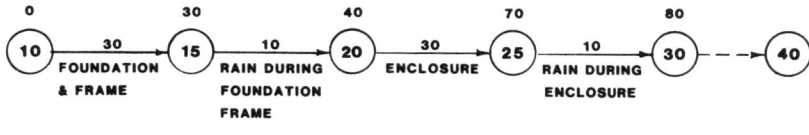

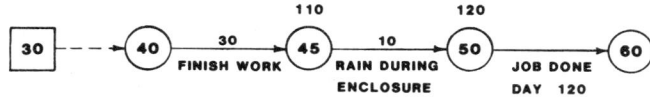

Again, one must realize there is no fixed way. Each problem requires judgement (and candor) to resolve. Let's go further, suppose that our desert job is such that the last scheduled 30 days consists of all finish work inside. On day 61 it starts to rain, the work is on schedule, the building is enclosed and weather tight, and all that is left is work inside. It rains 30 days. If either of the first two diagrams above is correct, then the contractor is due a 30-day extension. Does the contractor have the right to stay home? It never rained before in the desert. The contract says rain will be a reason for time extension. Silly you say? Come with us to the court room and see what is presented and argued and sustained.

CONSTRUCTION SCHEDULES

How about this approach? Imagine a $25,000,000 airport terminal. Now imagine the owner delays the pile foundations since the borings were found to be inaccurate and it takes two months longer to start piling; then the owner changes the roofing method eight months after the job started. It takes three extra months to get the new roof material. The day the job was originally scheduled to be completed, the owner adds what everyone agrees to be 16 months of new interior work. First look at the original schedule.

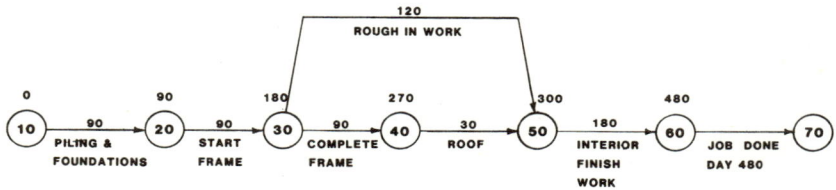

ORIGINAL SCHEDULE

We have seen the delay "proven" this way along with a $4,000,000 claim for acceleration and out-of-sequence work since the job was actually completed before the theoretical finish date.

PROVE TIME EXTENSIONS

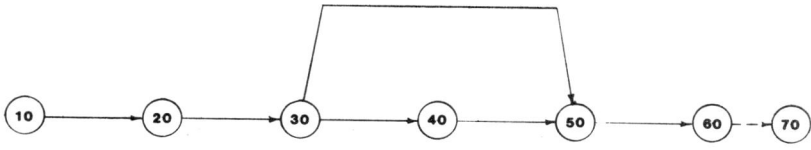

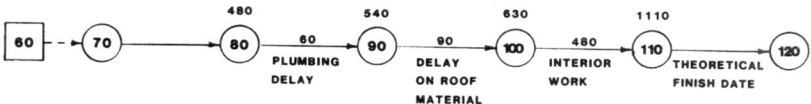

Seems silly and illogical. That very approach was used on another $2,000,000 claim on a Las Vegas Hotel. Indeed we see it all the time in spite of its being obviously wrong.

Another method would be to add 3 impact arrows.

1-10	Pile Delay by Owner	60 Days
1-40	Roof Start Delay by Owner	330 Days
1-120	Set Start Date of Added Work	480 Days
120-140	Added Work by Owner	480 Days

These have this effect.

CONSTRUCTION SCHEDULES

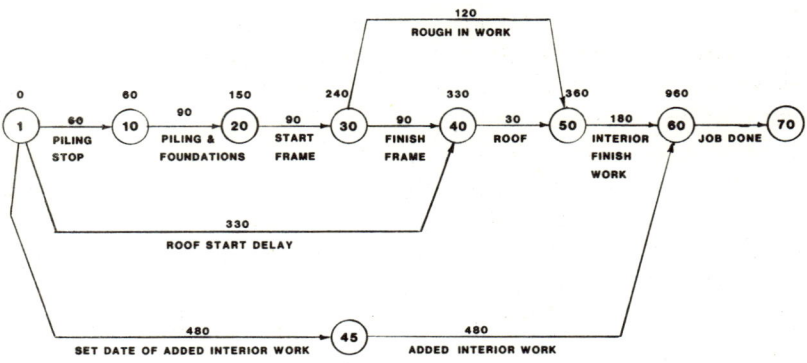

IMPACTED INITIAL CPM

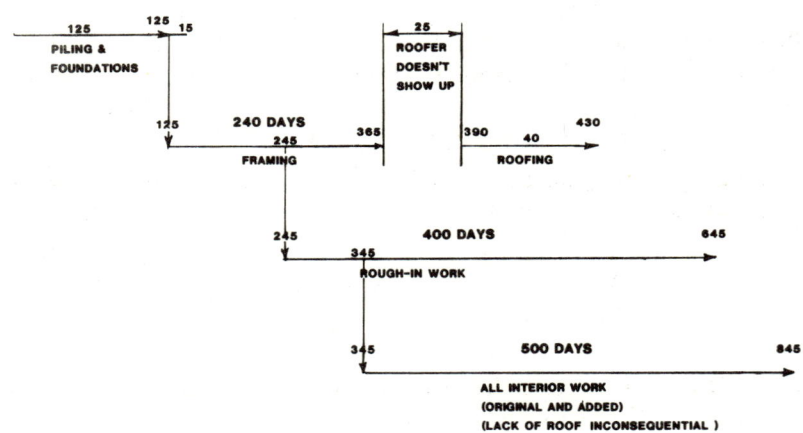

ACTUALLY BUILT SCHEDULE

PROVE TIME EXTENSIONS

Comparing the actually built diagram to the initial schedule shows the piling delay held the start of framing 35 days. Rough-in started 65 days late, 30 days were lost by the contractor. Interim finish work started 45 days later than first planned. The owner delayed the piling start by 60 days. Did the contractor accelerate to start the interior 15 days sooner? Was the acceleration to overcome its own time loss on the framing? Did the mechanical people show up early because they had nothing to do? Were the 480 days added to the new work really correct? How much is the contractor due?

Do you think this is incorrect? Why? Certainly four impact arrows are exactly correct. But their insertion into the CPM diagram no doubt will produce logic totally unlike the actual job progress. Nonetheless that is what the owner theoretically did to the job. There are times to make this theoretical argument. It is a lot easier and cheaper than other methods of trying to unscramble the who-struck-John. There are also times to analyze the job progress which is shown in the actually built diagram. This is better but a more more difficult and costly analysis.

Couple this type of conceptual approach problem along with inadequate records, attorneys and charts which don't really understand what is needed to really know who was doing what, when, and realize how very difficult it is to understand and present construction contract disputes.

How do you use a schedule to prove a delay or entitlement to a time extension? Again, one must realize there is no fixed way. Each situation requires judgement to resolve. There is, however, an ordered procedure which should be used to discipline the evaluator's judgement. The order provides a framework to which judgement can be applied in controllable and understandable increments.

First, define the job's status *at the time* the construction was delayed or performance was extended. Second, place each delay into the existing schedule in the *chronological order* in which the delay occurred. Third, determine the effect each delay had on the job schedule. Finally, analyze the effect each delay had on the construction performance. This means performing a new forward and backward pass to calculate the new critical path and to define each remaining activity's new float. This last step usually is completed through a narrative description of each "update" of the schedule to reflect the particular delay which has been added to the performance time.

Defining job status may be accomplished by a thorough job walk-through recording the progress in each area or floor if the period between the analysis and the occurrence of the delay was less than thirty days. This should be followed by an examination of the present material delivery schedules; a determination of the actual amount of materials available at the site or stored off-site; a review of present equipment availability and capacity; and a review of labor availability. A review of the project's progress history should also be made. The past progress rate may indicate the contractor's capability and the job's difficulty and may give a good indication of what can be expected in the future. By combining each examination the evaluator may confidently define the project's current status.

If the time between the analysis and the delay is greater than thirty days the current status of the job may be more difficult to define. Since the present condition of the job can no longer be seen, the evaluator must rely on the project's historical records. A variety of records *may* be available. The amount and quality of job records which any contractor (or owner or designer) will maintain will vary.

The first step in reviewing the job records will necessarily be one of survey. Who's records will be available? The contractor's? The owner's? The designer's? Where are they located? Project site? Home office? How many records are there? What records are available? Answers to these questions will assist the evaluator to estimate the time and travel necessary to study the various records; how long the review may take; how many people will be necessary to complete the review; and to determine whether all normally maintained records have been made available. (Are there any that have not been produced?) An investment in planning and organization before the review begins will shorten the review period, thus saving time and money.

Next, check the job's updated progress schedule closest to the occurrence of the delay. Actual start and completion dates may have been recorded at the time of the update; or perhaps completed activities were noted and an evaluation of each uncompleted activity's uncompleted status has been made (for instance, fifty-percent complete or seventy-five percent complete) in either situation the reviewer's task will be shortened. If actual dates have been recorded the evaluator may merely check them against other records to ensure accuracy. If partially or completed activities have been indicated, the evaluator will have been provided with a general frame of reference to which specific dates may be supplied (if found). A sufficiently detailed schedule with actual completion dates should be sufficient to define job status.

If no schedule is available or the available schedule is not adequate to measure status, the evaluator will find the job's progress meeting minutes a valuable source of information describing how the project was actually built. Progress meetings can be expected to discuss, naturally, the job's progress. Among items normally mentioned are subcontractor location; interference among the various subcontractor's crews; missing material or equipment that is needed to complete activities; and, perhaps design conflicts or omissions. All such information will permit the evaluator to identify the job's progress. The reader should

CONSTRUCTION SCHEDULES

note that progress meeting minutes may be kept by more than one group.

The contractor's job cost control system should also assist the reviewer to evaluate job status. Generally, progress will be related to the amount of and change in costs recorded on the cost report. Thus, as costs increase progress is made and can be measured to define delay. The interval between cost reports will vary from contractor to contractor. The smaller the interval (say, two weeks) the closer the reviewer can expect one cost report to come to the date the delay (or change) occurred. The cost report is intended to capture a picture of the project in numbers at a particular point in time. Therefore, the cost report can be relied upon and may provide a more reliable source of information than the progress meeting minutes. The most serious disadvantage the cost report presents is the inability to relate cost codes to the schedule's activities. It may be hard to relate a labor account for "concrete" to the construction activity for "fourth floor slab." Some cost reports will have greater detail than others. Regardless, the periodic cost reports should provide a relatively good basis to fix project status.

Progress photos can also be helpful to define job status. Unfortunately, progress photos are not always available. Even when available, the photos may have been taken at such a great distance that sufficient detail to see the status may be lacking. Further, the interval between photos may be too great to confidently measure progress at any one point in time. Combined with progress meeting minutes and job cost reports, however, progress photos provide a valuable reference.

Perhaps the least valuable source of information to define job status is the correspondence file. The regular job correspondence will not regularly discuss job progress. The evaluator can therefore expect to spend a great deal of time reading the exchange of letters or memos without finding

PROVE TIME EXTENSIONS

very much. In circumstances when job status must be established in a limited period of time, the reviewer should start his study elsewhere.

The reviewer may also consider interviewing the various people that actually participated in the construction when the delay occurred. Such interviews may provide a valuable source of information, depending, of course, on the memory of the one interviewed. If the parties have either considered or initiated litigation (or for that matter, arbitration) formal "statements" or perhaps depositions may be available. These should be studied.

It is important to recognize that the definition of job status at the time the delay occurred must be transferred to the job schedule. If no schedule exists, a schedule must be created. The effect of the delay on the job's progress will be measured by a schedule. The analysis depends upon one.

If an existing schedule is used to record the job status and measure delay, the remaining logic must be carefully reviewed to determine whether the project is built according to it. Durations must also be checked. If the sequence and order of construction has deviated from the original schedule's intent, it should be revised. Accuracy is important not only to support the schedule, but also to protect it from attack which claims the schedule cannot measure the effect of the delay because it does not accurately show how the project was (or is) being built. It is presumed that if a schedule was created when an insufficient schedule existed the logic will reflect the actual manner of construction or the contractor's intent if the project has not been completed. The reader will recall the Corps of Engineers manual "Modification Impact Evaluation Guide" made a similar suggestion.

Once the status of the project at the time the delays occurred has been defined, the evaluator can turn its attention to inserting the delay into the schedule. If more than one delay was experienced, they should be inserted in the order in which the delays were experienced. To insert the delay correctly, judgment is required. The delay must be placed at the correct place in the logic. More importantly, the remaining logic must be studied in order to revise it to reflect the change caused by the delay. Were activity durations increased? Decreased? Are labor requirements increased? Must more craftsmen work in the same area? Generally, how has the remaining work schedule been affected? As the effects are identified, logic and durations must be revised to indicate the new manner in which construction can be anticipated to be completed. This requires not only an understanding of the fundamentals of scheduling, but also an understanding of the construction process in order to exercise sufficient judgement to accurately insert the delays.

It is important that the effect of each delay be determined, the third step in the process, before any other delay is inserted in the schedule. Each delay must be measured separately. Since different parties may be responsible for different delays, the delays must be able to be allocated to assess responsibility. Additionally, a particular delay must be evaluated separately because its effect may be greater than the mathematical value of its duration. For instance, a two-week delay that forces an unanticipated winter shutdown will certainly impact the job more than two weeks. Each delay must also be evaluated separately because CPM is a dynamic method. It changes as assumption changes to fact. Thus we can see that each subsequent delay will affect the impact earlier delays had on the schedule.

The final step requires the schedule, now revised to show the effects of the delay, to be analyzed. What change has the delay force upon the project performance? This can be determined by a new forward and backward pass to calculate the remaining activities new float, define a new critical path, and project a new project completion date. Once these things have been defined, the evaluator should prepare a narrative description of the revised schedule. The narrative should describe in words the manner in which the project is now anticipated to be completed as indicated by the revised schedule's new logic and durations. If possible, a value for the change should also be provided.

Each delay should be inserted and analyzed separately. Each delay should have its own narrative description of effect and value. Each succeeding delay should not be inserted and analyzed until all preceding delays have been analyzed.

Evaluating the effect of schedule changes and delays is, in practice, difficult because all the needed information is not always available. Contractor records are incomplete, lost, or destroyed. Memories fade. Cost reports are inadequate and ignored. No attention is paid to original project schedule: work is completed when and as available. Every time needed information is missing, the evaluator must either interpolate the required facts from other sources or substitute its judgement. The more interpolation and judgement present, the less accurate the schedule analysis becomes.

But the most difficult obstacle the evaluator has to overcome is the utter impossibility to ever recreate a truly accurate historic job status. As-built schedules are impossible because of the inherent conflict between the I-J principles of scheduling (preceding activities must be complete before succeeding activities can begin) and the constant overlap of actual field construction. For example, lath and plaster are two almost inseparable activities. One will not be completed before the other is begun. They will be constantly complementing each other. They are not independent. A construction project is completed in a similar manner. Items of work may be left ninety-percent finished. Are they completed? Items may begin and immediately be abandoned in favor of other work. Have they started? If an activity takes five days to complete, but work was spread over a three-week period, how long has it taken to complete the activity? There are no answers applicable in all situations.

Demonstrating the effect which a delay has had on a project is sometimes as difficult as the initial calculation. A logic diagram, computer printout, and duration changes may be hard for one not familiar with scheduling techniques to understand. To an owner or attorney not familiar with construction it may be impossible. It is therefore advisable to convert the revised critical path schedule to an easy-to-read-and-understand bar graph. The bar chart can demonstrate extended performance easily when a line representing the originally anticipated performance is compared to a line representing the actual performance, both displayed on a time-scaled grid. The schedule analysis remains in the critical path method, however, rather than the bar chart. The bar chart merely illustrates the CPM study. The bar chart's contribution is in its ability to demonstrate in a simple manner, a complicated, interrelated activity delay.

Repeated efforts at measuring the effect of delays, naturally, have shown that contractors or owners can emphasize or reduce the effect of any delay or time extension even before it occurs by following certain scheduling techniques. A contractor may consider reducing the amount of float it puts in a schedule. The less float, the less time will be required before a delay will become critical. Owners, on the other hand, may wish to show more float since more time will be available for changes that may require additional time.

PROVE TIME EXTENSIONS

If this technique is considered, the reader is well-advised to remember the case of *C.H. Leavell & Co.*[171] The government had alleged that the contractor's schedule unrealistically provided excess durations in order to eliminate float. The government argued that these excessive durations, among other reasons, prevented accurate scheduling and proper analysis. The contractor argued that it was the person required to develop the schedule and that no specifications were present which defined the amount of time the activities were to take.

In *Leavell,* the contractor had allocated 285 days for "mechanical electrical rough-in." The government contended 120 days was a more reasonable duration. The duration of the mechanical electrical rough-in was important because the activity was delayed. At 120 days, however, the activity maintained sufficient float to be unaffected; at 285 days the delay to the activity delayed project completion. The Board of Contract Appeals in its decision found that the schedule analysis was made difficult by the lack of breakdown of the lengthy activity for mechanical electrical rough-in. The Board concluded the duration (and thus extent of delay) lay somewhere between the two positions and rendered a "jury verdict" decision. Manipulating durations is always risky. The authors' believe the best schedule is an accurate schedule. Good schedules do not shade or manipulate durations.

Another technique often used to emphasize or reduce the effect of a delay (depending upon one's position in a dispute) is to "adjust" the status of a job at the time a delay or change occurred. All commentators agree that delay or change must be measured at the time it occurred during the construction process. Earlier, however, we discussed how difficult it is to define the past status of a job especially if poor job records were kept. A considerable amount of judgment is often necessary to arrive at project status at any partic-

CONSTRUCTION SCHEDULES

ular time. The final judgment will influence the schedule's definition of delay or change.

As an example, assume three activities, *A, B,* and *C.* Each activity requires ten months to complete. The contractor loses $150,000 and five months during *A* due to its own fault and the owner changes the material during *C* causing further extensions of the project schedule. What is the contractor due for the owner-caused delay? Using the planned schedule without adjusting activity *A* for the contractor error, owner's responsibility may look like this:

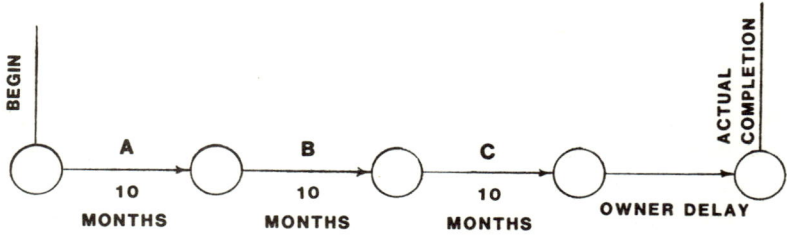

But adjusting *A* to reflect the contractor's delay changes the amount of owner delay:

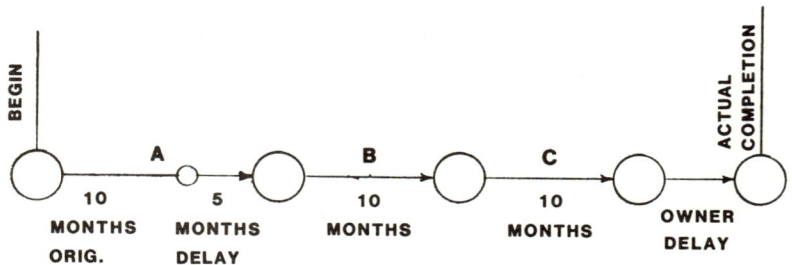

PROVE TIME EXTENSIONS

See the difference? Note further that any other *adjustment* to the duration of activity A will change the owner's responsibility. If the five-month, contractor-caused loss was not assumed, but had to be calculated from project records a year after it occurred, the potential for "favorable" adjustments giving either party "the benefit of the doubt" and the subsequent effect on the owner's responsibility can be readily seen. To the extent actual job status is ignored or delays are presented on artificial networks, the results of a computerized time study can be influenced.

The best technique to show the effect of a delay is to sequence the work correctly. Contractors generally fail to sequence the construction work. Instead, contractors tend to schedule activities independently, at the earliest time they can start, and tie the activity's early finish to project completion instead of another activity. Contractors should always attempt to tie the work together instead of project completion. Even when a particular group of related activities has been completed, sequencing can be continued by moving to another group of related activities instead of the end of the job. The schedule should reflect an interrelated work flow, not a series of parallel activities whose finish date is tied to project completion.

How do you use the schedule to define a time extension or delay? Our conclusion is that contractors and owners owe each other the best of cooperation and reasonable levels of skill in co-administrating the project. The use of the contract duration and the cost of additions to its length cannot be decided with preset rules, for even with preset rules, an inordinate loss by either party could lead to a challenge of the responsibility of reliance on the rules.

Sensible, concerned common sense treatment of each other's fortunes during the project is the best way to resolve disputes. Unfortunately most cannot accept blame, or voluntarily pay for one's own errors. Besides, it is a challenge to argue. Who knows? You may win a million dollar windfall; we have seen it happen before, but we have also seen some valid arguments fail to carry the day. We have even lost a few ourselves. That is called a "bad judge."

---

164. Modification Guide, *supra* note 45.
165. *Id.,* at 3-8.
166. *VACPM Handbook.* Veterans Administration, H-08-11 (January 1977).
167. *Id.* at 14.
168. *Id.* at 15.
169. *Id.*
170. *Blake Construction Co.* v. C.J. Coakley Co., *supra* note 126 at 575.
171. 70-2 BCA ¶ 8437 (1970).

CHAPTER 6

NETWORK SCHEDULES AS EVIDENCE

§ 6-1. Introduction.
§ 6-2. The Schedule as a Business Record.
§ 6-3. Schedules as Scientific Evidence.
§ 6-4. The Schedule as an Adversary's Testimony.
§ 6-5. The Schedule as Expert Testimony.

§ 6-1. Introduction.

Courts have regularly accepted Critical Path Method schedules as evidence of delay, out-of-sequence work, and lack of coordination. But on what basis does the court accept the schedules as evidence? In what form should the schedule be presented for the court to accept it as evidence? How can counsel defeat the introduction of a CPM as evidence?

To date, three main theories of accepting computer-generated material as evidence has been used to evaluate admissibility. Since schedules are for the most part computer-generated material, these theories will guide the acceptance of schedules as evidence. These theories see the computer's results as a type of business record, a kind of scientific evidence, and, in criminal trials, as the testimony of an adversary to be confronted.[172]

§ 6-2. The Schedule as a Business Record.

The first theory treats computer output as just another form of business or governmental record, and the computer system that printed it as a transcription device. The Federal Rules of Evidence, § 1001(1), defines "writings and records" to include "magnetic impulse, mechanical or electronic recording, or other form of data compilation." Section 1001(3) permits, when printed, data stored in a computer to be considered an "original."

A business record offered as proof of its contents is hearsay. It is admissible only when the records meet the usual tests of the business record exception to the Hearsay Rule. Considering CPM Schedules as business records requires similar treatment. The schedule must meet the business record exception to the Hearsay Rule. Generally, the exception requires a contemporaneous recording of facts about regularly conducted activity, following a regular recording practice. The Hearsay Rule exception for business records is justified by the element of reliability. In practice, regular business records have a comparatively high degree of accuracy (as compared to other memorandum) because such books are customarily checked as to correctness, because the regularity and continuity of records is calculated to train the recordkeeper in habits of precision; and because the entire business of the country constantly functions in reliance upon such entries.[173]

Considering a computer-generated construction schedule as a business record presumes that the scheduling process was merely a transcription of recorded business data stored in the computer to a printed form. But can computer-generated schedules be considered merely a transcription? Is it really only stored data in the computer or is it rather the judgment of the scheduler? Or more likely, a reflection of the circumstances under which the project must be built?

Let us compare the scheduling process to the business record exception. The exception first requires the contemporaneous recording of facts. The exception contemplates that the facts will be recorded as the event occurs which suggests accuracy — the recorder will not know future events that might influence the manner of the recording. A schedule, however, is based on assumption, not fact. The scheduler in preparing its schedule attempts to order the future and often to make the work "fit" into the time allowed for performance in the contract. A schedule is never based on fact. The future which the scheduler attempts to order is at best an estimate or educated guess. It is only in the updating process that the scheduler may contemporaneously record facts. In the updating process, actual start and finish dates for individual activities are noted. From this new data, projections of future performances are prepared. It is more accurate than the initial schedule because the update has some actual facts upon which to base a projected completion date. An initial schedule is based totally on professional judgment or guesses. Only the recording of actual start and finish dates during an update comes close to the requirement of a contemporaneous recording of facts.

In real life, however, these "actual" dates are far from "actual." In the confusion of a construction project, beginning and ending a particular activity often blend into the beginning of the succeeding activity or the ending of the preceding one. Does the masonry wall wait until the entire footing is poured? Or is just enough footing poured to permit some masonry to begin? To a great extent "actual" dates recorded in an update represent the scheduler's judgment.

However, even the updating process may not qualify as a *contemporaneous* recording. Most updates are not accomplished daily. Rather, they are usually monthly, with some performed bi-weekly. Thus the dates recorded at the update are present recollections of past occurrences, in some cases thirty days old — not a contemporaneous recording. Thus, only daily updated schedules are sufficiently contemporaneous to fit into the first part of the exception, but even those dates may be more the scheduler's judgment than actual start and finish dates.

Next, the exception requires that the record keeping be a regularly conducted activity. This part of the exception has its basis in the assumption that the regularity and continu-

§ 6-2   CONSTRUCTION SCHEDULES

ity of records is calculated to train the recordkeeper in habits of precision. Although the update may be completed regularly, the initial scheduling process is completed only once — at the beginning of the job (unless the scheduler only draws schedules for a living, producing them day-in, day-out but even then the scheduler does not record facts). Development of an initial schedule will not be a daily conducted activity, although it may be a regular activity in the sense that every schedule has an initial one to start.

Again, however, the updating portion of the scheduling process seems initially to apply. But the application of this part of the exception is limited to the regularity of the updating process and even that is limited to the precision of someone else's data. The updater may not witness the start and completion of activities, but rather receive and record reports from others in the "field." This part of the exception requires a regular recording practice. In other words, that the data be recorded in the same way, day after day. This part of the exception requires a regularity to insure accuracy. By recording the reports from "others" on the update, the update must rely on the regularity of the "others" information. The "others" are the first transcription of the data. The schedule is not a transcription of data but rather a transcription of a transcription of data.

In summary, a schedule has difficulty in meeting the business records exception to the Hearsay Rule. The initial schedule does not contemporaneously record facts; only the updating process *may* record facts, although even the updating process is usually based on what the updater learns from others. But neither the initial nor the updated schedule usually will *contemporaneously* record facts. Neither the initial nor updated schedule seem to be a regularly conducted recording activity, and yet even courts have schedules which are regularly recorded efforts for setting forth facts.

The business record exception developed because of the need to use regularly maintained records to prove commercial occurrences because of the "special trustworthiness of an entry made by a clerk of a party."[174] The customary accuracy of business records, vital to the survival of the business and backed by the usual training and experience of bookkeepers, provides the special reliability of the exception. But schedules are not considered by the construction industry to have the accuracy of business records. They may be vital to the survival of the business, but schedules are not the records of the business. Schedules do not meet the special circumstances of business records which provide the foundation of the exception.

It is the authors' opinion that CPM schedules do not meet the requirements of the business records exception to the Hearsay Rule.

Look at the Armed Services Board of Contract Appeals case *Lane-Verdugo*[175] for an example of a schedule which was not considered by the court as sufficiently reliable to prove the Government's responsibility for the claimed job delay. Lane-Verdugo, a joint venturer had requested a $162,000 equitable adjustment for Government delays to two contracts for renovation and addition to existing buildings at an air force base. Several CPM schedules were the primary evidence submitted by the contractor to establish the relationship of the claimed delays to the extended performance period. Some of the networks were prepared during performance and others subsequent to completion.

Although Lane-Verdugo made many allegations as to what the schedules established, the Board found no factual support for the purported results which the schedules demonstrated. The contractor's expert scheduling consultant testified that the critical path analysis was only as good as the information upon which it was based. But no evidence establishing the authenticity or validity of the data that was used in the preparation of the critical path charts and accompanying computer printouts was presented. The expert witness stated that the networks incorporated delay information only as furnished by Lane-Verdugo. The Board found the "charts as such cannot and do not directly depict responsibility." [176] The Board in *Lane-Verdugo* recognized that schedules are not business records themselves, but rather use information from business records which must be established independently from the schedule.

Look at *Chaney & James Construction Co.*[177] for another example. The Federal Aviation Agency Contract Appeals Panel found a critical path schedule could not be accepted as establishing either the facts protrayed or the reasonableness of the contractor's assertions as to the influence of specific incidences of work progress. Chaney and James submitted a bar chart as required by the contract. The bar chart schedule was approved by the contracting officer. Later, Chaney and James submitted a critical path schedule but failed to state why the CPM had been submitted. A CPM had not been required by the contract. At the hearing, no satisfactory evidence as to the origin of the data that went into the preparation of the chart, the purpose that the chart was to serve, or what use was actually made of the schedule was presented. The contractor's president and project manager testified that the CPM was not used either in preparing the bid or in managing the project.

During the hearing, Chaney and James submitted an updated version of the CPM and an additional critical path diagram purporting to show the relationship of the work elements and the impact on work progress of the specific instances of claimed Government caused delays. The contractor also presented expert testimony on the critical path method of scheduling. The expert had not seen the data from which the charts were prepared, but stated that from a casual study it appeared the logic of the charts was correct because activities appeared to be in a logical sequence. The expert could not verify the time estimates shown on the charts since the expert had no independent knowledge of the facts.

The Federal Aviation Agency Contract Appeals Panel, however, refused to consider the charts as "evidence of the facts they portray." [178] The Panel found the work sequence shown was not used in estimating or bidding the job and that the sequence on the critical path charts was not followed in performing the contract work. The Panel concluded that the CPM schedules cannot be accepted as establishing either the facts they portray or the reasonableness of the contractor's assertions as to the influence of specific incidents on work progress.

Both *Lane-Verdugo* and *Chaney & James* refused to accept a critical path method study without substantiation of the data upon which the schedule was based. Both courts recognized that a CPM schedule was not a business record but rather relies on business records. Both courts recognized in substance if not specifically that CPM schedules do not qualify for the business records exception to the Hearsay Rule.

When the schedule is created specifically for a construction dispute to offer opinions of past performances based on the construction and design records (the business records to which the exception refers), a different situation exists. The need to introduce the records as evidence and thus the need for the business record exception to the Hearsay Rule does not exist for analyses prepared after project completion. These schedules are not the record of the construction business. They are expert opinions based on selected parts of the record — dates when some of the work has been started or completed. The selection process of the expert witness reduces the amount of business records actually used and thus presents only part of the available data. Further, the selection process necessitates a manipulation of the data which the foundation of the business record exception does not contemplate. Post project, computer-generated scheduling analysis need not be treated as a business record within the business record exception of the Hearsay Rule. Post project, computer-generated scheduling analysis is expert testimony.

Even if the hearsay objection can be overcome, introduction of the schedule into evidence as computerized business records faces another hurdle: the best evidence rule.[179] It is a well-established rule of evidence that a party wishing to prove the contents of a writing must produce the original writing, if available, as the "best evidence" of what the writing says.[180] Interpretations of the voluminous writings exceptions to the best evidence rule may eliminate the hurdle, however.

Rule 1006 of the Federal Rules of Evidence provides this voluminous writing exception:

> The contents of voluminous writings, recordings, or photographs which cannot conveniently be examined in court may be presented in the form of a chart, summary, or calculation. The originals or duplicates shall be made available for examination or copying, or both, by other parties at a reasonable time and place. The court may order that they be produced in court.

Alternately, if the information stored in the computer originated from invoices or other paper records, it can be argued that the paper records constitute the best evidence.

Where the computer printout is not a complete copy but rather a summary of larger amounts of data in the computer, the best evidence rule can present an even greater problem. Although the printouts may be admissible, the summaries may not have been made in the regular course of business. Most jurisdictions, however, recognize the practicalities of the voluminous writings exception and permit introduction of the summary provided the underlying voluminous data is available for inspection.[181] Thus, since updated schedules rely almost exclusively on summaries of information, admission over objection based on the best evidence rule will require availability of the underlying data.

§ 6-3. Schedules as Scientific Evidence.

Critical Path Method Schedules can also be considered as scientific evidence. For any device, technique, or theory to be introduced as scientific evidence, the material must be shown to have won scientific acceptance before accepted by the court as evidence. The court which first faced the question of the admissibility of the results of a "lie detector" examination announced as a test for the admittance of scientific evidence whether the support of the theory had gained "general acceptance" among the scientific community.[182]

Most commentators, however, reject "general acceptance" as a means of accepting *scientific evidence.* General scientific acceptance may be a proper condition upon the courts' taking judicial notice of scientific technique or theory, but not a criterion for the admissibility of scientific evidence. Any relevant conclusions which are supported by a qualified expert witness should be received unless there are other reasons for exclusion.[183] Scientific theory supports the introduction of scientific data upon which an expert opinion may be based. The scientific theory supports the expert's connection of the scientific data to form an opinion.

The scientific theory of the Critical Path Method Schedule is in the creation of activity interrelationship to measure time. Although manual methods can be used, a computer is programmed to compute the mathematical distance between the activities and calculate early start, late start, early finish, and late finish times. Thus, the CPM schedule can be (and often is) offered as proof of a cause and effect relationship. The cause being a delay or out-of-sequence work; the effect being the extended project's completion date.

By the previous judicial acceptance and discussion of the Critical Path Method of scheduling, it is evident that courts have found the scheduling technique to be generally accepted by the construction industry experts who regularly utilize it to measure and coordinate construction projects. Thus, although the authors are unaware of any specific judicial recognition of the "general acceptance" of the schedule in the community of construction scientists, Critical Path Method scheduling should be entitled to be recognized as scientific technique or theory.

However, it is the author's opinion that schedules should not be considered as scientific evidence. A qualified expert witness should be required to base an opinion on the scheduling method's conclusions. The opinion on the arrangement of data according to the scientific theory of critical path method schedules is the evidence. For the opinion to be admitted, its probative value must be balanced against the familiar tests of the dangers of prejudicing or misleading the jury, unfair surprise, and undue consumption of time as any expert testimony must be.

§ 6-4. The Schedule as an Adversary's Testimony.

Computer output can also be offered as testimony of an adversary to be confronted as an element of an offense in a criminal trial or a cause of action in a civil trial. When used in this manner, the major question seems to be the defendant's right to discovery.[184] To what extent is the computer-generated evidence subject to discovery? In *Pearl Brewing Co. v. Jos. Schlitz Co.*[185] a civil, antitrust case, Pearl had permitted full discovery of the findings and opinions of their expert economists testifying to a computer econometric model, but refused to permit discovery of the non-testifying computer expert who developed the program. The court, after considering the necessity for full preparation by both parties in discovery and the extraordinary difficulty in assessing the computer, even with a full program listing available, without the explanation from the programmer, ordered the deposition of the non-testifying computer expert.

In *National Union Electric Corp. v. Matsushita Electric Industrial Co.*,[186] the court ordered plaintiff National Union Electric to create a computer tape of data previously supplied by National Union in printed form in answers to interrogatories. Although the printed answers could be read by defendant Matsushita's counsel, it could not be read by Matsushita's computer. Defense counsel contended they could not effectively analyze the data produced until the data could be read by their computer. The *National Union* court examined the 1970 amendments to Rule 34 of the Federal Rules of Civil Procedure which permitted computerized records subject to requests for production to be translated into reasonably usable form and concluded production of a computer tape of the information previously supplied to be the appropriate usable form.

The *Pearl Brewing* and *National Union* courts granted requests for additional discovery of computer tapes. Both recognized the importance of the computer programs to organize and analyze data. If computer evidence is an element of a cause of action, respondents should have the benefit of full discovery of the underlying data and programs since it is the programs which order and analyze the data. A computerized schedule analysis used as an element in a cause of action should be subject to the same discovery right. The computer programs which order the calculation and determination of the critical path and thus defines extensions of the project completion date to measure delay represent a significant part of the proof. Respondents should be able to study and use the same program to not only insure the accuracy of the program but also to facilitate their own calculations.

Pearl Brewing Co. v. Jos. Schlitz Co. and cases in which computer-generated evidence is used to establish an element of a criminal offense or cause of action bear a strong resemblance to the cases which have considered computer-generated schedules. Neither group of cases question the propriety of experts basing opinion on or court acceptance of the computer output. Rather, the courts seem more concerned with the reliability of the computer's results or opponent's discovery of it. Judicial acceptance of the computer-generated materials seems to be presumed without discussion, a presumption which the authors suggest should not be made. A justification for the admission of computer-generated schedules (or other data) within the Rules of Evidence should be required.

Merely because information comes from a computer should not automatically entitle it to judicial acceptance. The lay community already attributes far too much reliability to computer-generated data. The court system should require substantiation of the stored data. The computer as a machine should not be the focus of the evidentiary analysis [187] although the program (the manner in which the calculations are made) may be a worthwhile subject of examination. The evidence is the data which the computer uses to make its calculations.

§ 6-5. The Schedule as Expert Testimony.

So what is a critical path method schedule? While the project is under construction, the CPM schedule is a periodic "Management Report." The schedule may be produced periodically: every week, every month, or once a year depending upon when management wants to see a new schedule. It provides a sequence or order of activities in which management intends to proceed with construction. The schedule generally summarizes current operating data to assist decision making by those charged with managing the construction project. Such reports are, of course, only as reliable as the data on which they are based, and thus management can control the quality of the schedule as well. In other words, the schedule is an analytical report of the project's status and presents an opinion of the project's future.

What kind of evidence is a critical path method schedule? It is not a record of a construction business within the business record exception of the Hearsay Rule. It is not scientific evidence, but rather scientifically arranged data upon which opinions and management decisions can be based. A CPM schedule provides management information upon which an opinion can be given. The management *opinion* can then be accepted as evidence. The critical path method analysis permits the opinion and acts to direct the opinion. Thus, in many ways schedules used while the project is under construction are expert testimony. Although the computer exercises no judgment (the manager does that task) the analogy is appropriate.

Commentators have suggested that viewing the schedule as an expert's testimony has two important consequences. Rule 26(b) of the Federal Rules of Civil Procedure permits discovery of experts' opinions prior to trial. Characterizing the schedule as an expert's testimony would require discovery of the opinion pursuant to the Rules of Civil Procedure. Further, considering the schedule as an expert's opinion should permit opposing counsel to cross-examine the schedule by presenting alternate facts and obtaining an alternate opinion.[188] This means new and additional "adjusted" schedules through new computer runs with different facts supplied by opposing counsel may be necessary.

A post-completion schedule analysis prepared for litigation is not as much an expert's opinion as it is an advocate's tool to demonstrate a particular opinion. In many ways the CPM schedule prepared for litigation acts as an experiment as the expert arranges the data in various ways to produce alternate results. Hence the post completion schedule can be considered experimental evidence. By varying the durations of activities or their sequence, the project completion date may change. By changing the orders to the computer, its calculations may produce a new critical path and project end date. These "experiments" are completed before trial through the computer runs and presented to the court by those who conducted or witnessed the experiment's results.[189]

The evidentiary question involved in the submission of the "experiment" schedule is the probative value of the evidence of experiment versus the dangers of misleading the jury. The possibility of being mislead are great. The "trier of fact may be beguiled by the neat tabulations of a printout or the apparent precision of" six-digit numbers.[190] Who can dispute that stack of convincing computer paper? Would the computer lie?

Usually the best gauge of the probative value of an experiment is the extent to which the experiment was similar to the litigated happening.[191] The best gauge of the probative value of the scheduling analysis is the similarity of the data to actual occurrences on the project site — the accuracy of the records on which the schedule is based. In presenting post completion network scheduling analysis, one should accordingly make every effort to substantiate and document the source of the data. Counsel can best assure the introduction of the schedule by presenting it as support for the expert's opinion of the experiment's conclusion and substantiating the data on which the analysis is based by reference to documents or other forms of evidence.

An interesting question arises if the schedule is considered experimental evidence. Is opposing counsel entitled to discarded experiments? Can opposing counsel obtain abandoned computer runs which may indicate an unfavorable conclusion to the party presenting the schedule? In *Pearl Brewing Co. v. Jos. Schlitz Co.*[192] the Court refused Schlitz's requests for alternate computer models developed but rejected by plaintiff, Pearl Brewing Co. The court reasoned that the alternate non-testifying experts' reports are not normally discoverable under the Federal Rules of Civil Procedure. A similar result is most likely if abandoned CPM schedule runs are requested. What if, however, the CPM computer runs were prepared as a management report while the project was under construction? Could the printouts be considered a party opponent's admission against interest and be admissible under that exception to the Hearsay Rule?

A major problem in introducing computer printouts into evidence is laying the proper foundation to authenticate the printout and establish the foundation for the voluminous writings and business records exceptions. Cases and commentators indicate that laying the foundation is the most common difficulty encountered in attempting to introduce computer evidence.[193] One example of a successful foundation was the plaintiff insurance company's introduction of a computer printout to prove the amount of premiums due on an insurance policy in *Transport Indemnity Co. v. Seib.*[194] The insurance company's director of accounting gave foundational testimony showing that a printout was prepared for trial under his direction. The witness testified he had manually verified each of the calculations and reconciled the amounts shown as due on the printout. This foundational testimony required 141 pages of the record. The printout was admitted over defendant's objection.[195] When all foundational bases are touched by the witness, the court should accept the material into evidence regardless of the length of the foundation presentation.

How can counsel defeat the introduction of the schedule? Of course, the rules of evidence and civil procedure can successfully preclude the schedules. Such techniques are, however, beyond the scope of this chapter. The best way to substantively attack the veracity or accuracy of the schedule is to challenge the underlying data. By destroying the foundation of the analysis one not only destroys the schedule, but also the opinion which the schedule supports. However, care must be taken in attacking the foundation. The court must understand that the schedule analysis and opinion depend on the underlying data. The stack of computer paper can assume an aura of accuracy that is not necessarily present. The attack must consequently be linked to the schedule's computer calculations. Ask the opposition witness to estimate the change which will occur in the computer calculations if a particular duration or sequence is changed.

Counsel attempting to block the introduction can also attack the integrity of the computer equipment and programs, security of the data processing system, and integrity of the output. Humans have a significant role in the input process and consequently may be a source of error. Source information may be inaccurate or duplicate the entry. Errors may occur in the keystroke transfer. Malfunctions in the equipment may occur which may cause loss of data and impair the validity of any computer analysis of the remaining data. There may be errors in the program in which the study of the designing, coding, documenting and testing procedure may reveal.[196] Absence of complaints is not necessarily probative of the program's accuracy and reliability.[197]

Finally, there may be an opportunity for unauthorized access to the system. Someone familiar with the computer could change, delete, or create bogus new items without leaving a trace. Counsel should investigate the security of the system.[198]

All in all, the court has a long way to go to fully set forth the real meaning of the construction schedule. We think that the challenge we have found in using, scheduling, and interpreting the effects of delay over the years has been well-presented in this text.

We do not believe that rigid definitions can ever evolve on the real meaning of schedules. As long as people are different and dollars are at stake there will be opposing ideas about what the schedules mean. It is fun to argue, and more importantly, nothing can happen on this earth without a fair amount of debate.

---

172. A. Teubner, "The Computer as Expert Witness: Toward a Unified Theory of Computer Evidence," 19 Jurimetrics 283 (Spring, 1979).
173. C. McCormick, *Law of Evidence* 597 (1954).
174. *Id.,* at 599.
175. *Supra* note 55.
176. *Id.,* at 48,515.
177. 66-2 BCA ¶ 6066 (1966).
178. *Id.,* at 28,076.
179. W. Fenwick & G. Davidson, "Use of Computerized Business Records as Evidence," 19 Jurimetrics 10 (Fall, 1978).
180. *Id.,* at 13.
181. *Id.,* at 14.
182. Frye v. United States, 293 F. 1013, 1014 (C.A.D.C. 1923).
183. McCormick, *supra* note 169, at 363.
184. Teubner, *supra* note 168, at 285.
185. 415 F. Supp. 1122 (D.C. Texas 1976).
186. 494 F. Supp. 1257 (E.D. Pa. 1980).
187. Teubner, *supra* note 168, at 286.
188. Teubner, *supra* note 168, at 281-82.
189. McCormick, *supra* note 169, at 359.
190. Fenwick, *supra* note 175, at 21.
191. McCormick, *supra* note 169, at 360.
192. *Supra* note 181.

193. Fenwick, *supra* note 175, at 10.
194. 178 Neb. 253, 132 N.W.2d 871 (1965).
195. Fenwick, *supra* note 175, at 16.
196. *Id.,* at 21.
197. *Id.,* at 22.
198. *Id.*

APPENDIX

APPENDIX

EP 415-1-3

MODIFICATION IMPACT EVALUATION GUIDE

JULY 1979

DEPARTMENT OF THE ARMY
OFFICE OF THE CHIEF OF ENGINEERS
WASHINGTON, D.C. 20314

CONSTRUCTION SCHEDULES

DEPARTMENT OF THE ARMY
Office of the Chief of Engineers
Washington, DC 20314

DAEN-CWO-C
DAEN-MPC-E

Pamphlet
No. 415-1-3

EP 415-1-3
2 July 1979

Construction
MODIFICATION IMPACT EVALUATION GUIDE

		Paragraph	Page
Chapter 1.	INTRODUCTION		
	Purpose...............................	1-1	1-1
	Applicability.........................	1-2	1-1
	References............................	1-3	1-1
	Use of Neutral Language...............	1-4	1-1
	District Supplement...................	1-5	1-1
Chapter 2.	BACKGROUND		
	General...............................	2-1	2-1
	Settlement............................	2-2	2-1
	Reasons for Untimely Settlements......	2-3	2-1
	The Defense Acquisition Regulation....	2-4	2-1
	Estimate Preparation..................	2-5	2-2
	Alternatives to Agreement.............	2-6	2-2
	Need for Impact Estimates.............	2-7	2-2
	Scope.................................	2-8	2-2
Chapter 3.	IDENTIFICATION		
	Job Status............................	3-1	3-1
	Progress Schedule.....................	3-2	3-2
	Procedures............................	3-3	3-5
	Summary...............................	3-4	3-7
	Examples..............................	3-5	3-8
Chapter 4.	EVALUATION		
	General...............................	4-1	4-1
	Materials.............................	4-2	4-2
	Equipment.............................	4-3	4-2
	Manpower..............................	4-4	4-4
	Quantification........................	4-5	4-10

i

APPENDIX

EP 415-1-3
2 July 79

Chapter 5. THE GOVERNMENT ESTIMATE
General...................................... 5-1   5-1
Extended Overhead............................ 5-2   5-1
Examples..................................... 5-3   5-1

Chapter 6. THE CONTRACTOR'S PROPOSAL
The Request for Proposal..................... 6-1   6-1
Further Guidance............................. 6-2   6-1

Chapter 7. FINALIZING THE MODIFICATION
Format....................................... 7-1   7-1
Result....................................... 7-2   7-1

APPENDIX: IMPACT EVALUATION CHECKLIST

CONSTRUCTION SCHEDULES

EP 415-1-3
2 July 79

CHAPTER 1

INTRODUCTION

1-1. <u>Purpose</u>. This pamphlet provides information and guidance on the identification and evaluation of that portion of the fixed-price construction contract modification defined as "impact on the unchanged work."

1-2. <u>Applicability</u>. This pamphlet is applicable to all FOA having military and/or civil works construction responsibilities.

1-3. <u>References</u>.

    a. Defense Acquisition Regulation.

    b. ER 1-1-11.

    c. ER 415-1-303.

    d. ER 1180-1-1.

    e. EP 415-1-2.

    f. EP 415-1-260.

1-4. <u>Use of neutral language</u>. Wherever the words "man," "men," or their related pronouns appear, either as words or as parts of words (other than referring to a specific individual), they have been used for literary purposes and are meant in their generic sense to include both sexes.

1-5. <u>District supplement</u>. Districts should supplement this guide with District guidance and pertinent literature.

APPENDIX

EP 415-1-3
2 July 79

CHAPTER 2

BACKGROUND

2-1. General.

    a. Because each contract modification presents a unique set of circumstances, this pamphlet will not deal specifically with all possible combinations; consequently, the following material describes basic procedures which may be applied to "impact" analysis for any modification. Personnel having detailed knowledge of the specific modification being evaluated should adapt these procedures and their underlying principles to the prevailing circumstances.

    b. This pamphlet is to be considered as a guide only. It is not intended to supersede any regulations or contract requirements; neither is it intended to abridge command authority or responsibility in any respect.

2-2. Settlement. The Corps of Engineers has long recognized that it is desirable to settle the terms of a contract modification before issuing the Notice to Proceed (NTP). This settlement requires timely action by both the Corps of Engineers and the contractor, culminating in an agreement on the fair and reasonable price and time for accomplishing the changed work. Although it will occasionally be in the best interests of the Government to issue an NTP before the exact price of the change is determined, these cases are the exception rather than the rule.

2-3. Reasons for untimely settlements. It has recently become more difficult to attain a timely settlement on modification costs. The reasons include: lack of contractor incentive to agree before the work is accomplished; the increasing number of modifications being processed; and lack of guidance or experience in developing reasonably reliable estimates of cost/time for impact on the unchanged work "before the fact." Only the latter problem will be dealt with in this pamphlet.

2-4. The Defense Acquisition Regulation (DAR). DAR prescribes the exact wording of the General Provision (GP) clauses for construction contracts. In 1968, revisions to DAR caused like revisions to GP clauses, "Changes," and "Differing Site Conditions" (fig. 2-1 and 2-2). Before the 1968 revisions to the GP clauses, estimating the cost/time for a modification was straightforward, with only the directly changed work to consider. The revised clauses have added a new dimension to the estimate; it must now address all of the remaining work -- not only the

2-1

CONSTRUCTION SCHEDULES

EP 415-1-3
2 July 79

directly changed work, but also the effect that the modification may have on the unchanged work.

2-5. <u>Estimate preparation</u>. Preparing the estimate takes longer now as the techniques for evaluating impact on the unchanged work before performance are still in the formative stage and the evaluation requires an in-depth analysis. Delays in developing the Government estimate or receiving the contractor's proposal can cause increases in the ultimate cost of a contract modification. During negotiation, the Corps of Engineers approaches with a figure it believes to be reasonable, and the contractor approaches with a figure he believes is sufficient to protect him in case everything goes wrong that possibly could. Reaching an equitable agreement under these circumstances is difficult and time consuming.

2-6. <u>Alternatives to agreement</u>. If an agreement cannot be reached, the Corps of Engineers is forced to fall back on its alternatives; that is, to either issue a change order with NTP now and settlement of price/time at a later date (Alternative 1), or issue a unilateral modification (Alternative 2). Using Alternative 1 immediately renders the progress schedule ineffective as a management tool and useless for determining the extent of impact for future modifications. In effect, Alternative 1 provides the contractor a cost-plus contractual relationship on the modification work. Alternative 2 establishes (at least tentatively) the modification cost and time factors, and allows prompt revision of the progress schedule, thus maintaining its usefulness. The use of Alternative 2 requires a high degree of confidence in the Government Estimate. Neither of the alternatives can adequately replace the achievement of an equitable agreement before the NTP is issued for a modification.

2-7. <u>Need for impact estimates</u>. To be more successful in processing modifications, the Corps of Engineers must be able to develop estimates that consider the impact, if any, for the ordered change. The Corps of Engineers must develop logical methods and techniques for before-the-fact impact evaluation, since entering into negotiations armed with a tenable estimate certainly enhances the prospects of coming out with a fair and reasonable agreement.

2-8. <u>Scope</u>. This pamphlet provides information and procedures fundamental to the identification of impact. Although too many possible combinations of circumstances affect the distribution and severity of impact to cover each specifically, this pamphlet will provide insights which can be adapted to most situations.

APPENDIX

EP 415-1-3
2 July 79

DIFFERING SITE CONDITIONS (1968 FEB)
(a) The Contractor shall promptly, and before such conditions are disturbed, notify the Contracting Officer in writing of: (1) subsurface or latent physical conditions at the site differing materially from those indicated in this contract, or (2) unknown physical conditions at the site, of an unusual nature, differing materially from those ordinarily encountered and generally recognized as inhering in work of the character provided for in this contract. The Contracting Officer shall promptly investigate the conditions, and if he finds that such conditions do materially so differ and cause an increase or decrease in the Contractor's cost of, or the time required for, performance of any part of the work under this contract, whether or not changed as a result of such conditions, an equitable adjustment shall be made and the contract modified in writing accordingly.
(b) No claim of the Contractor under this clause shall be allowed unless the Contractor has given the notice required in (a) above; *provided,* however, the time prescribed therefor may be extended by the Government.
(c) No claim by the Contractor for an equitable adjustment hereunder shall be allowed if asserted after final payment under this contract. (ASPR 7-602.4)

Figure 2-1. "Differing Site Conditions" Specification.

CHANGES (1968 FEB)

(a) The Contracting Officer may, at any time, without notice to the sureties, by written order designated or indicated to be a change order, make any change in the work within the general scope of the contract, including but not limited to changes:

    (i) in the specifications (including drawings and designs);
    (ii) in the method or manner of performance of the work;
    (iii) in the Government-furnished facilities, equipment, materials, services, or site; or
    (iv) directing acceleration in the performance of the work.

(b) Any other written order or an oral order (which terms as used in this paragraph (b) shall include direction, instruction, interpretation or determination) from the Contracting Officer, which causes any such change, shall be treated as a change order under this clause, *provided* that the Contractor gives the Contracting Officer written notice stating the date, circumstances, and source of the order and that the Contractor regards the order as a change order.

(c) Except as herein provided, no order, statement, or conduct of the Contracting Officer shall be treated as a change under this clause or entitle the Contractor to an equitable adjustment hereunder.

(d) If any change under this clause causes an increase or decrease in the Contractor's cost of, or the time required for, the performance of any part of the work under this contract, whether or not changed by any order, an equitable adjustment shall be made and the contract modified in writing accordingly: *Provided, however,* That except for claims based on defective specifications, no claim for any change under (b) above shall be allowed for any costs incurred more than 20 days before the Contractor gives written notice as therein required: *And provided further,* That in the case of defective specifications for which the Government is responsible, the equitable adjustment shall include any increased cost reasonably incurred by the Contractor in attempting to comply with such defective specifications.

(e) If the Contractor intends to assert a claim for an equitable adjustment under this clause, he must, within 30 days after receipt of a written change order under (a) above or the furnishing of a written notice under (b) above, submit to the Contracting Officer a written statement setting forth the general nature and monetary extent of such claim, unless this period is extended by the Government. The statement of claim hereunder may be included in the notice under (b) above.

(f) No claim by the Contractor for an equitable adjustment hereunder shall be allowed if asserted after final payment under this contract. (ASPR 7-602.3)

Figure 2-2. "Changes" Specification.

APPENDIX

EP 415-1-3
2 July 79

CHAPTER 3

IDENTIFICATION

3-1. Job status.

a. Knowing the current status of a job is important when making an estimate for the changed work portion of a contract modification, and absolutely vital to estimating impact. Data on current job status should be developed without influence from the contractor's formal progress schedule. In many cases, the contractor's real plan for pursuing the work is not the same as indicated on the schedule, the schedule may not have been revised to reflect the effects of previous modifications, or both. In analyzing the current status of a job, accurate data must be compiled on the following:

   (1) Activities completed.

   (2) Activities in progress (including percent complete).

   (3) Activities to start soon (not necessarily from progress schedule).

   (4) Onsite manpower (divided into supervisory, administrative, Quality Control (QC), and various crafts; the employer, contractor, subcontractor, and numbers and types employed on each activity in progress must be indicated).

   (5) QC and Quality Assurance (QA) reports must be reviewed to determine production efficiency and past delaying factors.

   (6) Materials onsite (for future incorporation in the facility); materials submitted, approved, and ordered (anticipated delivery date).

   (7) Materials submitted, approved, but not ordered.

   (8) Materials submitted, disapproved, and not resubmitted.

   (9) Materials not submitted, where approval and procurement lead time is such that they may not be delivered to the site in time to avoid delaying a part of the work.

3-1

(10) Construction equipment and special tools; the status, i.e., working or not working, must be indicated. If working, activities for which used must be shown; if not working, whether or not future need exists (indicate specific activity) must be shown.

b. Current job status information must be developed early in the estimating process for a modification. However, since the status of a job changes from day to day, the information must be updated to reflect any significant change right up to the date negotiations are conducted.

3-2. Progress schedule.

a. The GP clause, "Progress Charts and Requirements for Overtime Work (1965 Jan)," establishes the basis for requiring the contractor to submit his progress schedule for approval (fig. 3-1). The contract Special Provisions (SPs) will include a clause, supplementing the GP, to indicate the type of schedule required. Corps of Engineers construction contracts will use either a Network Analysis System (NAS), as defined in Appendix I of ER 1-1-11 and ER 415-1-303; or a Bar Chart, per ENG Form 2454. For the identification of impact, the NAS, more commonly known as the CPM (Critical Path Method), is more detailed than the Bar Chart. To develop such detail from a Bar Chart may require breaking the relatively large units of work shown on the chart into networks of individual activities with corresponding duration and dollar value. Fortunately, the Bar Chart schedule is specified for small, routine, straightforward projects where the presence or absence of impact may be more evident. This pamphlet assumes that the project specifies NAS scheduling; or, if not, that the estimator will have developed a reasonable network from the Bar Chart information for identifying impact-susceptible activities.

b. When it approved the contractor's progress schedule, the Corps of Engineers accepted the information it conveyed as defining a practicable way to accomplish the work within the contract completion time. As long as actual progress meets or exceeds that schedule, the originally approved progress schedule remains valid. Very few, if any, construction projects are completed according to the original schedule. Something usually happens along the way that makes the subsequent portion of the original plan undesirable to the contractor, or just plain unworkable. The causes for this arise from three areas:

(1) <u>The Contractor</u>. The contractor fails to diligently pursue the work, plans poorly, or the prime contractor, subcontractor, or suppliers fail to perform the work in the sequence scheduled.

APPENDIX

EP 415-1-3
2 July 79

(2) <u>The Corps of Engineers</u>. The Corps of Engineers changes the work, gives inaccurate site condition data, fails to take timely actions, etc.

(3) <u>Other delays</u>. Delays caused by events defined in the contract as "excusable" delays.

c. Item b (1) does not justify a contract time extension, but does require the contractor to revise the schedule, indicate how he proposes to recoup the lost time and complete the work within the remaining contract time. Item b (2) provides for contract price and time adjustment equitable for the effect the Corps of Engineers action had on the contractor. Item b (3) allows an extension of time for the delay.

d. Paragraph 3-2b emphasizes that if the progress schedule is to be a valid tool for identifying and evaluating impact, it must reflect all changes to the original schedule regardless of the reasons for them. The most frequent cause for revising the progress schedule is to accommodate contract modifications initiated by the Corps of Engineers. The importance of settling each modification as it is identified and immediately making appropriate revisions to the progress schedule should be obvious. This goal is not impossible, but its achievement does require diligent efforts by the Corps of Engineers and the contractor.

e. The purpose for requiring the contractor to submit a progress chart is primarily to assure the Corps of Engineers that the contractor has a reasonable plan for accomplishing the work within the specified time. The progress chart provides both the Corps of Engineers and the contractor with a common basis for evaluating the acceptability of the actual rate of progress as the work proceeds. The progress schedule often must be revised for reasons other than contract modifications. The contractor is responsible for providing the job with the materials, manpower, equipment, and supervisory expertise required to maintain scheduled progress. Many unforeseen delays may occur in the original progress schedule. Even minor delays should be closely monitored by the Corps of Engineers; persistent delays may become critical and affect other future activities. The Corps of Engineers must take immediate action when a critical activity is delayed to the extent that the existing schedule no longer represents a viable plan for accomplishing the remaining work within the specified time. The basis for the Corps of Engineers' action in this case is found in the GP clause, "Progress Charts and Requirements for Overtime Work (1965 Jan)," which, in addition to giving the Corps of Engineers the right to order the contractor to take actions to improve his progress, also requires the contractor to submit for approval a revised progress schedule showing how he plans to

3-3

CONSTRUCTION SCHEDULES

EP 415-1-3
2 July 79

regain the lost time and complete the project on schedule (fig. 3-1). The contractor must bear the cost of complying with directions issued by the Corps of Engineers, pursuant to the provisions of the Progress Chart clause. Consequently, the Corps of Engineers is justified in using this clause only when the delaying factor(s) are attributable solely to the contractor. If the progress schedule, used to determine that the contractor is behind schedule, is not up to date, including allowance for all time extensions, the contractor may have grounds for claiming reimbursement for costs incurred due to Corps of Engineers directions even though the delay is mostly caused by the contractor. Here again, the urgency of settling modifications quickly is apparent. If the Corps of Engineers has issued an NTP on a modification before the settlement terms are agreed upon, until such time as that modification is settled, there is no up-to-date, realistic progress schedule and the pertinent contract provisions cannot be enforced.

f. Cases where it is essential that the contractor be allowed to proceed on modification work before the price/time terms are settled must be kept to an absolute minimum. The attitude that the urgency for reaching a settlement no longer exists once the NTP has been issued is self-defeating. For many reasons, it is advantageous to the contractor to delay final settlement of all modifications until the work is finished:

(1) The contractor can be less cost conscious in doing the work.

(2) Some of the risks contractually assigned to the contractor are shifted to the Corps of Engineers.

(3) The contractor will have actual cost data with which to confront the Corps of Engineers. (Actual cost under this circumstance does not necessarily represent reasonable cost.)

g. The Corps of Engineers' goal, on the other hand, is to settle modifications before performance so:

(1) The contractor has more incentive to accomplish the work in the most efficient manner.

(2) The risks stay with the contractor.

(3) The burden of proving that the price is reasonable remains on the contractor.

APPENDIX

EP 415-1-3
2 July 79

h. A major benefit of settling modifications before performance is that it encourages prompt revision of the progress schedule, thus maintaining accurate knowledge of the sequencing of the remaining work, the final contract price, and the final completion date. The schedule then remains a realistic tool for determining the impact of changes on the contractor's operations. An up-to-date CPM schedule is a prerequisite to forecasting the presence and extent of impact. If a CPM schedule is not available, the work of the estimator is more difficult.

3-3. Procedures.

a. The data on job status (para 3-1) show what activities remain to be accomplished, and whether the necessary materials can be expected onsite to support these activities as scheduled. Except for Government Furnished Property (GFP), the contractor is responsible for obtaining the materials in a timely manner. If some materials will not be available when needed to maintain scheduled progress, the schedule should be marked up by the estimator to reflect this situation. The next step is to analyze the scope of the modification to determine which remaining activity(ies) will be <u>directly</u> affected; that is, identify the activity(ies) having less work, more work, or other revisions. Using the estimate of <u>direct changes</u>, assign to the affected activity(ies) revised durations that reflect the sum of the duration assigned by the contractor and the duration now estimated as required to accommodate the modification. When part or all of the work to be performed under a modification does not fit an existing activity, the estimator can create a new activity(ies) tied into existing nodes. Many factors must be considered when selecting the start and finish nodes for the new activity: (1) other activities which restrain its start, (2) material procurement lead time (this could be a new activity itself), (3) weather (if the work is outdoors), (4) duration of changed work, and (5) other activities restrained by the new activity(ies). The challenge is to find where the addition of changed work will least disrupt the other remaining work. Since the impact costs originate in activities that are not directly changed by the modification, the fewer unchanged activities remaining when the changed work starts, the less potential there is for impact. Unfortunately, completion of at least some of the unchanged work will depend on completion of the modification work. So the estimator accepts these limitations, inserts the modification work into the network, and starts to identify unchanged activities that represent potential impact points. As soon as the estimator is satisfied that the modification work is correctly placed in the schedule, he should discuss it with the contractor. A mutual understanding of the schedule for accomplishing the modification work is necessary to provide the Corps of Engineers and the contractor a common basis upon which to develop impact cost estimates.

3-5

CONSTRUCTION SCHEDULES

EP 415-1-3
2 July 79

b. The revised progress schedule now shows the remaining work and the changes introduced by the modification. Using the durations previously assigned, and taking advantage of any float time, new early start (ES), early finish (EF), late start (LS), and late finish (LF) dates are calculated. These new calculations show the schedule for completing the modified work and the other remaining work. The critical path may have changed, and it is likely that the earliest completion date is now later.

c. If the modified work affects only activities off the critical path, with enough float to absorb the modified work, the completion date will not change. In this case, all of the remaining activities, including those directly affected by the modification, have stayed within their contract timeframe; consequently, the modification does not justify additional completion time. This fortunate result is more likely for a modification issued early in the job, before float time is depleted.

d. If rescheduling the remaining work to include the modification, as described above, has changed the final completion date, a time extension is justified. The negative difference between the previously scheduled final completion date and the newly developed completion date represents only the time extension caused by direct changes to the work. Now the scheduling changes that have occurred to the unchanged activities must be analyzed. So far, originally assigned durations have been retained, but impact may require assigning longer durations to at least some of the activities.

e. The revised schedule must now be analyzed to see how the modification has affected unchanged work activities. Answer questions such as:

(1) Has any activity been moved from where the contractor had it scheduled into a season where normal weather is more unfavorable or makes it impractical to do this type of work?

(2) Are there now more activities in progress at a given time than indicated by the schedule before revision?

(3) Have any activities slipped to the extent that significant phases of the work, such as closing in a building for winter, providing necessary utilities, completing an access road, building a coffer dam, etc., will not be accomplished before some overriding factor (winter, high water stages, unavailability of site) prevent it, thus making it necessary to defer a portion of the work until the next favorable season?

3-6

APPENDIX

EP 415-1-3
2 July 79

f. The durations of the impacted activities should be increased to reflect the time now realistically required for their accomplishment. The schedule should also be revised to show any activity(ies) which require a dormant period. (Such dormant period(s) shall be defined in the finalized modification documents.) The schedule should be updated to show the logical sequence and timing of activities representing the work directly changed by the modification, and all other unchanged work. Further slippage of the final completion from the date developed in para d above, justifies an extension of contract completion time because of impact. The total amount of the time extension for a modification is the sum of delay attributable to direct changes and that attributable to impact.

3-4. <u>Summary</u>.

a. Paragraph 3-3 defined procedures for developing the time requirements portion of a CPM schedule to reflect the changes necessary to accommodate the work as directly changed by a modification, and its effects on the unchanged work. These procedures are:

(1) <u>Define current job status</u>. Compile data on actual progress, status of materials, manpower, equipment, and any other pertinent factors. (para 3-1)

(2) <u>Analyze progress schedule</u>. The process of accurately identifying and evaluating impact depends largely on an up-to-date CPM progress schedule. To effectively fulfill its contract administration responsibilities, the Corps of Engineers must exercise the authorities and options available to maintain progress schedule validity throughout the life of the project (para 3-2).

(3) <u>Procedures for developing a revised schedule (para 3-3)</u>.

(a) Revise the schedule to show actual job status.

(b) Insert the directly changed work.

(c) Recalculate affected unchanged work (retaining presently assigned durations).

(d) Reestablish critical path, and note time extension justified by direct changes.

(e) Analyze schedule for impacted unchanged activities; assign new durations to these activities as appropriate.

3-7

CONSTRUCTION SCHEDULES

EP 415-1-3
2 July 79

(f) Reestablish critical path, and note any slippage of final completion date indicated in (d), above. Difference is amount of time extension justified because of impact.

b. The above effort will develop a logical schedule for the remaining work (i.e., work changed by the modification and all other work remaining at the time the modification is effective). Developing this schedule is not merely a mechanical exercise. Many judgments must be made, and the schedule's reliability depends largely on their quality. Personnel making such judgments must have thorough knowledge of the jobsite conditions, the contractor's capabilities and methods of operation, the schedule applicable before the modification occurred, the CPM scheduling system, and the Corps of Engineers' contractual liabilities pertaining to impact on the unchanged work.

c. The revised schedule represents a realistic sequencing and timing of the remaining work, but is only a working tool for the estimator's use, with no other contractual implications. It represents one method, but not necessarily the only method, for completing the remaining work. It has quantified the time considered reasonable, without acceleration, for the contractor to accomplish the work.

3-5. Examples. To help demonstrate the procedures described in paragraph 3-3, an NAS progress schedule has been prepared for a hypothetical construction project. The contractor's original schedule, approved by the Corps of Engineers, is shown in figures 3-2a through 3-2o. This schedule is used as the basis for analyzing the impact caused by various modifications. In actual practice, the original schedule would be revised after each modification, and the new schedule would become the basis upon which the next modification would be evaluated; however, to avoid complicating the examples shown here, each situation will be dealt with as though the original schedule was valid when the modification occurred.

a. Example 1.

(1) Assume that it is necessary to modify the contract to correct a dimension controlling the building location. The contractor had just completed Activity 201-203, Layout, when the error in the plans was detected. Almost all of the critical Activity 201-203 must now be redone. Since the correct information is available, and to avoid further delays, the Request for Proposal (RFP) has been issued with a simultaneous NTP.

(2) The estimator begins the analysis by marking up the network to indicate actual job status (fig. 3-3). The figure shows Activities 1-201, 1-207, and 201-203 complete, and Activity 201-207 50 percent

3-8

APPENDIX

EP 415-1-3
2 July 79

complete. The modification directly changes the work and duration of critical path Activity 201-203 only. Critical path Activity 203-207, Excavation 1/2, depends on the completion of Activity 201-203 for its start. Likewise, the start dates for all subsequent critical path activities will be delayed for whatever length of time is determined reasonable to now complete Activity 201-203. Looking further at the schedule, it can be determined that increasing the duration of Activity 201-203 will not affect the completion of Activity 201-207; and Activity 205-225 has sufficient float to absorb the delay to its early start date.

(3) A review of the status of materials submittals and deliveries indicates that they are proceeding essentially on schedule, so materials do not affect the remaining work, nor become a cost factor for this modification.

(4) Onsite manpower is not significant in this case, except for Activity 201-203. The crew assigned to this activity will be the basis for determining the direct labor costs applicable to this modification.

(5) Except for some powered hand tools being used on Activity 201-207, the only equipment onsite is a contractor-owned backhoe to be used in the excavation work, Activity 203-207. Since the modification has delayed the completion of Activity 201-203, the date the backhoe can be placed in service is also delayed. This is an impact cost which will be included in the impact portion of the estimate. (See fig. 5-1.)

(6) The estimator and the contractor agree that Activity 201-203, as modified, can best be accomplished using the existing crew assigned to that work, and that the additional work will require 5 calendar days to complete. Therefore, the schedule is modified to indicate a new duration of 13 calendar days (8 plus 5) for Activity 201-203 (fig 3-3). This actually causes the time frame of all remaining critical activities to slip 5 calendar days; but for this example, it is not considered necessary to provide a printout showing this result.

(7) A review of the remaining work -- which in this case amounts to nearly the entire project -- indicates that a slippage of the 5 calendar days does not impact on the unchanged activities that would require further rescheduling. The slippage in the final completion date is acceptable to the Using Agency. Consequently, the revised schedule developed by the estimator to analyze the effects of the modification shows only two pertinent factors; i.e., Activity 201-203 will incur the direct costs of the modification and have its duration increased 5 calendar days, and Activity 203-207 will sustain impact costs for equipment standby time. The estimate will be prepared accordingly.

CONSTRUCTION SCHEDULES

EP 415-1-3
2 July 79

b. Example 2. For this example, the effects of Example 1 on the progress schedule will be disregarded. The original schedule will be considered applicable.

(1) Assume that on 15 September 1978, the District Office issues an RFP on a change order which proposes the following:

(a) Increasing the size of exterior doors.

(b) Reducing the air-to-air roof U-Value from 0.07 to 0.05.

(c) Adding 50 lineal feet of 4-ft-wide concrete sidewalks.

(2) The first step toward identifying impact and preparing the estimate is to mark up the progress chart to show actual progress to date. (See fig. 3-4a and 3-4b.) The project is on schedule with Activity 223-227, Backfill Foundation Walls, 50 percent complete; and Activity 205-225, Underground Water and Sewer Lines, 60 percent complete. Procurement activities are also proceeding according to plan, with no delays foreseen.

(3) From the NAS it can be seen that the modification will directly affect Activity 231-235, Door Frames, Windows, and Louvers; and Activity 243-245, Roofing and Sheet Metal (roof insulation is included in this activity). Since there is no existing activity for sidewalks, a new activity will need to be created to include this work.

(4) The schedule mark-up reflects the effects of this modification, and begins with the first activity to be changed, i.e., Activity 231-235. As figure 3-4a indicates, the doors and frames are now on the job site, but because of this modification they are unusable. Activity 231-235 has 14 days of float indicated; however, this does not apply to the door frames. The door frames must be available very shortly after the start of critical Activity 227-235, Exterior Masonry, to avoid delaying that activity. The contractor is consulted to establish the quickest way to obtain new door frames, and the following factors are identified: the door size now specified is not standard with the manufacturer who supplied the ones onsite; the best date received from other manufacturers is 45 days after receipt of an order; the manufacturer of the doors and frames onsite will rework the doors and frames to meet the new size requirement, at a cost of $50 per frame and $100 per door; and reworking the frames at the manufacturer's plant will require 5 work days after receipt. Reworking the doors will require 20 work days after receipt. (The cost of shipment will be borne by the contractor.) The District (which issued the change) is contacted and it is confirmed that

3-10

APPENDIX

EP 415-1-3
2 July 79

the modification is mandatory. Since the overall cost of the modification is expected to be within the Resident Contracting Officer's (RCO's) authority, an NTP for reworking the doors and frames is issued by the RCO. The contractor proceeds to deliver the doors and frames to the manufacturer in his own truck. The contractor will also use his own truck to pick up the reworked materials when ready, since this is considered faster and less expensive than using commercial carriers. The estimator decides that 2 work days will be required to deliver the frames and doors, 5 work days to remanufacture the frames, 2 work days to return the frames to the site, 13 work days more to rework the doors, and 2 work days to return the doors to the site. It is concluded that only the frames are critical, so the 9 work days required to obtain them is considered first. Converting from work to calendar days produces a 13 calendar day delay in receipt of the new door frames. Rather than change the duration of Activity 73-105, Doors and Windows (procurement), which is complete and carries no monetary value, a new Activity 105-106, Rework Frames (Mod 2), is created and assigned a duration of 13 calendar days (fig. 3-4a). The activity has a start date of 16 September 1978 (the date NTP on this work was issued), and a finish date of 28 September 1978. Since Activity 105-106 constrains the start of Activity 231-235, the early start of Activity 231-235 is adjusted to 29 September 1978. (The original early start date for Activity 231-235 was 18 September 1978, and the late start date was 2 October 1978.) It now appears that Activity 231-235 has plenty of float to absorb the delay caused by its early start date without affecting Critical Activity 227-235. But the float in Activity 231-235 is misleading. The door frames must be available within a short time following the start of the masonry work. The estimator now faces two choices on how to schedule Activity 227-235, Exterior Masonry:

(a) **Option A.** Allow the exterior masonry work to start as scheduled on 17 September 1978 and let it proceed as far as it can (estimated 4 calendar days) before door frames are needed, then shut down and wait for door frames (29 September 1978). Following delivery of door frames, resume operations and complete the activity.

(b) **Option B.** Delay the start of the exterior masonry work until such time that once started it can proceed to completion without interruption. This adjusts the start date for Activity 227-235 to 25 September 1978, or 4 calendar days before the door frames are due at the site.

(5) Both Options A and B will cause work on the critical path to slip the same amount -- 8 calendar days, i.e., 29 September minus 17 September 1978 plus 4 calendar days. Although both options must address

3-11

CONSTRUCTION SCHEDULES

EP 415-1-3
2 July 79

any impact costs arising from the 8 day delay, only Option A introduces the additional impact liabilities associated with disruption of the masonry work after it is underway. Therefore, Option B is selected, since it represents the least impact on the contractor's operations.

   (6) The estimator must remember to include the time (and later the cost) for reworking the doors on the schedule. Since the installation of exterior doors does not really represent a constraint on masonry work completion or any other activity scheduled in the near future, reworking the doors is an extension of procurement Activity 73-105. However, this does not coincide with new Activity 105-106; another new activity must be created. If node 105 is used as the starting point and node 235 is used as the finishing point, a new Activity 105-235, Rework Doors (Mod 2), is created. This activity has an early start date of 16 September 1978, and a duration of 34 calendar days. Its early finish will be 19 October 1978 and its late finish is 24 October 1978 (coinciding with the finish date of critical Activity 227-235). Activity 105-235 has been placed between nodes 105 and 235 for convenience, and to locate it in a realistic time frame.

   (7) The result of the foregoing analysis and revision to the progress schedule caused by the first part of the modification is as follows:

   (a) New Activity 105-106, Rework Door Frames (Mod 2), was created. It has an early start of 16 September 1978 and a duration of 13 calendar days. Its completion is prerequisite to the start of Activity 231-235.

   (b) Existing Activity 231-235's early start date has been slipped to 28 September 1978. Its duration remains unchanged, because the time and effort required to install the revised frames and doors is not much different from that required for the originally specified materials.

   (c) Existing critical path Activity 227-235's start date has been slipped 8 calendar days, to 25 September 1978. Its duration remains unchanged.

   (d) New Activity 105-235, Rework Doors (Mod 2), was created to show the time frame for this noncritical activity. It has an early start of 16 September 1978, a 34 calendar day duration, and 5 days of float.

   (e) Since a delay of 8 calendar days has been placed in the critical path at Activity 227-235, all subsequent activities will also slip 8 calendar days. In actual practice, a new mathematical analysis would

3-12

APPENDIX

EP 415-1-3
2 July 79

report revised sets of dates for the remaining activities, including a new final completion date. Since the only purpose of this example is to demonstrate effect, a revised mathematical analysis is not included.

(8) The second part of the modification requires a change in the roof insulation. The current job status of Activities 1-13, 13-45, 45-77, and 77-109 shows that the material has been submitted, approved, and ordered (fig. 3-4 a). However, as of 16 September 1978 the material has not been delivered to the site, although it is scheduled to arrive not later than 29 October 1978. The October deadline is necessary because the second part of the modification constrains the start date of critical Activity 243-245. This activity contains the installation of roof insulation, and is scheduled to start on 30 October 1978 (fig. 3-4 a). In view of the 8 calendar day slippage in the schedule caused by the first part of the modification, the revised start date for critical Activity 243-245 is 7 November 1978. Consequently, the late finish date for Activity 77-109 is 6 November 1978.

(9) The estimator collected the following information:

(a) The roof insulation, roof membrane materials, and roof sheet metal items included in Activity 77-109 are to be provided and installed by a subcontractor.

(b) The modification does not affect roof membrane materials.

(c) The originally specified roof insulation is promised for delivery at the job site on or before 15 October 1978. The subcontractor plans to achieve the modified U-value by placing another layer of the same brand of insulation on top of the original.

(d) The insulation manufacturer will not guarantee a delivery date or price for the required additional material until a purchase order is received.

(e) The prime contractor's purchasing agent has contacted all known insulation distributors, and found that none of them have the required types and thickness of insulation in stock. These manufacturers are filling orders as fast as they can, but the average wait is 60 days.

(f) The subcontractor has received the necessary sheet metal stock and is fabricating gutters and fascia in accordance with approved shop drawings. The fascia detail, however, will require revision because the modification has increased the insulation thickness.

3-13

CONSTRUCTION SCHEDULES

EP 415-1-3
2 July 79

(10) In view of the above, the Resident Engineer (RE) takes the following actions:

   (a) An NTP ordering the additional insulation is issued to the contractor.

   (b) The contractor is informed that resubmittal of U-value calculations will not be required, because the original submittal provides sufficient data to indicate that the proposed additional thickness will produce the required 0.05 U-value.

   (c) A voluntary commitment is obtained from the contractor to stop fabricating sheet metal fascia and to resubmit revised shop drawings.

   (d) A copy of the contractor's purchase order is forwarded to the District Expediter, requesting action to obtain the best possible delivery date for the additional insulation; it is emphasized that the material is essential to job progress and must be received by 6 November 1978.

(11) Information is obtained from the expeditor and the contractor, indicating that the insulation manufacturer promises delivery of the additional materials on or before 1 November 1978 at $0.35/sq ft, FOB job site.

(12) The estimator returns to the progress schedule and creates an Activity 78-109, Procure Additional Roof Insulation (Mod 2), with an early start date of 17 September 1978, and a duration of 46 calendar days (fig. 3-4 a). The late finish date of this activity will be 6 November 1978, to provide 5 calendar days of float. New Activity 80-109, Fascia Rework (Mod 2), is also created. Activity 80-109 has an early start date of 17 September 1978, a duration of 30 calendar days (which includes resubmittal and approval of revised shop drawings, and refabrication of fascia), a late finish date of 6 November 1978, which provides 21 calendar days of float (see fig. 3-4 a). By placing the modified work in the two new activities, the NAS now shows that the start of critical Activity 243-245 will not be delayed beyond 7 November 1978 (the date it was slipped to by the first part of the modification).

(13) When the first part of the modification was inserted into the progress schedule, Activity 243-245 was an affected unchanged activity -- its time frame slipped 8 calendar days. The second part of the modification directly affects Activity 243-245, since another layer of insulation, deeper plates, and revised fascia must be added. The estimator must now evaluate the combined effect of the first and second part of the modification on critical Activity 243-245.

3-14

APPENDIX

EP 415-1-3
2 July 79

(a) The activity is now scheduled for a time period later than the contractor originally planned; i.e., 7 November through 17 November 1978 instead of 30 October through 9 November 1978. The estimator must decide whether or not this will cause the contractor's cost and/or time required to accomplish the work to increase. Weather is the primary factor in this case. In many parts of the country, the approach of winter reduces the number of days suitable for roofing operations. It is likely -- but not certain -- that more days unsuitable for roofing will occur during the period 7 November through 17 November 1978 than 30 October through 9 November 1978. Probabilities developed using historical weather data are not specific enough for this situation. The real issue is the actual difference, this year, at this project site, between the weather conditions during the original period planned for the roofing work, and the period into which it will be delayed. Any attempt to predict an increase in the duration of Activity 243-245 before the fact would be conjecture. The estimator decides to document the actual weather conditions that occur during the originally planned time period and the actual performance period, and use these data as the basis for granting or not granting a time extension after-the-fact for Activity 243-245 under GP clause "Termination for Default Damages for Delay -- Time Extensions" (fig. 3-5).

(b) The work in Activity 243-245 has been increased since the contractor must now place an additional layer of insulation, and build up the nailers and plates. The time and cost of reworking the sheet metal fascia is covered in Activity 80-109; its installation, covered in Activity 243-245, requires no time or cost adjustment. One additional day is considered reasonable by the estimator for doing the revised insulation and associated work. The duration of Activity 243-245 is increased to 12 calendar days, extending the finish date of the activity to 18 November 1978. This extension causes an equal slippage in all subsequent activities. As the estimate develops, appropriate monetary values for Activities 78-109, 80-109, and 243-245 will be established. (Chapter 5 provides examples of estimates pertaining to these situations.)

(14) The third part of the modification described in paragraph 3-5b adds some sidewalk work. There was no sidewalk in the contract before; consequently, there is no applicable existing activity in the network. The estimator must now study the progress schedule and determine where this new work will best fit. The following are pertinent considerations:

EP 415-1-3
2 July 79

(a) The time required to grade, form, and place the sidewalk is 3 calendar days.

(b) The sidewalk work must be completed before inclement weather arrives.

(c) Underground Utilities, Activity 205-225, should be in and backfilled in the sidewalk area before sidewalk construction starts.

(d) Fine Grading the Site, Activity 247-253, should (preferably) be completed after the sidewalks are constructed.

(e) Exterior Masonry, Activity 227-235, will probably obstruct at least part of the sidewalk construction area. So Activity 227-235 should be finished before starting sidewalks.

(15) Based on the above analysis, the estimator decides that creating new Activity 235-247, Sidewalks (Mod 2), is appropriate. The new activity has a duration of 3 calendar days with an early start date of 25 October 1978, a late finish date of 17 November 1978, and 21 calendar days of float (fig. 3-4a). New Activity 235-247, Sidewalks (Mod 2) permits the contractor to perform the work any time between 25 October and 17 November 1978, without causing any impact on the unchanged work.

c. Example 3.

(1) The original approved progress schedule, figures 3-2a through 3-2o, is used as the basis for analyzing the effects of this example. Note that in actual practice, a schedule revised to reflect previous modifications would account for the cumulative effect of multiple modifications.

(2) For this example, assume that:

(a) The contract calls for the contractor to construct an area of thickened floor slab within the building, and to install Government-furnished anchor bolts in a pattern to be determined by a Government-furnished template.

(b) The contract further stipulates that the anchor bolts and template will be furnished to the contractor within 90 days after notice to proceed on the contract (in this case, by 22 September 1978.)

3-16

APPENDIX

EP 415-1-3
2 July 79

(c) The contractor's approved progress schedule indicates that possession of the GFP is prerequisite to the start of Activity 239-245, Floor Slab Subgrade. The early start date for Activity 239-245 is 28 October 1978, well beyond the date scheduled for delivery of the bolts and template. Although the contractor does not really require the GFP to begin subgrade preparation, it is necessary for the completion of that activity. GFP is prerequisite to starting Activity 251-255, Floor Slab Concrete. (See fig. 3-2g.)

(d) On 2 October 1978, the District advised the RE that there will be some delay in obtaining the GFP because equipment revisions by the Using Agency will change the anchor bolt configuration. Therefore, even though every effort is being made to obtain the revised bolts and template, there will be a minimum delay of 30 days.

(e) The RE advised the contractor of the anticipated delay, and discussed the possibility of blocking out the anchor bolt area so the remainder of the floor slab could proceed uninterrupted.

(f) On 1 November 1978, the contractor advised the RE by letter that the Government's failure to furnish the GFP as stipulated in the contract will generate additional costs and if the GFP is not received by 15 November 1978, he will be required to shut down the job. The letter further advised that the contractor will submit a claim for all additional costs and delays after the GFP arrives and the actual costs/delays can be calculated.

(g) The claim letter is forwarded to the District with RE comments verifying the claim's validity. The District indicates that the Using Agency expects to ship the GFP on 15 November 1978 directly to the RE. The Using Agency has indicated that a slippage in the final completion date is not acceptable. They also object to blocking out the anchor bolt area for placing the bolts later.

(h) On 17 November 1978, the contractor is finishing Activity 249-251, Floor Concrete-1st 1/2, and advises the RE that he will shut down the job the next day unless directed differently. Although the contractor does not normally work on weekends (18 and 19 November 1978 are Saturday and Sunday), he correctly points out that his schedule calls for critical Activity 251-255, Floor Concrete-2nd 1/2, to be accomplished on those days, so they have been added to the work schedule. It is confirmed that the GFP was shipped on 15 November 1978, but its exact whereabouts is unknown.

CONSTRUCTION SCHEDULES

EP 415-1-3
2 July 79

(i) The RE agrees that working on the weekend would be unproductive under the circumstances, but indicates to the contractor that since no stop order has been issued, the contractor is expected to staff the job on Monday, 20 November 1978. No work was performed on 18 and 19 November 1978. The RE kept the office open on Saturday, but the GFP did not arrive.

(j) On Monday, 20 November 1978, the contractor had workers on the job, but there was little to be done and the contractor reminded the RE that the Government is responsible for paying his costs. At 11 a.m., the GFP arrived and was immediately turned over to the contractor. That afternoon the bolts were set to template and made ready for concrete. On 21 and 22 November 1978, the concrete was placed, finished, and placed under cure. Critical Activity 251-255 was completed on 22 November 1978, 3 days later than scheduled.

(k) While the estimator was developing cost/time data to represent the Government's liability in this case, the RE was looking for a means to get the work back on schedule. After the first half of the floor slab had been curing for 5 days, the RE authorized the contractor to begin stockpiling masonry materials on it and to remove the curing from the second half slab concrete on 28 November 1978. These actions shortened the duration of critical Activity 255-259, Cure Floor Slab, enough to permit the critical interior masonry work, Activity 259-267, to start when originally scheduled (29 November 1978).

(3) The following conclusions were reached by the estimator in the case described in subparagraphs (a) through (k), above.

(a) The contractor incurred no additional cost; in fact, the premium labor costs which would have occurred had the weekend remained on the work schedule were saved.

(b) No time was lost on the critical path, because the delay in completing the second half slab was immediately offset by shortening the subsequent curing period. And since the required curing period was less than the duration assigned to the activity by the contractor, the RE did not waive any contract requirement.

(4) The contractor's claim, which arrived at the RE's office on 1 December 1978, asked for an increase in contract price equaling the cost of the entire onsite crew for 4 hours, plus half the crew for 4 hours on 20 November 1978. In addition, the contractor claimed a 3-day time extension, the cost of 3 days' temporary heating, and markup because the start of Activity 251-255 was delayed from 18 to 21 November 1978.

APPENDIX

EP 415-1-3
2 July 79

(5) On 4 December 1978, the RE and contractor met to discuss the claim. The RE explained that while the late delivery of the GFP was acknowledged, the real issue was whether the delay increased the contractor's cost of performing the work and/or whether it constrained the completion of any phase of the work to the extent that final completion of the project was affected. The estimator's conclusions as outlined in (3) above were also explained to the contractor by the RE; with respect to the contractor's claim for additional temporary heating, the RE reminded the contractor of his commitment to provide temporary heating continuously after the subgrade was prepared. Therefore, it seemed that charges for additional heating costs were not justified. The contractor made a token protest, but had no real argument with the decision. The contractor finally agreed to drop the claim and indicated that a letter would be sent to the RE rescinding the 1 November and 1 December 1978 claim letters.

(6) This is a case where the Government was at fault and the contractor protected his rights by promptly notifying the RE of an intent to claim. However, circumstances developed wherein the RE was able to almost totally mitigate the effect on the contractor. A "No Change in Price or Time" modification was issued to provide written evidence of the specifications change and to protect the Government.

(7) The example described above points out an important element of contract administration; i.e., that it is the duty of the RE (and staff) to use every available means to reduce the cost of each claim and modification. By no means should this be construed to suggest it is good practice to attempt forcing the contractor into unreasonable settlements. The principle of "equity" is as severely violated by settlements that are too low as it is by ones too high. The interests of the Corps of Engineers and the contractor are best fulfilled when there exists a working relationship based upon mutual respect and trust. It is the RE's responsibility to initiate such a relationship, and demonstrate the Corps of Engineers' desire for fairness in the way controversial issues are handled. Before-the-fact estimating of the effect a modification will have on the contractor requires indepth knowledge of the contractor's operations. Keeping the cost of a modification to the minimum requires planning the additional work so it causes the least possible disruption to the contractor's work flow. Factual input from the contractor can be of great help to the Resident Office. Creating an environment where the exchange of information is routinely accomplished in the planning, payment, and execution of modifications serves the interests of all parties involved.

CONSTRUCTION SCHEDULES

EP 415-1-3
2 July 79

PROGRESS CHARTS AND REQUIREMENTS FOR OVERTIME WORK (1965 JAN)

(a) The Contractor shall within 5 days or within such time as determined by the Contracting Officer, after date of commencement of work prepare and submit to the Contracting Officer for approval a practicable schedule, showing the order in which the Contractor proposes to carry on the work, the date on which he will start the several salient features (including procurement of materials, plant and equipment) and the contemplated dates for completing the same. The schedule shall be in the form of a progress chart of suitable scale to indicate appropriately the percentage of work scheduled for completion at any time. The Contractor shall enter on the chart the actual progress at such intervals as directed by the Contracting Officer, and shall immediately deliver to the Contracting Officer three copies thereof. If the Contractor fails to submit a progress schedule within the time herein prescribed, the Contracting Officer may withhold approval of progress payment estimates until such time as the Contractor submits the required progress schedule.

(b) If, in the opinion of the Contracting Officer, the Contractor falls behind the progress schedule, the Contractor shall take such steps as may be necessary to improve his progress and the Contracting Officer may require him to increase the number of shifts, or overtime operations, days of work, or the amount of construction plant, or all of them, and to submit for approval such supplementary schedule or schedules in chart form as may be deemed necessary to demonstrate the manner in which the agreed rate of progress will be regained, all without additional cost to the Government.

(c) Failure of the Contractor to comply with the requirements of the Contracting Officer under this provision shall be grounds for determination by the Contracting Officer that the Contractor is not prosecuting the work with such diligence as will insure completion within the time specified. Upon such determination the Contracting Officer may terminate the Contractor's right to proceed with the work, or any separable part thereof, in accordance with the clause of the contract entitled "Termination for Default – Damages for Delay – Time Extensions." (ASPR 7-603.48)

Figure 3-1. "Progress Charts and Requirements for Overtime Work" Specification.

3-20

APPENDIX

EP 415-1-3
2 July 79

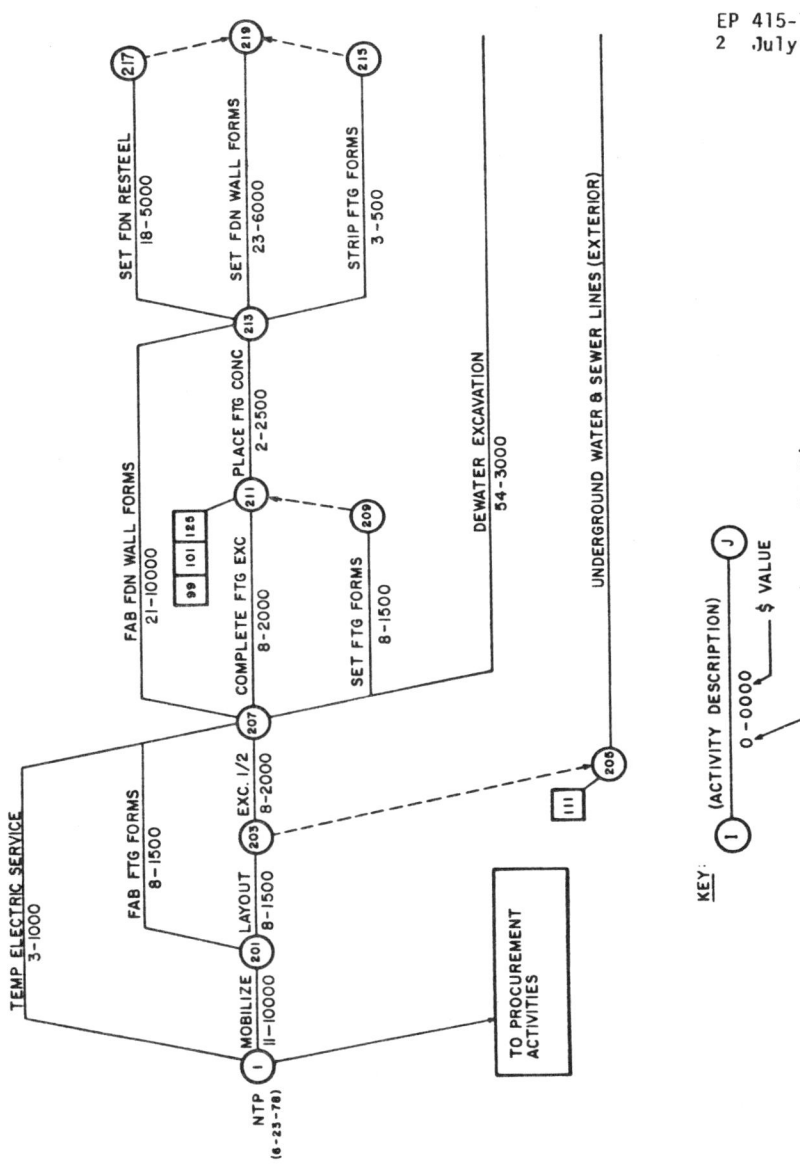

Figure 3-2a. Example of contractor's original schedule.

CONSTRUCTION SCHEDULES

EP 415-1-3
2 July 79

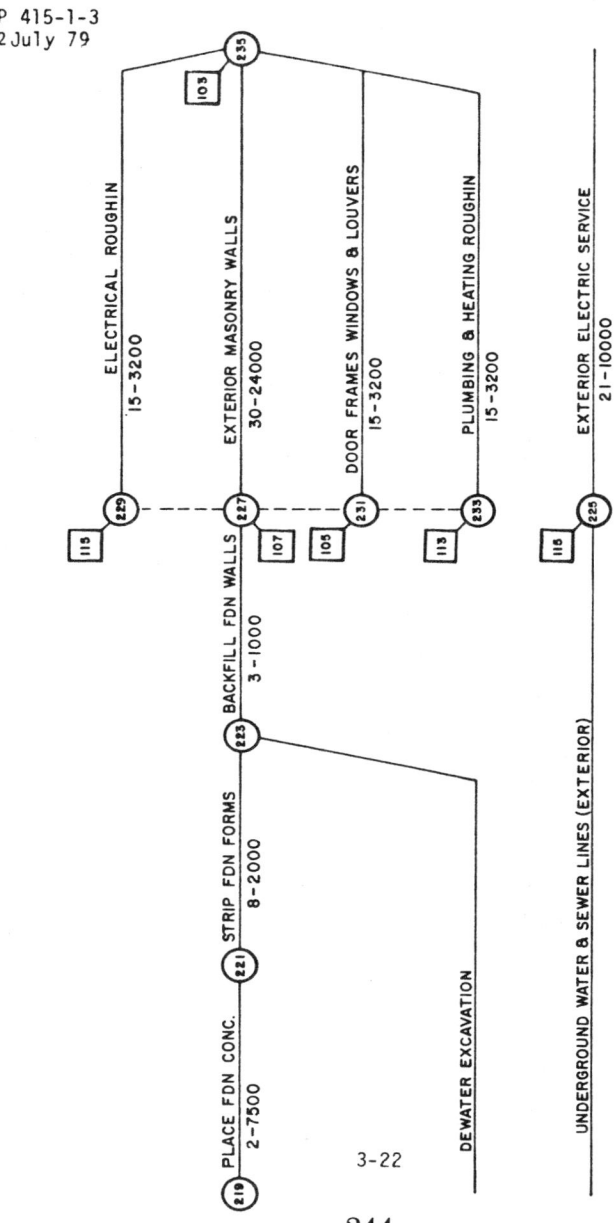

Figure 3-2b. Example of contractor's original schedule--continued.

APPENDIX

EP 415-1-3
2 July 79

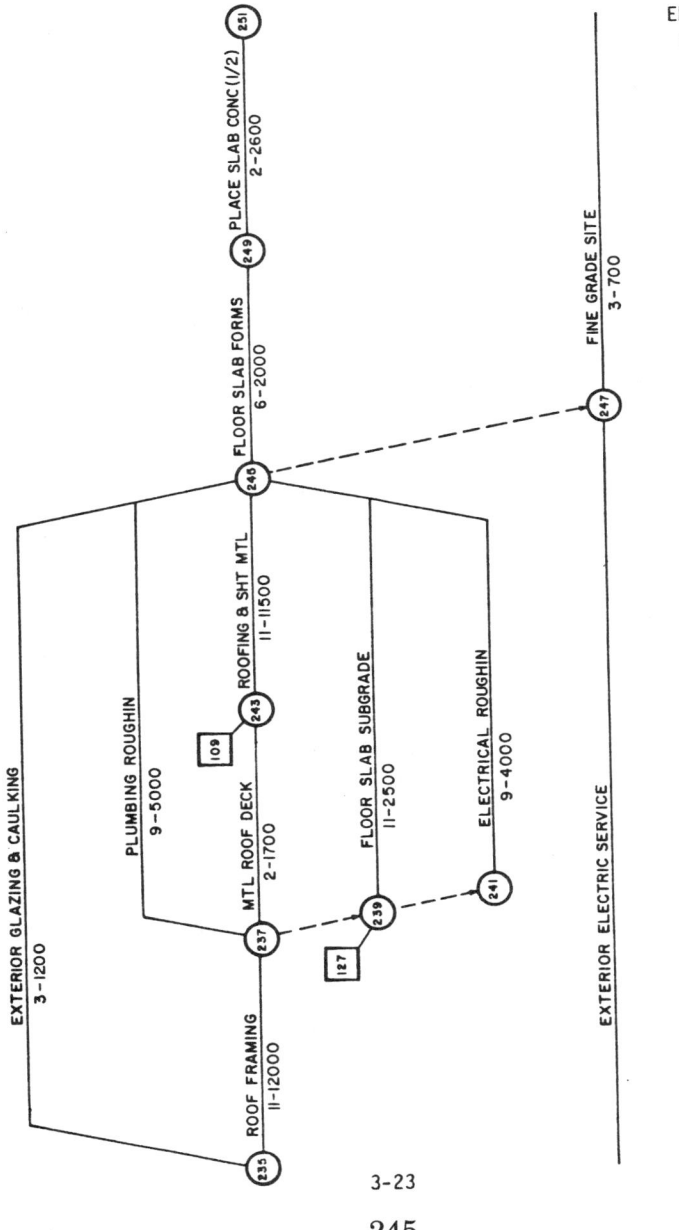

Figure 3-2 c. Example of contractor's original schedule--continued.

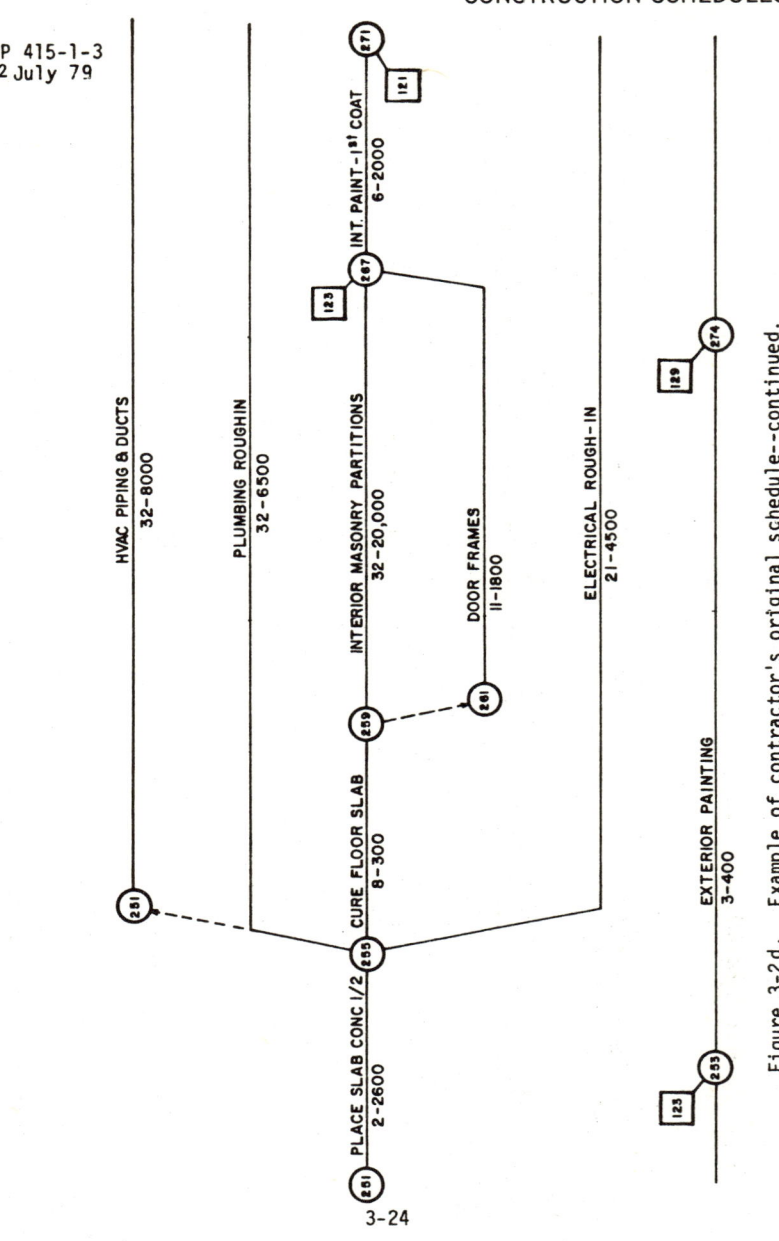

Figure 3-2d. Example of contractor's original schedule--continued.

APPENDIX

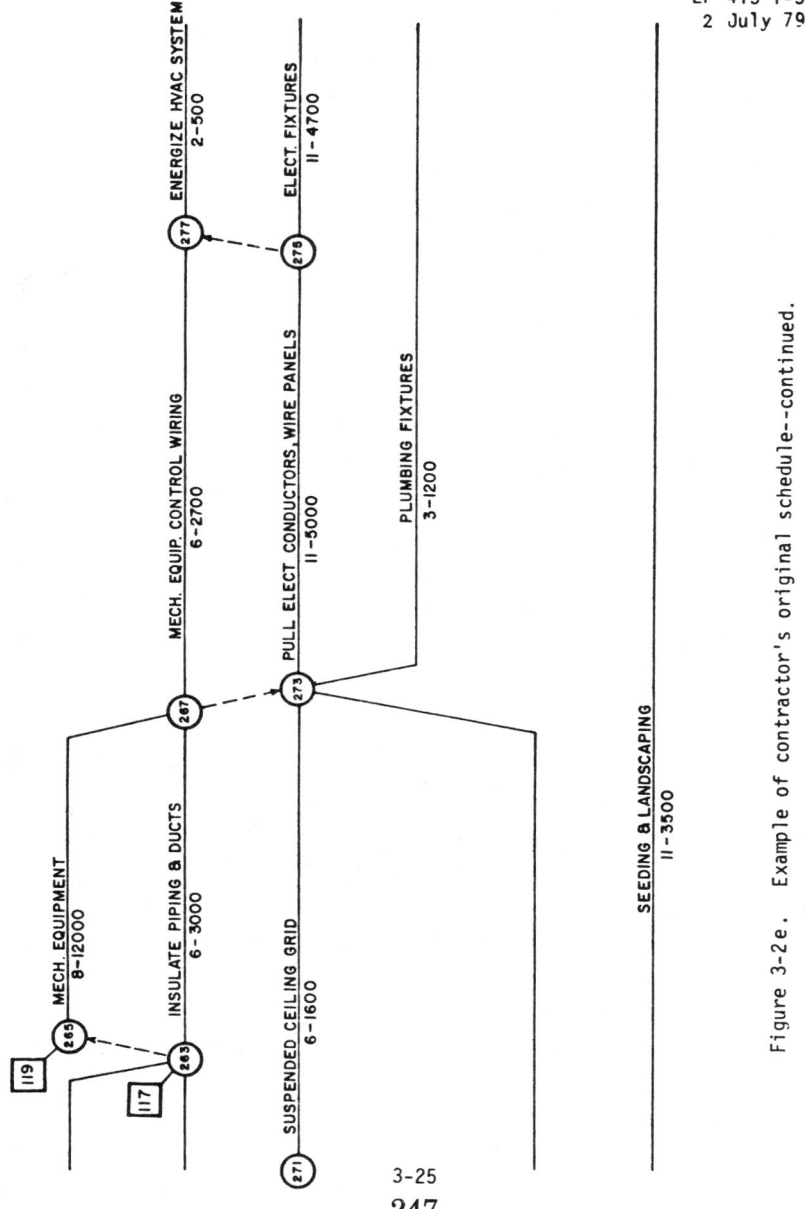

Figure 3-2e. Example of contractor's original schedule--continued.

CONSTRUCTION SCHEDULES

EP 415-1-3
2 July 79

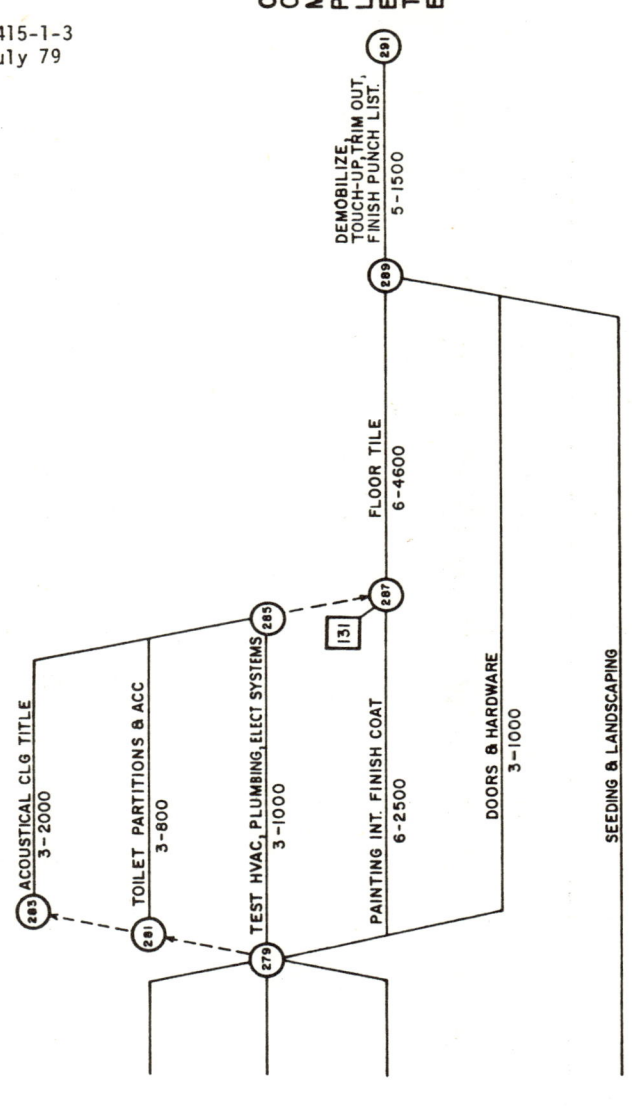

Figure 3-2 f. Example of contractor's original schedule--continued.

APPENDIX

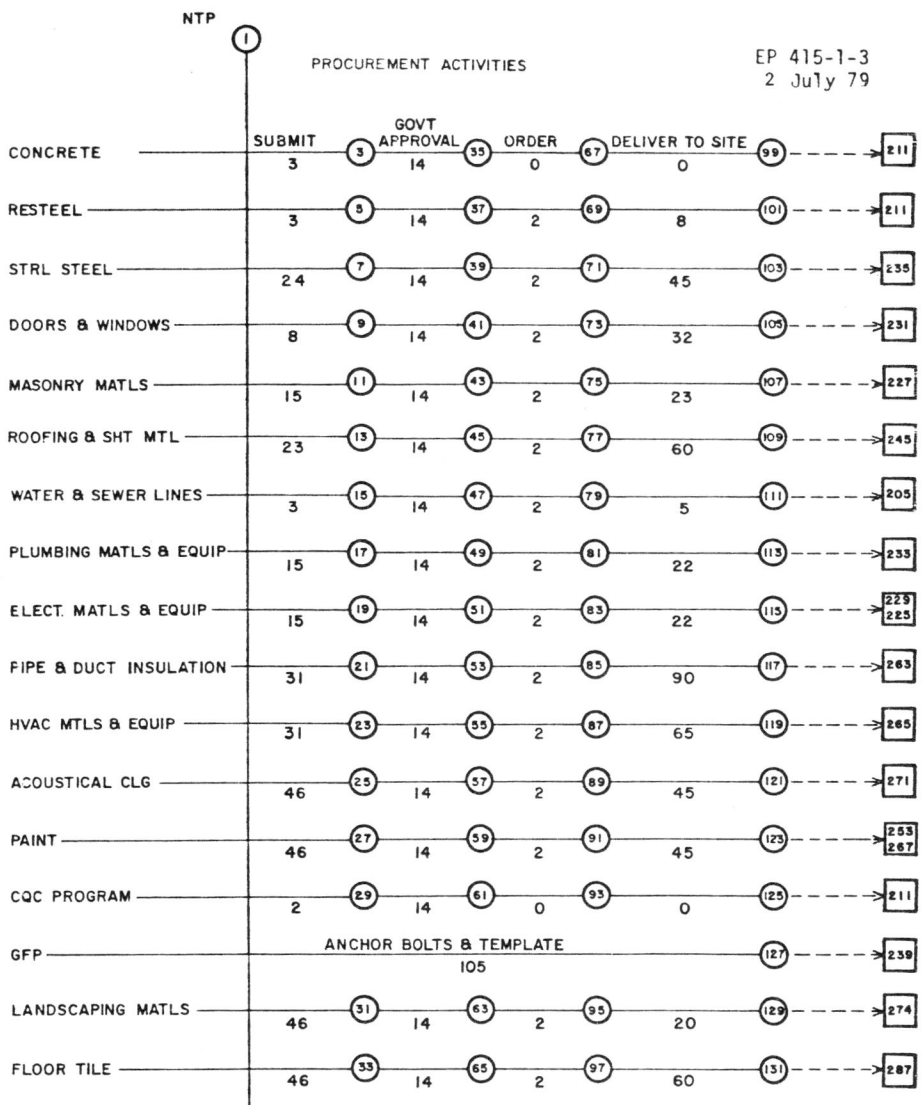

Figure 3-2g. Example of contractor's original schedule--continued.

CONSTRUCTION SCHEDULES

EP 415-1-3
2 July 79

PROCUREMENT ACTIVITIES
(SUBMIT - APPROVE - ORDER - DELIVER)

ACTIVITY	DESCRIPTION	DURATION (CAL. DAYS)	VALUE ($)	ES	EF	LS	LF	FLOAT (CAL. DAYS)
1-3	S-CONCRETE	3	0	23 JUN 78	25 JUN 78	12 JUL 78	14 JUL 78	18
3-35	A-CONCRETE	14	0	26 JUN 78	10 JUL 78	15 JUL 78	28 JUL 78	18
35-67	O-CONCRETE	0	0	-	-	-	-	-
67-99	D-CONCRETE	0	0	-	-	-	-	-
1-5	S-RESTEEL	3	0	23 JUN 78	25 JUN 78	15 JUL 78	17 JUL 78	21
5-37	A-RESTEEL	14	0	26 JUN 78	10 JUL 78	18 JUL 78	31 JUL 78	21
37-69	O-RESTEEL	2	0	11 JUL 78	12 JUL 78	01 AUG 78	02 AUG 78	21
69-101	D-RESTEEL	8	0	13 JUL 78	20 JUL 78	03 AUG 78	10 AUG 78	21
1-7	S-STR STEEL	24	0	23 JUN 78	17 JUL 78	24 JUL 78	16 AUG 78	30
7-39	A-STR STEEL	14	0	18 JUL 78	31 JUL 78	17 AUG 78	30 AUG 78	30
39-71	O-STR STEEL	2	0	01 AUG 78	02 AUG 78	31 AUG 78	01 SEP 78	30
71-103	D-STR STEEL	45	0	03 AUG 78	17 SEP 78	02 SEP 78	16 OCT 78	30
1-9	S-DRS & WINDOWS	8	0	23 JUN 78	30 JUN 78	24 JUL 78	31 JUL 78	30
9-41	A-DRS & WINDOWS	14	0	01 JUL 78	15 JUL 78	01 AUG 78	14 AUG 78	30
41-73	O-DRS & WINDOWS	2	0	16 JUL 78	17 JUL 78	15 AUG 78	16 AUG 78	30
73-105	D-DRS & WINDOWS	32	0	18 JUL 78	18 AUG 78	17 AUG 78	17 SEP 78	30
1-11	S-MASONRY MATLS	15	0	23 JUN 78	08 JUL 78	25 JUL 78	08 AUG 78	31
11-43	A-MASONRY MATLS	14	0	09 JUL 78	22 JUL 78	09 AUG 78	22 AUG 78	31
43-75	O-MASONRY MATLS	2	0	23 JUL 78	24 JUL 78	23 AUG 78	24 AUG 78	31
75-107	D-MASONRY MATLS	23	0	25 JUL 78	16 AUG 78	25 AUG 78	16 SEP 78	31

Figure 3-2h. Example of contractor's original schedule--continued.

APPENDIX

EP 415-1-3
2 July 79

ACTIVITY	DESCRIPTION	DURATION (CAL.DAYS)	VALUE ($)	ES	EF	LS	LF	FLOAT (CAL.DAYS)
1-13	S-ROOFING & SHT MTL	23	0	23 JUN 78	16 JUL 78	13 JUL 78	09 AUG 78	19
13-45	A-ROOFING & SHT MTL	14	0	17 JUL 78	30 JUL 78	05 AUG 78	18 AUG 78	19
45-77	O-ROOFING & SHT MTL	2	0	31 JUL 78	01 AUG 78	19 AUG 78	20 AUG 78	19
77-109	D-ROOFING & SHT MTL	60	0	02 AUG 78	10 OCT 78	21 AUG 78	29 OCT 78	19
1-15	S-WATER & SWR LINE	3	0	23 JUN 78	25 JUN 78	28 JUN 78	30 JUN 78	5
15-47	A-WATER & SWR LINE	14	0	26 JUN 78	10 JUL 78	01 JUL 78	15 JUL 78	5
47-79	O-WATER & SWR LINE	2	0	11 JUL 78	12 JUL 78	16 JUL 78	17 JUL 78	5
79-111	D-WATER & SWR LINE	5	0	13 JUL 78	17 JUL 78	17 JUL 78	21 JUL 78	5
1-17	S-PLMB MATLS & EQ.	15	0	23 JUN 78	08 JUL 78	27 JUL 78	10 AUG 78	32
17-49	A-PLMB MATLS & EQ.	14	0	09 JUL 78	22 JUL 78	11 AUG 78	24 AUG 78	32
49-81	O-PLMB MATLS & EQ.	2	0	23 JUL 78	24 JUL 78	25 AUG 78	26 AUG 78	32
81-113	D-PLMB MATLS & EQ.	22	0	25 JUL 78	15 AUG 78	27 AUG 78	17 SEP 78	32
1-19	S-ELECT. MATLS	15	0	23 JUN 78	08 JUL 78	28 JUN 78	13 JUL 78	5
19-51	A-ELECT. MATLS	14	0	09 JUL 78	22 JUL 78	14 JUL 78	27 JUL 78	5
51-83	O-ELECT. MATLS	2	0	23 JUL 78	24 JUL 78	28 JUL 78	29 JUL 78	5
83-115	D-ELECT. MATLS	22	0	25 JUL 78	15 AUG 78	30 JUL 78	20 AUG 78	5
1-21	S-PIPE & DUCT INSL	31	0	23 JUN 78	24 JUL 78	04 AUG 78	04 SEP 78	42
21-53	A-PIPE & DUCT INSL	14	0	25 JUL 78	07 AUG 78	05 SEP 78	19 SEP 78	42
53-85	O-PIPE & DUCT INSL	2	0	08 AUG 78	09 AUG 78	20 SEP 78	21 SEP 78	42
85-117	D-PIPE & DUCT INSL	90	0	10 AUG 78	08 NOV 78	22 SEP 78	22 DEC 78	42
1-23	S-HVAC EQUIP	31	0	23 JUN 78	24 JUL 78	30 AUG 78	30 SEP 78	67
23-55	A-HVAC EQUIP	14	0	25 JUL 78	07 AUG 78	01 OCT 78	15 OCT 78	67
55-87	O-HVAC EQUIP	2	0	08 AUG 78	09 AUG 78	15 OCT 78	16 OCT 78	67

Figure 3-21. Example of contractor's original schedule--continued.

3-29

CONSTRUCTION SCHEDULES

EP 415-1-3
2 July 79

ACTIVITY	DESCRIPTION	DURATION (CAL.DAYS)	VALUE ($)	ES	EF	LS	LF	FLOAT (CAL.DAYS)
87-119	D-HVAC EQUIP	65	0	10 AUG 78	14 OCT 78	17 OCT 78	22 DEC 78	67
1-25	S-ACOUSTICAL CLG	46	0	23 JUN 78	08 AUG 78	29 AUG 78	15 OCT 78	66
25-57	A-ACOUSTICAL CLG	14	0	09 AUG 78	22 AUG 78	16 OCT 78	30 OCT 78	66
57-89	O-ACOUSTICAL CLG	2	0	23 AUG 78	24 AUG 78	31 OCT 78	01 NOV 78	66
89-121	D-ACOUSTICAL CLG	45	0	25 AUG 78	09 OCT 78	02 NOV 78	07 JAN 79	66
1-27	S-PAINT	46	0	23 JUN 78	08 AUG 78	26 JUL 78	11 SEP 78	32
27-59	A-PAINT	14	0	09 AUG 78	22 AUG 78	12 SEP 78	25 SEP 78	32
59-91	O-PAINT	2	0	23 AUG 78	24 AUG 78	25 SEP 78	26 SEP 78	32
91-123	D-PAINT	45	0	25 AUG 78	09 OCT 78	27 SEP 78	12 NOV 78	32
1-29	S-CQC PROGRAM	2	0	23 JUN 78	24 JUN 78	14 JUL 78	15 JUL 78	20
29-61	A-CQC PROGRAM	14	0	25 JUN 78	09 JUL 78	16 JUL 78	29 JUL 78	20
61-93	O-CQC PROGRAM	0	0	-	-	-	-	-
93-125	D-CQC PROGRAM	0	0	-	-	-	-	-
1-127	D-GOVT FURN EQUIP	105	0	23 JUN 78	07 OCT 78	13 JUL 78	27 OCT 78	19
1-31	S-LANDSCAPING	46	0	23 JUN 78	08 AUG 78	23 AUG 78	09 OCT 78	60
31-63	A-LANDSCAPING	14	0	09 AUG 78	22 AUG 78	10 OCT 78	23 OCT 78	60
63-95	O-LANDSCAPING	2	0	23 AUG 78	24 AUG 78	24 OCT 78	25 OCT 78	60
95-129	D-LANDSCAPING	20	0	25 AUG 78	14 SEP 78	26 OCT 78	15 NOV 78	60
1-33	S-FLOOR TILE	46	0	23 JUN 78	08 AUG 78	04 OCT 78	21 NOV 78	105
33-65	A-FLOOR TILE	14	0	09 AUG 78	22 AUG 78	22 NOV 78	07 DEC 78	105
65-97	O-FLOOR TILE	2	0	23 AUG 78	24 AUG 78	08 DEC 78	09 DEC 78	105
97-131	D-FLOOR TILE	60	0	25 AUG 78	24 OCT 78	10 DEC 78	10 FEB 78	105

Figure 3-2 j. Example of contractor's original schedule--continued.

3-30

APPENDIX

EP 415-1-3
2 July 79

PROCUREMENT CONSTRAINTS TO CONSTRUCTION:

ACTIVITY	DESCRIPTION	DURATION (CAL.DAYS)	VALUE ($)	ES	EF	LS	LF	FLOAT (CAL.DAYS)
99-211	DUMMY	0	0	-	-	-	-	-
101-211	DUMMY	0	0	-	-	-	-	-
103-235	DUMMY	0	0	-	-	-	-	-
105-231	DUMMY	0	0	-	-	-	-	-
107-227	DUMMY	0	0	-	-	-	-	-
109-243	DUMMY	0	0	-	-	-	-	-
111-205	DUMMY	0	0	-	-	-	-	-
113-233	DUMMY	0	0	-	-	-	-	-
115-225	DUMMY	0	0	-	-	-	-	-
115-229	DUMMY	0	0	-	-	-	-	-
117-263	DUMMY	0	0	-	-	-	-	-
119-265	DUMMY	0	0	-	-	-	-	-
121-271	DUMMY	0	0	-	-	-	-	-
123-253	DUMMY	0	0	-	-	-	-	-
123-267	DUMMY	0	0	-	-	-	-	-
125-211	DUMMY	0	0	-	-	-	-	-
127-239	DUMMY	0	0	-	-	-	-	-
129-274	DUMMY	0	0	-	-	-	-	-
131-287	DUMMY	0	0	-	-	-	-	-

Figure 3-2k. Example of contractor's original schedule--continued.

3-31

CONSTRUCTION SCHEDULES

FP 415-1-3
2 July 79

CONSTRUCTION ACTIVITIES:

ACTIVITY	DESCRIPTION	DURATION (CAL. DAYS)	VALUE ($)	ES	EF	LS	LF	FLOAT (CAL. DAYS)
1-201	MOBILIZE	11	10,000	23 JUN 78	03 JUL 78	23 JUN 78	03 JUL 78	0
1-207	TEMP ELECT	3	1,000	23 JUN 78	25 JUN 78	18 JUL 78	20 JUL 78	24
201-203	LAYOUT	8	1,500	05 JUL 78	12 JUL 78	05 JUL 78	12 JUL 78	0
201-207	FAB FTG FORMS	8	1,500	05 JUL 78	12 JUL 78	13 JUL 78	20 JUL 78	8
203-205	DUMMY	0	0	-	-	-	-	-
203-207	EXC FTG 1/2	8	2,000	13 JUL 78	20 JUL 78	13 JUL 78	20 JUL 78	0
205-225	UNGRND WATER & SWR	30	9,000	13 JUL 78	11 AUG 78	09 DEC 78	09 JAN 79	147
207-209	SET FTG FORMS	8	1,500	21 JUL 78	28 JUL 78	01 AUG 78	08 AUG 78	11
207-211	EXC FTG 1/2	8	2,000	21 JUL 78	28 JUL 78	01 AUG 78	08 AUG 78	11
207-213	FAB FDN FORMS	21	10,000	21 JUL 78	10 AUG 78	21 JUL 78	10 AUG 78	0
207-223	DEWTR EXC	54	3,000	21 JUL 78	13 SEP 78	21 JUL 78	13 SEP 78	0
209-211	DUMMY	0	0	-	-	-	-	-
211-213	PLACE FTC CONC	2	2,500	29 JUL 78	30 JUL 78	09 AUG 78	10 AUG 78	11
213-215	STRIP FTG FORMS	3	500	11 AUG 78	13 AUG 78	30 AUG 78	01 SEP 78	19
213-217	SET FDN RESTL	18	5,000	11 AUG 78	28 AUG 78	15 AUG 78	01 SEP 78	4
213-219	SET FDN FORMS	23	6,000	11 AUG 78	02 SEP 78	11 AUG 78	02 SEP 78	0
215-219	DUMMY	0	0	-	-	-	-	-
217-219	DUMMY	0	0	-	-	-	-	-
219-221	PLACE FDN CONC	2	7,500	03 SEP 78	05 SEP 78	03 SEP 78	05 SEP 78	0
221-223	STRIP FDN FORMS	8	2,000	06 SEP 78	13 SEP 78	06 SEP 78	13 SEP 78	0

Figure 3-21. Example of contractor's original schedule--continued.

3-32

APPENDIX

EP 415-1-3
2 July 79

ACTIVITY	DESCRIPTION	DURATION (CAL. DAYS)	VALUE ($)	ES	EF	LS	LF	FLOAT (CAL. DAYS)
223-227	BFILL FDN	3	1,000	14 SEP 78	16 SEP 78	14 SEP 78	16 SEP 78	0
225-247	EXT ELECT	21	10,000	16 AUG 78	06 SEP 78	10 JAN 79	30 JAN 79	143
227-229	DUMMY	0	0	-	-	-	-	-
227-231	DUMMY	0	0	-	-	-	-	-
227-233	DUMMY	0	0	-	-	-	-	-
227-235	EXT MASONRY	30	24,000	17 SEP 78	16 OCT 78	17 SEP 78	16 OCT 78	0
229-235	ELECT RI	15	3,200	18 SEP 78	02 OCT 78	02 OCT 78	16 OCT 78	14
231-235	DRS & WINDOWS	15	3,200	18 SEP 78	02 OCT 78	02 OCT 78	16 OCT 78	14
233-235	PLMB & HTG RI	15	3,200	18 SEP 78	02 OCT 78	02 OCT 78	16 OCT 78	14
235-237	ROOF FRMG	11	12,000	17 OCT 78	27 OCT 78	17 OCT 78	27 OCT 78	0
235-245	EXT GL & CAULK	3	1,200	17 OCT 78	19 OCT 78	07 NOV 78	09 NOV 78	21
237-239	DUMMY	0	0	-	-	-	-	-
237-241	DUMMY	0	0	-	-	-	-	-
237-243	MTL ROOF DECK	2	1,700	28 OCT 78	29 OCT 78	28 OCT 78	29 OCT 78	0
237-245	PLMB RI	9	5,000	28 OCT 78	05 NOV 78	01 NOV 78	09 NOV 78	4
239-245	FLR SUBGRADE	11	2,500	28 OCT 78	07 NOV 78	30 OCT 78	09 NOV 78	2
241-245	ELECT RI	9	4,000	28 OCT 78	05 NOV 78	01 NOV 78	09 NOV 78	4
243-245	ROOF & SHT MTL	11	11,500	30 OCT 78	09 NOV 78	30 OCT 78	09 NOV 78	0
245-247	DUMMY	0	0	-	-	-	-	-
245-249	SET FLR FORMS	6	2,000	10 NOV 78	15 NOV 78	10 NOV 78	15 NOV 78	0
247-253	GRADE SITE	3	700	10 NOV 78	12 NOV 78	31 JAN 79	02 FEB 79	79
249-251	PLACE FLR CONC 1/2	2	2,600	16 NOV 78	17 NOV 78	16 NOV 78	17 NOV 78	0
251-255	PLACE FLR CONC 1/2	2	2,600	18 NOV 78	19 NOV 78	18 NOV 78	19 NOV 78	0

Figure 3-2 m. Example of contractor's original schedule--continued.

CONSTRUCTION SCHEDULES

EP 415-1-3
2 July 79

ACTIVITY	DESCRIPTION	DURATION (CAL. DAYS)	VALUE ($)	ES	EF	LS	LF	FLOAT (CAL. DAYS)
253-274	EXT PAINT	3	400	13 OCT 8	15 OCT 78	03 FEB 79	05 FEB 79	79
255-257	DUMMY	0	0	-	-	-	-	-
255-259	CURE FLR CONC	8	300	20 NOV 78	28 NOV 78	20 NOV 78	28 NOV 78	0
255-263	PLMB RI	32	6,500	20 NOV 78	22 DEC 78	02 DEC 78	04 JAN 79	11
255-273	ELECT RI	21	4,500	20 NOV 78	11 DEC 78	22 DEC 78	13 JAN 79	31
257-263	HVAC PIPE & DUCT	32	8,000	20 NOV 78	22 DEC 78	02 DEC 78	04 JAN 79	11
259-261	DUMMY	0	0	-	-	-	-	-
259-267	INT MASONRY	32	20,000	29 NOV 78	31 DEC 78	29 NOV 78	31 DEC 78	0
261-267	SET DOOR FRAMES	11	1,800	29 NOV 78	09 DEC 78	20 DEC 78	31 DEC 78	21
263-265	DUMMY	0	0	-	-	-	-	-
263-269	INSUL PIPE & DUCTS	6	3,000	23 DEC 78	29 DEC 78	07 JAN 79	12 JAN 79	13
265-269	INSTL MECH EQUIP	8	12,000	23 DEC 78	31 DEC 78	05 JAN 79	12 JAN 79	11
267-271	INT PAINT (1)	6	2,000	02 JAN 79	07 JAN 79	02 JAN 79	07 JAN 79	0
269-273	DUMMY	0	0	-	-	-	-	-
269-277	WIRE MECH EQUIP	6	2,700	02 JAN 79	07 JAN 79	28 JAN 79	02 FEB 79	26
271-273	CLG GRID	6	1,600	08 JAN 79	13 JAN 79	08 JAN 79	13 JAN 79	0
273-275	ELECT CONDUCTORS	11	5,000	14 JAN 79	24 JAN 79	14 JAN 79	24 JAN 79	0
273-279	PLMB FIXTURES	3	1,200	14 JAN 79	16 JAN 79	02 FEB 79	04 FEB 79	19
274-289	LNDSCP & SEED	11	3,500	16 NOV 78	27 NOV 78	06 FEB 79	16 FEB 79	79
275-277	DUMMY	0	0	-	-	-	-	-
275-279	ELECT FIXTURES	11	4,700	25 JAN 79	04 FEB 79	25 JAN 778	04 FEB 79	0
277-279	ENERGIZE HVAC	2	500	25 JAN 79	26 JAN 79	03 FEB 79	04 FEB 79	9
279-281	DUMMY	0	0	-	-	-	-	-

Figure 3-2 n. Example of contractor's original schedule--continued.

3-34

APPENDIX

EP 415-1-3
2 July 79

ACTIVITY	DESCRIPTION	DURATION (CAL.DAYS)	VALUE ($)	ES	EF	LS	LF	FLOAT (CAL.DAYS)
279-283	DUMMY	0	0	-	-	-	-	-
279-285	TEST SYSTEMS	3	1,000	05 FEB 79	07 FEB 79	07 FEB 79	09 FEB 79	2
279-287	INT PAINT (2)	6	2,500	05 FEB 79	10 FEB 79	05 FEB 79	10 FEB 79	0
279-289	DOORS & HDWRE	3	1,000	05 FEB 79	07 FEB 79	14 FEB 79	16 FEB 79	9
281-285	TOILET PRTN	3	800	05 FEB 79	07 FEB 79	07 FEB 79	09 FEB 79	2
283-285	ACSTL CEILING	3	2,000	05 FEB 79	07 FEB 79	07 FEB 79	09 FEB 79	2
285-287	DUMMY	0	0	-	-	-	-	-
287-289	FLOOR TILE	6	4,600	11 FEB 79	16 FEB 79	11 FEB 79	16 FEB 79	0
289-291	PUNCH OUT & DEMOB	5	1,500	17 FEB 79	21 FEB 79	17 FEB 79	21 FEB 79	0

TOTAL CONTRACT PRICE = $246,500
START DATE = 23 JUN 78
FINISH DATE = 21 FEB 79

Figure 3-2 o. Example of contractor's original schedule--continued.

3-35

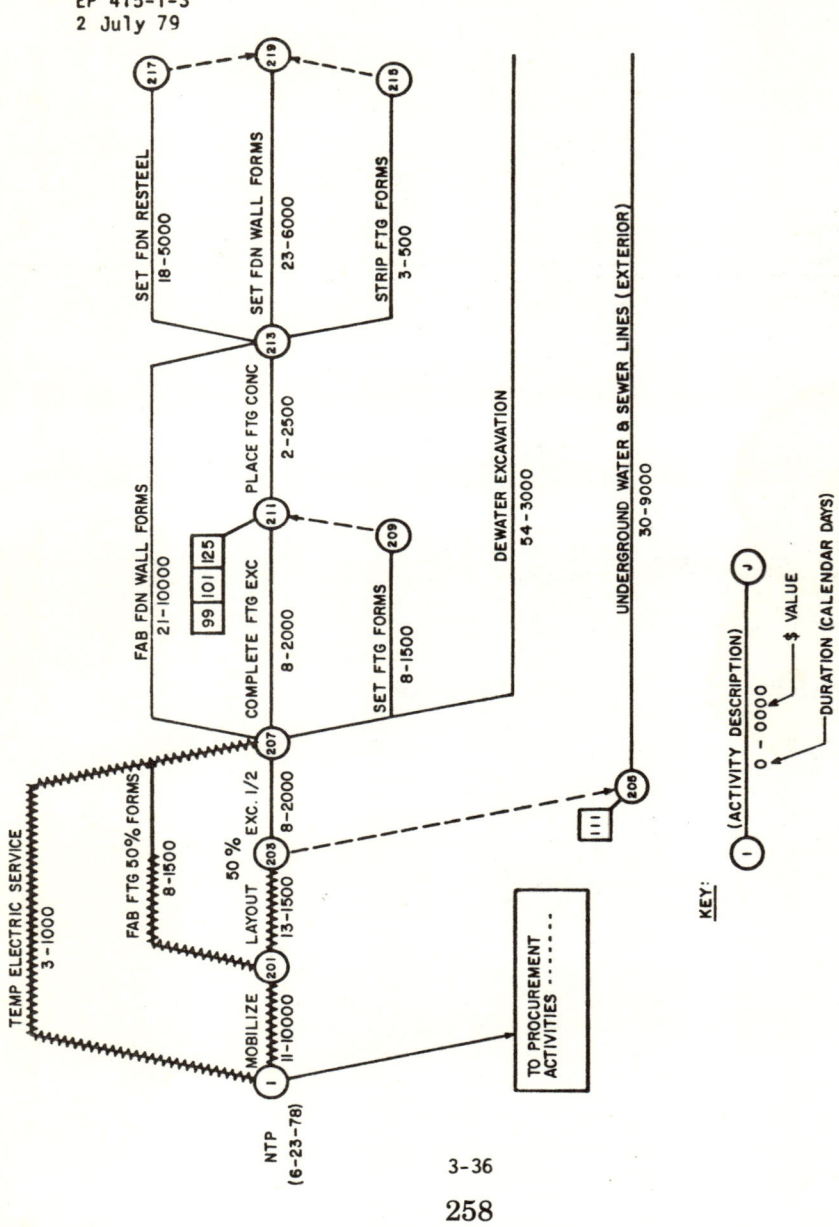

Figure 3-3. Progress chart analysis for modification 1 (example 1).

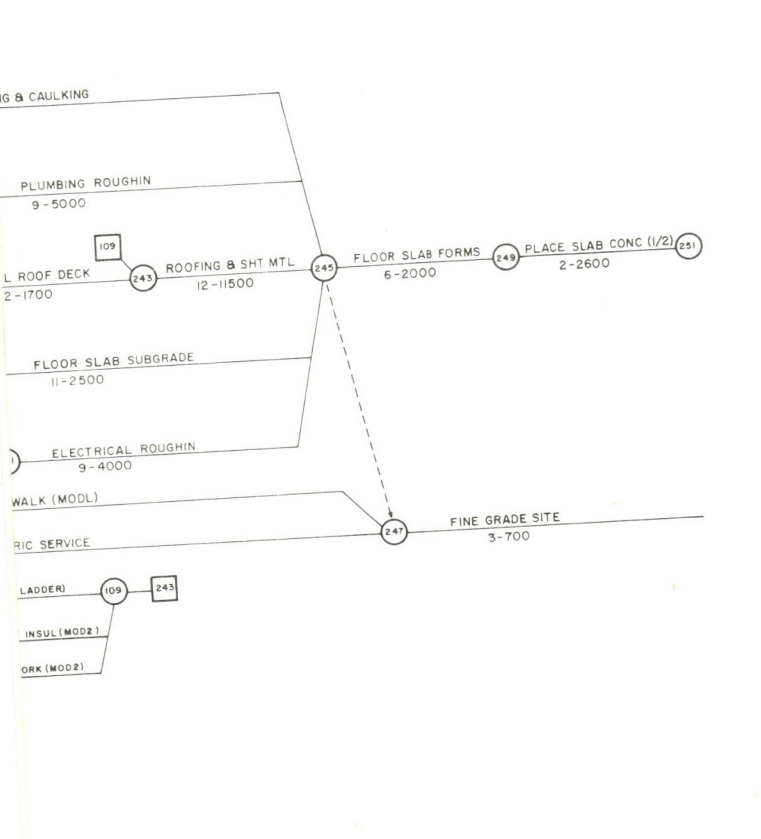

CONSTRUCTION SCHEDULES

EP 415-1-3
2 July 79

CHAPTER 4

EVALUATION

4-1. General.

a. The revised time schedule developed in Chapter 3 assumes that the contractor will proceed with the unchanged work using the same number of work days per week, the same number of shifts, and the same manpower density as planned before the modification. This approach will minimize, but not eliminate, impact costs; however, its application is limited to those situations where the resulting completion date slippage is acceptable. Nevertheless, even when the Using Agency has indicated that a given completion date is mandatory, it is beneficial to first estimate the modification costs based on this approach, followed by an estimate of the modification costs required to meet the Using Agency's mandatory date. A comparison of the two amounts will enable the Using Agency to reevaluate their position before becoming committed to a course of action that might be economically unjustifiable.

b. When the schedule developed in Chapter 3 is incompatible with an immovable interim or final completion date, the estimator must compress the schedule into the time available by reducing, as required, the duration of activities. This requires that the rate of progress be increased on some -- perhaps most -- activities. In other words, acceleration becomes an element of impact. When acceleration enters the picture, the principle of diminishing returns adversely alters the normal labor cost/productivity ratio. Situations may occur where the impact costs amount to more than the cost of accomplishing the directly changed work. It is likely that the credibility of an estimate producing such results will be questioned by those unfamiliar with the facts; it is therefore important for the estimator's work to be thoroughly documented so its rationale can be defended. The following are applicable to developing the estimate for impact of any cost item:

(1) Has, or will the contractor actually incur an increase in costs?

(2) Is the modification the sole cause of the increase?

(3) Have all feasible actions been taken to reduce or eliminate this cost?

(4) Has it been established that this item does not duplicate any other compensable item included in the estimate for this modification?

APPENDIX

EP 415-1-3
2 July 79

c. An affirmative answer is required on all four questions before the item can be included in the cost estimate. The above questions are equally applicable to that portion of the estimate dealing with the direct costs; however, this pamphlet is only concerned with the impact.

4-2. Materials.

a. The effect of impact on construction materials can take several forms. The more common of these are:

(1) Partially completed construction.

(a) Cost of additional temporary protection.

(b) Cost of rehandling.

(2) Materials stored offsite (cost of additional storage time).

(3) Materials shipments (situations may arise where it is desirable to have vendors defer material shipments beyond the originally scheduled date. In these cases, storage costs may be charged by the vendor, and/or freight rates may increase the contractor's cost of obtaining the material. These additional costs are impact-related).

b. The above situations are not all-inclusive since it is impractical to attempt a listing of every possible way that any modification could increase the material-related aspects of a contractor's unchanged work.

4-3. Equipment.

a. Impact costs arising from equipment are similar to those arising from materials in that both are relatively easy to quantify once their applicability is determined. Equipment in this context encompasses all the tools, large and small, assembled by the contractor in support of a construction effort. Typical of modification impacts on equipment are:

(1) Temporarily taken out of service; standby costs.

(2) Rescheduling work causing workspace limitations; reduced productivity.

CONSTRUCTION SCHEDULES

EP 415-1-3
2 July 79

(3) Disruption of continuity; increased travelling; loss of production time.

(4) Increased iterations of mobilization and demobilization.

b. Only affected equipment is considered in determining the Government's liabilities for impact costs related to equipment. For example, if the contractor has 10 scrapers on the site, but five are down for repairs or deadlined awaiting removal, only the operational five are subject to impact -- and therefore are the only ones included in the cost estimate.

c. The costs of standby time can be developed in a relatively straightforward manner from the applicable equipment rate schedules cited in the contract. (If the contract does not include an equipment rate schedule, costs will be based upon the Contractors' Equipment Ownership Expense Schedule, Sixth Edition, published by the Associated General Contractors of America, Inc. [1966]. Standby costs will not exceed 50 percent of the equipment ownership expense.)(DAR 15-402.1).

d. Reduction in productivity because of equipment crowding or increased travelling time requires a study of the individual situation. The objective of such a study is to define the production time lost to travelling (hours) and the loss of productivity caused by crowding (converted to hours), plus equivalent additional costs for operators and oilers (when applicable).

e. In cases where one or more pieces of major equipment will be removed from service for a long period due to the modification, it is advisable to compare the cost of standby time for the entire period vs. the cost of demobilization and remobilization; whichever amount is smallest should be used in the estimate.

f. Mobilization is defined as the gathering of materials and equipment necessary to accomplish some phase of the construction operation. Demobilization is defined as the equipment removal and cleanup operation following completion of some phase of the work. Since mobilization and demobilization cycles occur frequently on a project, the time and costs required to mobilize and demobilize should be included in the estimate for a modification only when that modification caused the additional cycle. If the additional mobilization/demobilization cycle is related to an unchanged activity, the costs are attributed to impact.

4-3

APPENDIX

EP 415-1-3
2 July 79

4-4. Manpower.

    a. The two major impacts upon manpower are reduced productivity and pay scale increases. The latter is a factor when modifications delay progress to the point that work which would have otherwise been completed must now be performed at a time when higher wages are in effect. Reduced productivity takes many forms, and is therefore more difficult to quantify before the fact.

    b. Reduced labor productivity implies a loss from some established normal or anticipated level of productivity. Although construction does not lend itself to definitive measurement of labor productivity, there are methods a contractor can use to quantify anticipated labor costs when preparing a bid. The most common technique draws heavily on data derived from the contractor's past experiences, including any indicated trends, present labor pay rates, and anticipated labor rate increases during the life of the project.

    c. The contractor's NAS progress schedule carries lump sum values for each construction activity. However, the ratio of labor costs vs. material and equipment costs varies widely for different activities, so it is impractical to apply a universal rule-of-thumb ratio. Nevertheless, a fairly accurate breakout of labor costs for any activity can be obtained by subtracting from the total activity value all the cost items which are not direct labor. These items are material costs, equipment costs, and overhead and profit. The remaining costs are production labor costs, including wages paid, fringe benefits, insurance and taxes, and overhead and profit markups. Through a process of elimination, a reasonably accurate determination of the manhours represented by the dollar amount of labor cost for an activity can be reached. The Government estimate for the project and data from the contractor's payroll submittals can also be helpful in projecting manpower levels on future activities.

    d. That portion of the contract price devoted to labor costs indicates the contractor's anticipated level of labor productivity. Whether or not the anticipated profit can be realized from the completed project depends to a great extent on the contractor's ability to maintain the planned labor productivity level. With expert management and some good luck, the contractor may achieve labor productivity exceeding original expectations. Conversely, labor productivity or effectiveness can fall below expectations as a result of many uncontrollable factors.

CONSTRUCTION SCHEDULES

EP 415-1-3
2 July 79

e. The actual labor productivity of a project affects the cost of labor for modifications. On projects where actual labor productivity is running at or better than the contractor's anticipated level, data developed from the analysis described in c above is appropriate for prepricing direct and impact costs of modifications. However, when the contractor's actual labor costs are higher (productivity lower) than those anticipated by the bid, actual experience data should be considered. Depending on the degree to which contractor mismanagement has contributed to the higher labor costs, the estimator may find it expedient to use a combination of actual and anticipated productivity projections in arriving at a reasonable labor cost figure for the modification. This does not imply that a modification should be priced to reimburse the contractor for excess labor costs incurred because of his inept management; however, it is possible to incur labor costs higher than those anticipated. The higher costs can occur through no fault of the contractor. The estimator must therefore take this into account when forward-pricing direct or impact-related modification labor costs.

f. This pamphlet deals specifically with the estimation of the costs arising from impact on the unchanged work. It also encourages the settlement of contract modifications before the work is accomplished.

g. Prepricing of impact costs arising from labor is the most difficult aspect of the estimating process for two reasons. First, the estimator must verify that these determinations are reasonable and well founded. Second, when negotiating it is necessary to convince the contractor that the determinations are reasonable. Most contractors (and many personnel within the Corps of Engineers) would prefer to leave the settlement of impact cost/time until after the modification work is performed. However, for the reasons stated earlier, such a procedure is not recommended. The preferred approach is to anticipate the costs before the fact, and to include them in the cost estimate. Figures 4-1a through 4-4 illustrate the effects of various situations on construction manpower efficiency. These figures are included as a source of general information and some estimators may find them helpful in supplementing other data generated in the development of modification cost estimates. However, the validity of the graphs has not been sufficiently tested to warrant their use in preference to established methodologies.

h. The lowest reasonable price for modifications is estimated by basing the direct and impact costs of labor upon the productivity level established in e above. (Allowances for labor impact costs compensate the contractor for losses in productivity.) Typical causes of labor productivity loss on the unchanged work resulting from modifications are as follows.

4-5

APPENDIX

EP 415-1-3
2 July 79

(1) <u>Disruption</u>. The contractor's progress schedule represents the planned sequence of activities leading to final completion of the project. Workers who know what they are doing, what they will be doing next, and how their activities relate to the successful completion of the project develop a "job rhythm." Labor productivity is at its optimum when there is good job rhythm. When job rhythm is interrupted (i.e., when a contract modification necessitates a revision of the progress schedule), it affects workers on both the directly changed and/or unchanged work and may result in a loss of productivity.

(a) Disruption occurs when workers are prematurely moved from one assigned task to another. Regardless of the competency of the workers involved, some loss in productivity is inevitable during a period of orientation to a new assignment. This loss is repeated if workers are later returned to their original job assignment. Learning curves which graph the relationship between production rate and repeated performance of the same task have been developed for various industrial tasks. The basic principle of all learning curve studies is that efficiency increases as an individual or team repeats an operation over and over; assembly lines are excellent demonstrations of this principle. However, although construction work involves the repetition of similar or related tasks, these tasks are seldom identical. Skilled construction workers are trained to perform a wide variety of tasks related to their specific trade. Therefore, in construction it is more appropriate to consider the time required to become oriented to the task rather than acquiring the skill necessary to perform it. One of the attributes of the construction worker is the ability to perform the duties of his trade in a variety of environments. How long it will take the worker to adjust to a new task and environment depends on how closely related the task is to his experience or how typical it is to work usually performed by his craft. Figure 4-1a assumes that the worker will always be assigned to perform work within the scope of his trade, and that the average worker will require a maximum of one shift (8 hours) to reach full productivity. Full productivity (100 on the Theoretical Productivity Scale) represents optimum productivity for a given project. Figure 4-1b is a tabulation of productivity losses derived from figure 4-1a.

(b) The time required for a worker (or crew) to reach full productivity in a new assignment is not constant. It will vary with skill, experience, and the difference between the old and new task. In using the chart or its tabulation, the estimator must decide what point on the Theoretical Productivity Scale represents a composite of these factors. For example, an ironworker is moved from placing reinforcing bars to the structural steel erection crew. The ironworker is qualified by past training to work on structural steel, but the vast majority of his

CONSTRUCTION SCHEDULES

EP 415-1-3
2 July 79

experience has been with rebars, and the two tasks are significantly different. In view of this, a starting point of "0" is appropriate. The estimator can determine from the chart that a "0" starting point indicates the ironworker will need 8 hours to reach full productivity, with a resulting productivity loss of 4 hours. The Government's liability is then 4 hours times the hourly rate times markups. As a second example, assume the same ironworker is moved from placing reinforcing bars for Building A to placing reinforcing bars for Building B. The buildings are similar but not identical. A starting point of "90" is appropriate. The duration of only 0.8 hours is required to reach full productivity, and the productivity loss is 0.4 hours. The Government's liability would then be 0.4 hours times the hourly rate times markups.

(c) The contractor normally absorbs many orientation/learning cycles as his labor forces are moved from task to task in the performance of the work. Only those additional manpower moves, caused solely by a contract modification, represent labor disruption costs for which the contractor is entitled extra payment.

(2) <u>Crowding</u>. If a contractor's progress schedule is altered so that more activities must be accomplished concurrently, impact costs caused by crowding can result. Crowding occurs when more workers are placed in a given area than can function effectively. Crowding causes lowered productivity; it can be considered a form of acceleration because it requires the contractor either to accomplish a fixed amount of work within a shorter time frame, or to accomplish more work within a fixed time frame. Granting additional time for completion of the project can eliminate crowding. When the final completion date cannot be slipped, increased stacking of activities must be analyzed and quantified.

(a) Activity stacking does not necessarily result in crowding -- when concurrent activities are performed in areas where working room is sufficient, crowding is not a factor. But, if the modification forces the contractor to schedule more activities concurrently in a limited working space, crowding does result. Both increased activity stacking and limited (congested) working space must be present for crowding to become an item of impact cost.

(b) Crowding can be quantified by using techniques similar to those used for acceleration. Figure 4-2 illustrates the curve developed to represent increases in labor costs from crowding. Before applying this curve, the estimator must determine whether crowding will occur and to what degree. For example, the assumption that the contractor's scheduling of the activities in question is the most efficient

4-7

APPENDIX

EP 415-1-3
2 July 79

sequencing of the work must be verified. Perhaps more workers can work effectively in the applicable work space than the contractor has scheduled; if they cannot, perhaps the crowding is not severe enough to justify using the full percentage of loss indicated by the graph. (The graph should be interpreted as representing the upper limit of productivity loss.) In this case, the estimator's judgment of the specific circumstances may indicate that some lower increase factor is appropriate.

(c) For example, assume that the estimator decides that severe crowding will occur in the following situation: The contractor's schedule indicates three activities concurrently in progress in a limited area of the project. Each of these activities employs five workers, placing a total of 15 workers in the area. One of these activities has a duration of 10 days; the other two have 20-day durations. The modification has required that a fourth activity be scheduled concurrently in the same limited area. This additional activity requires three workers; it has a normal duration of 5 days. There are now 18 workers in an area which can only efficiently accommodate 15. The percent of crowding is 3/15 or 20 percent. On the graph (figure 4-2), 20 percent crowding intersects the curve opposite 8 percent loss of efficiency. To find the duration of crowding, the estimator multiplies the normal duration of the added activity by 100 percent plus the percent loss of efficiency. For this example, 5 days times 1.08 equals 5.4 days. Therefore, because of the inefficiency introduced by crowding, the added activity will require 5.4 days to complete. Likewise, on the three affected activities, the first 5 days of normal activity will now require 5.4 days. All four activities will experience loss of productivity resulting from an inefficiency factor equivalent to 0.4 of a single day's labor cost. This is calculated as follows:

Average hourly rate x hours worked per day x number of workers x 0.4 = $ loss

or

$12.00 x 8 x 18 x 0.4 = $691 plus normal labor markups.

3/18 x $691 = direct crowding cost; and should be included in the Direct Cost section of the modification estimate

15/18 x $691 = crowding on unchanged activities, and should be placed in the Impact on Unchanged Work section of the modification estimate.

CONSTRUCTION SCHEDULES

EP 415-1-3
2 Jul 79

(3) <u>Acceleration</u>. Acceleration occurs when a modification requires the contractor to accomplish a greater amount of work during the same time period even though he may be entitled to an extension of time to accomplish the changed work. This is sometimes referred to as "buying back time." Acceleration should be distinguished from expediting. Expediting occurs whenever the modification would require the contractor to complete the work before the original completion date included in the contract. Per DAR 18-111, expediting is not permissible in the absence of approval by the Assistant Secretary of Defense (Manpower, Reserve Affairs and Logistics). Acceleration may be accomplished in any of the following ways:

(a) <u>Increasing the size of crews</u>. The optimum crew size (for any construction operation) is the minimum number of workers required to perform the task within the allocated time frame. Optimum crew size for a project or activity represents a balance between an acceptable rate of progress and the maximum return from the labor dollars invested. Increasing crew size above optimum can usually produce a higher rate of progress, but at a higher unit cost. As more workers are added to the optimum crew, each new worker will increase crew productivity less than the previously added worker. Carried to the extreme, adding more workers will contribute nothing to overall crew productivity. Figures 4-3a through 4-3d indicate the effect of crew overloading.

(b) <u>Increasing shift length and/or days worked per week</u>. The standard work week is 8 hours per day, 5 days per week (Monday through Friday). Working more hours per day or more days per week introduces premium pay rates and efficiency losses. Workers tend to pace themselves for longer shifts and more days per week. An individual or a crew working 10 hours a day, 5 days a week, will not produce 25 percent more than they would working 8 hours a day, 5 days a week. Longer shifts will produce some gain in production, but it will be at a higher unit cost than normal hour work. When modifications make it necessary for the contractor to resort to overtime work, some of the labor costs produce no return because of inefficiency. Costs incurred due to loss of efficiency created by overtime work are an impact element because the increase in overtime results from the introduction of the modification. Contractors occasionally find that to attract sufficient manpower and skilled craftsmen to the job, it is necessary to offer overtime work as an incentive. When this is done, the cost must be borne by the contractor; however, if overtime is necessary to accomplish modification work, the Government must recognize its liability for introducing efficiency losses. Figure 4-4 is the result of study which attempted to graphically demonstrate efficiency losses over a 4-week period for several combinations of work schedules. These data are included merely

4-9

APPENDIX

EP 415-1-3
2 Jul 79

as information on trends rather than firm rules which might apply to any project. Although figure 4-4 data do not extend beyond the fourth week, it is assumed that the curves would flatten to a constant efficiency level as each work schedule is continued for longer periods of time.

(c) Multiple shifts. The inefficiencies in labor productivity caused by overtime work can be avoided by working two or three 8-hour shifts per day. However, additional shifts introduce other costs. These costs would include additional administrative personnel, supervision, quality control, lighting, etc. Modifications that cause the contractor to implement shift work should price the impact cost as appropriate for the activity being accelerated. Environmental conditions such as lighting and cold weather may also influence labor efficiency.

(4) Morale. The responsibility for motivating the work force and providing a psychological environment conducive to optimum productivity rests with the contractor. Morale does exert an influence on productivity, but so many factors interact on morale that their individual effects defy quantification. A project's contract modifications, particularly a large number, have an adverse effect on the morale of the workers. The degree to which this may affect productivity, and consequently the cost of performing the work, would normally be very minor when compared to the other causes of productivity loss. A contractor would probably find that it would cost more to maintain the records necessary to document productivity losses from lowered morale than justified by the amount he might recover. Modification estimates do not consider morale as a factor because whether morale becomes a factor is determined by how effective the contractor is in his labor relations responsibilities.

4-5. Quantification. The following example demonstrates how to use figures 4-3a through 4-3d to quantify the impact costs of crew overloading. Assume that the contractor has planned a construction operation with a duration of 15 working days and an optimum crew size of 10. The modification now requires that the contractor accomplish this operation in 10 working days. The rate of production is the unit of work per amount of effort in mandays. The percent increase is new rate minus original rate divided by original rate times 100. Thus,

$$\frac{(1 \text{ job} \div 100 \text{ MD}) - (1 \text{ job} \div 150 \text{ MD})}{1 \text{ job} \div 150 \text{ MD}} \times 100 =$$

$$\frac{.01 - .0067}{.0067} \times 100 = 50 \text{ percent}$$

4-10

CONSTRUCTION SCHEDULES

EP 415-1-3
2 Jul 79

This represents a 50 percent increase in the crew's rate of production. From figure 4-3a or 4-3d, it appears likely that 50 percent production gain can be achieved by increasing the size 80 percent. Other options could be implemented to speed up production: the optimum crew could work longer shifts, more days per week; a second crew could be placed in operation (if allowed by the nature of the work). However, for this example only increasing crew size is considered. The way to quantify the impact cost before the fact is:

	Original Plan	Accelerated Plan
Manpower	10	18
Hourly Rate	$12	$12
Crew Cost/Day (8 hours)	$960	$1,728
Duration (Working Days)	15	10
Crew Cost (Cost/Day x Duration)	$14,400	$17,280
Taxes, Insurance, Fringes (18 percent)	$2,595	$3,110
Total Crew Cost	$16,992	$20,390

Impact Cost (Accelerated-Original) = $3,398 ($3,400)

    - or -

Impact Cost (Accelerated Plan x Efficiency Loss) =
    $20,390 x 16.7 percent (from fig. 4-3b), = $3,405 ($3,400)

The amount of $3,400 would be placed in the modification estimate, under "Impact on Unchanged Work" and identified by the activity involved. Increased cost of supervision, if necessary, is not included in this crew overloading analysis. Supervision must be costed separately, either as a separate item or as an element of Job Site Overhead, as appropriate.

4-11

APPENDIX

EP 415-1-3
2 July 79

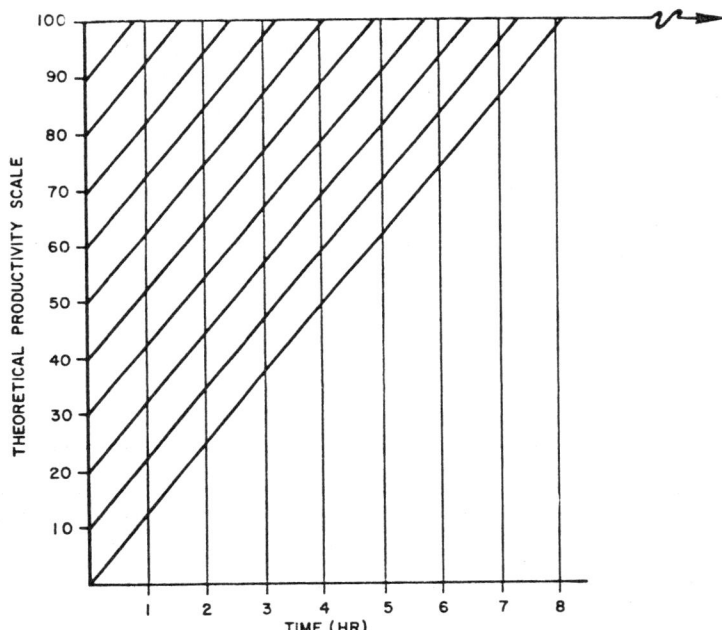

*100 REPRESENTS THE PRODUCTIVITY RATE REQUIRED TO MAINTAIN SCHEDULED PROGRESS

Figure 4-1a. Construction operations orientation/
learning chart.

CONSTRUCTION SCHEDULES

EP 415-1-3
2 July 79

(BASED ON CONSTRUCTION OPERATIONS
ORIENTATION / LEARNING CHART)

PRODUCTIVITY STARTING POINT	DURATION (HR)	AVERAGE LOSS (HR)
100	0	0
90	0.8	0.4
80	1.6	0.8
70	2.4	1.2
60	3.2	1.6
50	4.0	2.0
40	4.8	2.4
30	5.6	2.8
20	6.4	3.2
10	7.2	3.6
0	8.0	4.0

Figure 4-1b. Productivity losses derived from figure 4-1.1.

APPENDIX

EP 415-1-3
2 July 79

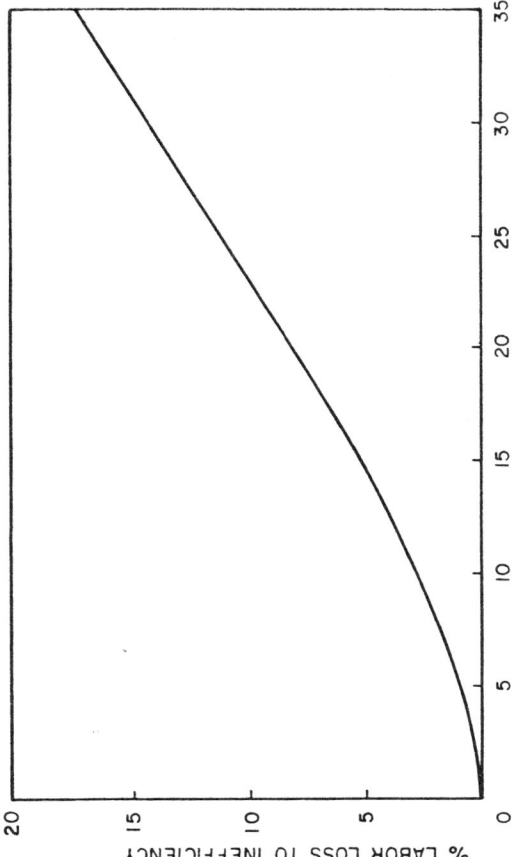

Figure 4-2. Effect of crowding on labor efficiency.

CONSTRUCTION SCHEDULES

EP 415-1-3
2 July 79

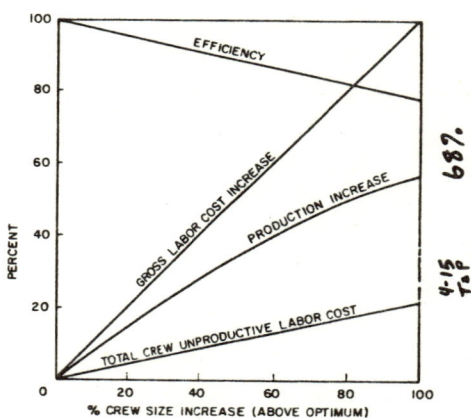

Figure 4-3 a. Composite effects of crew overloading

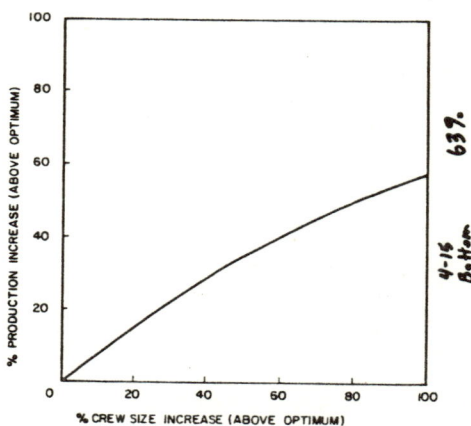

Figure 4-3 b. Unproductive labor at crew overloading.

4-15

APPENDIX

EP 415-1-3
2 July 79

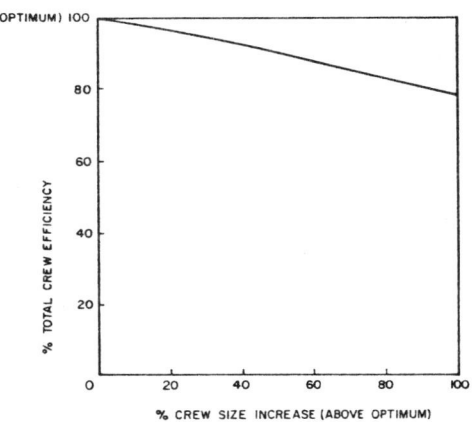

Figure 4-3 c.   Efficiency of crew overloading.

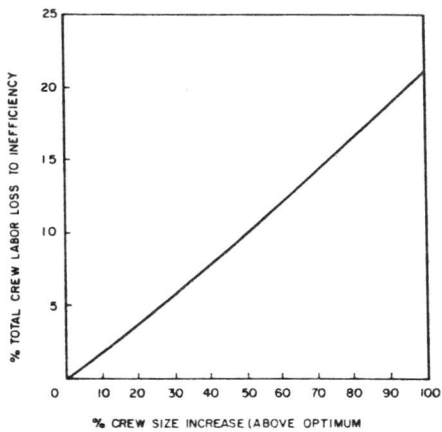

Figure 4-3 d.   Production gain of crew overloading.

4-16

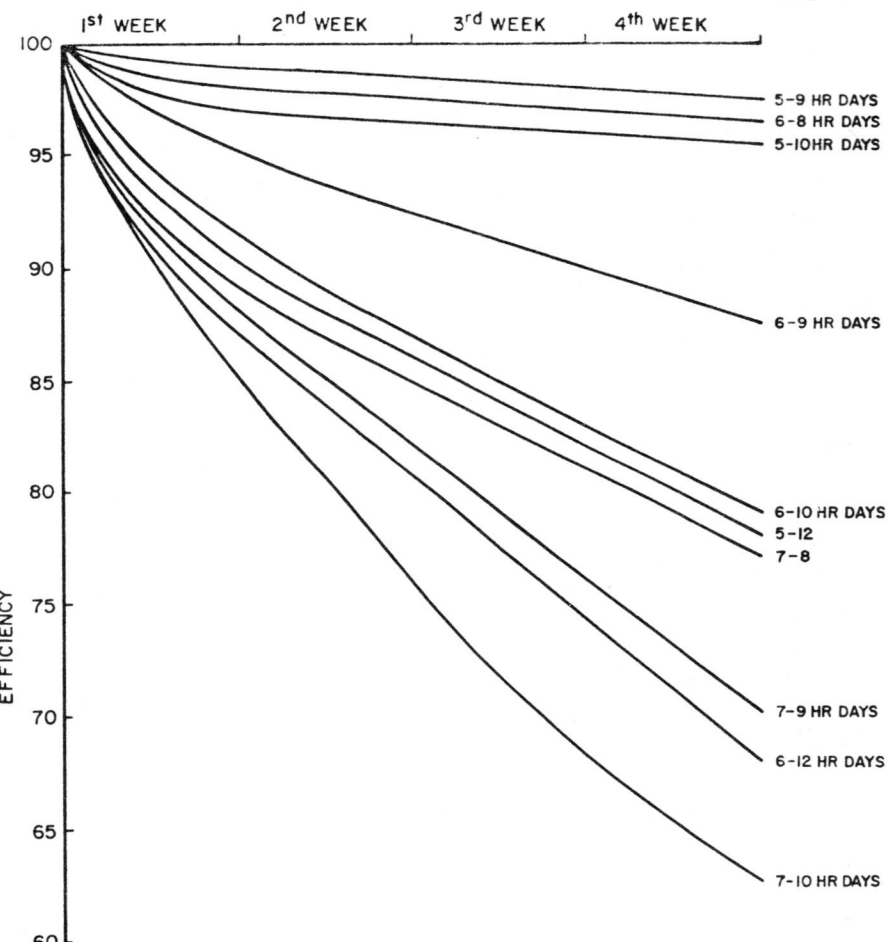

Figure 4-4. Effect of work schedule on efficiency.

APPENDIX

EP 415-1-3
2 July 79

CHAPTER 5

THE GOVERNMENT ESTIMATE

5-1. <u>General</u>. Government estimates should contain two general cost headings, <u>Directly Changed Work</u>, and <u>Impact on Unchanged Work</u>. Even though no Impact on Unchanged Work exists, <u>the heading should be included in the estimate with "0" costs, or "none," indicating that an analysis was made</u>. All Government estimates should be started as soon as the scope of the modification is defined, and should be completed as quickly as possible -- certainly before receipt of the contractor's proposal. When the NTP is issued concurrently with the RFP, work on the Government estimate should not be deferred, but should be completed as soon as possible so the modified price and time may be settled quickly. There is nothing to be gained by delaying the settlement until the work is completed. In fact, waiting gives the contractor an unwarranted advantage.

5-2. <u>Extended overhead</u>. Overhead is defined as the costs incurred for the general operation of the business that cannot be directly identified as resulting from a specific activity. Extended overhead is the indirect cost the contractor is entitled to receive when a time extension to the contract is granted. Extended overhead should be a separate item on the cost estimate and should be based on an analysis of the nature of the operations during the period extended. In some cases, an audit may be conducted to provide this information. District policy will provide guidance when audits are required to determine Extended Overhead.

5-3. <u>Examples</u>.

    a. The examples (fig. 5-1, 5-2a, 5-2b, and 5-3) show only the arrangement of the estimate. Costs pertaining to impact on the unchanged work are separated from direct costs. (Quantities and labor/material unit costs are for illustration only.)

    b. The estimates in the figures correspond to the hypothetical change orders described in paragraphs 3-5a, 3-5b, and 3-5c.

CONSTRUCTION SCHEDULES

EP 415-1-3
2 July 79

CONSTRUCTION COST ESTIMATE				DATE PREPARED 14 Sep 78			SHEET 1 OF 1	
PROJECT: MODIFICATION EXAMPLE P00001				BASIS FOR ESTIMATE				
LOCATION				☐ CODE A (No design completed)				
ARCHITECT ENGINEER				☐ CODE B (Preliminary design) ☐ CODE C (Final design) ☒ OTHER (Specify) Example 1				
DRAWING NO.			ESTIMATOR			CHECKED BY		
SUMMARY	QUANTITY			LABOR		MATERIAL		TOTAL COST
	NO. UNITS	UNIT MEAS	PER UNIT	TOTAL	PER UNIT	TOTAL		
Scope of Work:	Revised Building Layout							
DIRECTLY CHANGED WORK:								
Act 201-203 (Layout)								
Labor	84	MH	$7.30	613.20				
Ins, Taxes, Fringes on Labor	(18%)			110.38				
Materials	1	LS			$10.00	10.00		
								733.58
Revise NAS Schedule	1	LS						300.00
								1033.58
				Extended Overhead				**
						Subtotal		1188.62
					Profit			**
					TOTAL COSTS			1307.48
Time Analysis: Layout has been increased 5 calendar days. Since it is a critical activity, 5 additional calendar days are needed for the project completion date.								
IMPACT ON UNCHANGED WORK:								
Act 203-207 (Excav)								
Backhoe Standby	29	HRS			$4.43	128.47		128.47
				Extended Overhead				**
								147.74
					Profit			**
					TOTAL IMPACT ON UNCHANGED WORK			162.51
Time Analysis: No additional time required for impact.								
			TOTAL INCREASED COST MOD P00001					$1469.99

ENG FORM 150
1 AUG 39   (ER 1110-345-730)   PREVIOUS EDITION MAY BE USED   (TRANSLUCENT)

Figure 5-1. Modification example.

5-2

APPENDIX

EP 415-1-3
2 July 79

CONSTRUCTION COST ESTIMATE							
DATE PREPARED:				SHEET 1 OF 2			
PROJECT: MODIFICATION EXAMPLE: P00002				BASIS FOR ESTIMATE: OTHER (Specify) Example 2			
LOCATION:							
ARCHITECT ENGINEER:							
DRAWING NO.			ESTIMATOR		CHECKED BY		
SUMMARY	QUANTITY			LABOR		MATERIAL	TOTAL COST
	NO. UNITS	UNIT MEAS	PER UNIT	TOTAL	PER UNIT	TOTAL	
A. Scope of Work: This modification provides for the following items							
1. Increased size of exterior doors							
2. Increased roof insulation thickness							
3. Addition of concrete sidewalk							
B. Estimate Assumptions							
1. Job site prevailing wages							
2. Manufacture quotes for materials used							
DIRECTLY CHANGED WORK:							
1 Increase Size of Exterior Doors							
Act 105-106 (new)							
Truck and Driver	32	Mh	$5.25	168.00			
Subsistence	2	Ea	$25.	50.00			
Rework Frames	5	Ea			$50	250.00	
Act 105-235 (New)							
Truck & Driver	16	Mh	$5.25	84.00			
Subsistence	1	Ea	$25.	25.00			
Rework Doors	5	Ea			$100	500.00	
2 Increase Roof Insulation Thickness							
Act 78-109 (New)							
Addn'l Insulation	5000	SF			.35	1750.00	
Act 80-109 (New)							
Rework Fascia	100	LF	$1.50	150.00			
Act 243-245							
Install Addn'l Insulation	5000	SF	.10	500.00	.05	250.00	
Addn'l nailers	300	LF	.15	45.00	.15	45.00	

ENG FORM 150
1 AUG 59   (ER 1110-345-730)   PREVIOUS EDITION MAY BE USED   (TRANSLUCENT)

Figure 5-2a. Modification example.

5-3

CONSTRUCTION SCHEDULES

EP 415-1-3
2 July 79

CONSTRUCTION COST ESTIMATE		DATE PREPARED		SHEET 2 OF 2		
PROJECT			BASIS FOR ESTIMATE			
LOCATION			☐ CODE A (No design completed)			
			☐ CODE B (Preliminary design)			
ARCHITECT ENGINEER			☐ CODE C (Final design)			
			☐ OTHER (Specify)			
DRAWING NO.	ESTIMATOR			CHECKED BY		
SUMMARY	QUANTITY			LABOR		MATERIAL	TOTAL COST
	NO. UNITS	UNIT MEAS.	PER UNIT	TOTAL	PER UNIT	TOTAL	
3 New Sidewalk							
Act 235-249 (New)							
4" conc x 4' x 50'	200	SF	.60	120.00	.50	100.00	
4" sand base							
SUBTOTALS							
Item 1				327.00		750.00	
Item 2				695.00		2045.00	
Item 3				120.00		100.00	
				1142.00		2895.00	
Ins, Taxes, Fringes on				206.00			
Labor (18%)				1348.00			
Revise NAS Schedule						400.00	
				Total Direct Changes			4643.00
				Total Impaction Unchanged Work			0.00
				Extended Overhead			**
						Subtotal	5497.00
				Profit			**
						Subtotal	6027.00
				Bond (1%)			60.00
				TOTAL COSTS			6087.00
Time Analysis							
Critical Activity (229-235), Exterior Masonrys' start date has been slipped							
8 calendar days due to door frame delivery. This will cause an 8 calendar							
day delay in final completion of the project. This modification does not							
cause any other delay.							
Recommend additional time of 8 calendar days to the project final completion							
date.							

ENG FORM 150

Figure 5-2b. Modification example--continued.

5-4

APPENDIX

EP 415-1-3
2 July 79

CONSTRUCTION COST ESTIMATE			DATE PREPARED 14 Sep 78			SHEET 1 OF 1	
PROJECT Modification Example P00003				BASIS FOR ESTIMATE			
LOCATION				☐ CODE A (No design completed)			
				☐ CODE B (Preliminary design)			
ARCHITECT ENGINEER				☐ CODE C (Final design)			
				☒ OTHER (Specify) Example 3			
DRAWING NO.			ESTIMATOR		CHECKED BY		

SUMMARY	QUANTITY			LABOR		MATERIAL		TOTAL COST
	NO. UNITS	UNIT MEAS.	PER UNIT	TOTAL	PER UNIT	TOTAL		
SCOPE OF WORK: Change delivery time of Government Furnished Property (anchor bolts and template) from 90 calendar days after NTP to 141 days after NTP.								
Direct Costs								
Costs based on original delivery date								
Act 251-255 (conc floor slab)								
Labor	96	Mh	$15.00	1440.00				
Material	20	Cy			$30.00	600.00		
								2040.00
Ins, Taxes, fringes on labor								**
								2299.00
				PROFIT				**
				TOTAL				2529.00
Costs based on actual work								
Act 251-255								
Labor	96	Mh	$10.00	960.00				
Labor Standby	40	Mh	$10.00	400.00				
Material	20	Cy			$30.00	600.00		
								1960.00
Ins, Taxes, Fringes on labor								**
							Subtotal	2205.00
				Profit				**
				Total				2426.00
Analysis: No Significant change in contract cost due to change. No additional time required for impact.								

ENG FORM 150
1 AUG 59

5-3. Modification example.

5-5

CONSTRUCTION SCHEDULES

EP 415-1-3
2 July 79

CHAPTER 6

THE CONTRACTOR'S PROPOSAL

6-1. _The Request for Proposal_. Whether or not the RFP carries an immediate notice to proceed, the contractor should be requested to submit the proposal by a specified date. The time allowed for the contractor to prepare the proposal will vary with the complexity of the change. GP clause, Modification Proposals -- Price Breakdown (1968 APR), specifies the detail in which the contractor's proposal is to be submitted (fig. 6-1).

6-2. _Further guidance_. Further guidance for the contractor may be necessary when issuing RFPs. For instance, the contractor's proposal should identify the activities to which cost items are applicable on the CPM schedule. It should also separate direct costs from impact costs; a cost item for revising the CPM schedule should be included. Additional instructions in the RFP should produce proposals that can be readily analyzed and compared to the Government estimate.

APPENDIX

EP 415-1-3
2 July 79

SUSPENSION OF WORK (1968 FEB)

(a) The Contracting Officer may order the Contractor in writing to suspend, delay, or interrupt all or any part of the work for such period of time as he may determine to be appropriate for the convenience of the Government.

(b) If the performance of all or any part of the work is, for an unreasonable period of time, suspended, delayed, or interrupted by an act of the Contracting Officer in the administration of this contract, or by his failure to act within the time specified in this contract (or if no time is specified, within a reasonable time), an adjustment shall be made for any increase in the cost of performance of this contract (excluding profit) necessarily caused by such unreasonable suspension, delay, or interruption and the contract modified in writing accordingly. However, no adjustment shall be made under this clause for any suspension, delay, or interruption to the extent (1) that performance would have been so suspended, delayed, or interrupted by any other cause, including the fault or negligence of the Contractor or (2) for which an equitable adjustment is provided for or excluded under any other provision of this contract.

(c) No claim under this clause shall be allowed (1) for any costs incurred more than 20 days before the Contractor shall have notified the Contracting Officer in writing of the act or failure to act involved (but this requirement shall not apply as to a claim resulting from a suspension order), and (2) unless the claim, in an amount stated, is asserted in writing as soon as practicable after the termination of such suspension, delay, or interruption, but not later than the date of final payment under the contract. (ASPR 7-602.46)

MODIFICATION PROPOSALS — PRICE BREAKDOWN (1968 APR)

The Contractor, in connection with any proposal he makes for a contract modification, shall furnish a price breakdown, itemized as required by the Contracting Officer. Unless otherwise directed, the breakdown shall be in sufficient detail to permit an analysis of all material, labor, equipment, subcontract, and overhead costs, as well as profit, and shall cover all work involved in the modification, whether such work was deleted, added or changed. Any amount claimed for subcontracts shall be supported by a similar price breakdown. In addition, if the proposal includes a time extension, a justification therefor shall also be furnished. The proposal, together with the price breakdown and time extension justification, shall be furnished by the date specified by the Contracting Officer. (ASPR 7-602.36)

PRICING OF ADJUSTMENTS (1970 JUL)

When costs are a factor in any determination of a contract price adjustment pursuant to the "Changes" clause or any other provision of this contract, such costs shall be in accordance with Section XV of the Armed Services Procurement Regulation as in effect on the date of this contract. (ASPR 7-103.26)

Figure 6-1. GP clause, modification proposal--price breakdown.

CONSTRUCTION SCHEDULES

EP 415-1-3
2 July 79

CHAPTER 7

FINALIZING THE MODIFICATION

7-1. <u>Format</u>. Regardless of the document used to execute a contract modification (SF-30 or ENG Form 3938), the settlement terms should show impact costs on the unchanged work as a defined element or a statement that impact has been considered, even if only a lump sum amount is shown. For example, the portion of the document indicating the price/time agreement for a modification having impact costs could be completed as follows:

> "This Modification constitutes compensation in full on behalf of the contractor and its subcontractors and suppliers for all costs and markups directly or indirectly attributable to the changes ordered herein, for all delays related thereto, and for performance of the changes within the time stated."

7-2. <u>Result</u>. This kind of information on the official modification document makes it apparent to everyone that the contractor has been compensated for impact costs, and has agreed that the amounts shown are reasonable and acceptable, and can deter the contractor from later claiming additional compensation for the modification because the settlement ignored impact costs. (In cases where no impact on the unchanged work is involved, "0" or "none" should be noted for the impact costs.)

FOR THE CHIEF OF ENGINEERS:

THORWALD R. PETERSON
Colonel, Corps of Engineers
Executive Director, Engineer Staff

1 Appendix
APP A - Modification Impact Checklist

APPENDIX

EP 415-1-3
2 July 79

APPENDIX

MODIFICATION IMPACT CHECKLIST

1. Justification for change order

    a. Is change essential for proper function of facility?

    b. Is contract modification preferable to accomplishing change work under separate contract?

    c. Is funding available to accomplish the changed work, including impact costs?

2. Request for Proposal

    a. Is scope of work clearly defined?

    b. Is a specific date stipulated for receipt of the proposal?

    c. Is the request accompanied by sufficient instructions on format, detail desired, etc?

3. Government Estimate

    a. Are both direct and indirect costs considered?

    b. Are both direct and indirect delaying factors considered?

    c. Are cost/time for direct work and affect on unchanged work itemized separately?

    d. Is the impact on unchanged work based upon current project status and the approved progress schedule?

    e. If no impact exists, does estimate so indicate?

    f. Is appropriate allowance for revising progress schedule included?

CONSTRUCTION SCHEDULES

EP 415-1-3
2 July 79

4. Review of Contractor's Proposal

   a. Is proposal in required format, with items adequately identified and justified?

   b. Does proposal reflect a thorough understanding of the scope of work?

   c. Is impact on the unchanged work, if applicable, identified separately from direct costs/time?

   d. Does the proposal use current job status and the approved progress schedule as the basis for justifying additional cost/time, both direct and impact?

5. Audit

   a. Was the audit agency given advance notice of impending request for audit?

   b. Did the request include desire for verification of specific items in addition to routine audit procedures?

6. Negotiations

   a. Was impact discussed (even if none exists) and this fact included in the record of negotiations?

BIBLIOGRAPHY

BOOKS

Callahan, Michael. "The Law Behind Construction Schedules," *Deskbook of Construction Contract Law — With Forms*, edited by H. Murray Hohns, Englewood Cliffs, New Jersey, Prentice-Hall, Inc., 1981.

Clough, R. *Construction Project Management*, New York: Wiley Interscience, 1972.

Corbin, A.L. *Contracts*, St. Paul: West Publishing Co., 1960.

Hohns, H. Murray. *Preventing and Solving Construction Contracts Disputes*, New York: Van Nostrand, Reinholt, 1979.

Lockyer, K. *An Introduction to Critical Path Analysis,* London: Pitman Publishing, 1964.

McCormick, C. *Law of Evidence*, St. Paul: West Publishing Co., 1954.

Moder, T. and Phillips, C. *Project Management with CPM and PERT*, New York: Van Nostrand, Reinholt, 1979.

O'Brien, J. *CPM in Construction Management*, New York: McGraw-Hill, 1971.

ARTICLES AND PRESENTATIONS

Fenwick, W. and Davidson, G. "Use of Computerized Business Records as Evidence," *Jurimetrics*, Chicago: ABA, 1979.

Garner, Borcherding, and Samelson. "Factors Influencing the Motivation and Productivity of Craftsmen and Foremen on Large Construction Projects," United States Department of Energy, EQ-78-G-01-6333, 1979.

"Modifications Impact Evaluation Guide," Department of the Army, Office of the Chief of Engineers, EP-415-1, Federal Publications, Inc, 1979.

Tuebner, A. "The Computer as Expert Witness: Toward a Unified Theory of Computer Evidence," *Jurimetrics*, Chicago: ABA, 1979.

Wickwire, T., Walstead, Paul, and Asselin, Tom. "Project Scheduling," *The Briefing Papers Collection*, Washington, D.C., Federal Publications, Inc., 1975.

BIBLIOGRAPHY

Wickwire, T., and Smith. "The Use of Critical Path Method Techniques in Contract Claims," *Public Contract Law Journal*, Chicago: ABA, 1974.

MANUALS

CPM in Construction, Washington, D.C.: Associated General Contractors of America, 1965.

Construction Claims and Disputes — 1978, Chicago: Engineering News-Record Conference and Exposition Management Co., Inc., 1978.

TABLE OF CASES

A

American Sanitary Sales Co. v. New Jersey, 429 A.2d 403 (N.J. Super. 1981) — Ch. 4, n. 50.

B

Baltimore Contractors, Inc., Vermont Marble Co. v.
Blackhawk Heating & Plumbing Co., 75-1 BCA ¶ 11,261 (1975) — Ch. 4, nn. 40, 41, 53, 94, 113, 114.
Blackhawk Heating & Plumbing Co., 76-1 BCA ¶ 11,649 (1975) — Ch. 4, n. 134.
Blake Constr. Co. v. C. J. Coakley Co., 431 A.2d 569 (D.C. App. 1981) — Ch. 4, nn. 126, 136, 149, 150; Ch. 5, n. 166.
Brooks Tower Corp. v. Hunkin-Conkey Constr. Co., 454 F.2d 1203 (10th Cir. 1972) — Ch. 4, n. 96.
Brown v. Rugo, 436 F.2d 632 (1st Cir. 1971) — Ch. 4, n. 73.
Burgess Constr. Co. v. M. Morrin & Son Co., 526 F.2d 108 (10th Cir. 1975) — Ch. 4, nn. 89-91, 143-145.

C

Carney Gen. Constructors, Inc., 79-1 BCA ¶ 13,855 (1979), Ch. 4, n. 121.
Central Sur. & Ins. Corp., Freeman Contractors, Inc. v.
Chaney & James Constr. Co., 66-2 BCA ¶ 6066 (1966) — Ch. 4, n. 54; Ch. 6, nn. 173, 174.
C. H. Leavell & Co., 70-2 BCA ¶ 8437 (1970) — Ch. 4, n. 115; Ch. 5, n. 167.
Chouteau v. United States, 95 U.S. 61, 24 L. Ed. 371 (1877) — Ch. 1, n. 4.
C. J. Coakley Co., Blake Constr. Co. v.
Continental Consol. Corp., 67-2 BCA ¶ 6624 (1967) — Ch. 4, nn. 34, 35, 102, 128.

D

Dawson Constr. Co., 75-2 BCA ¶ 11,563 (1975) — Ch. 4, nn. 46, 130.

TABLE OF CASES

Dobson v. Rutgers, 157 N.J. Super. 357, 384 A.2d 1121 (1978) — Ch. 4, nn. 36, 37; nn. 57, 64, 120.
Dover, J. A. Jones Constr. Co. v.
Drew Brown, Ltd. v. Joseph Rugo, Inc., 436 F.2d 632 (1st Cir. 1971) — Ch. 4, nn. 51, 52, 73.

E

E. C. Ernst, Inc. v. Koppers Co., 476 F. Supp. 729 (W.D. Pa. 1979) — Ch. 4, nn. 81-87, 106, 107, 122, 123.
E. C. Ernst, Inc. v. Manhattan Constr. Co., 387 F. Supp. 1001 (S.D. Ala. 1974) — Ch. 4, nn. 99, 105, 161-163.
Economy Mechanical Indus., Inc., 79-1 BCA ¶ 13,571 (1979) — Ch. 4, nn. 58, 59, 77-80.

F

Franchise Equities, Inc., Kroeger v.
Freeman Contractors, Inc. v. Central Sur. & Ins. Corp., 205 F.2d 607 (8th Cir. 1953) — Ch. 4, n. 138.
Frye v. United States, 293 F. 1013 (C.A.D.C. 1923) — Ch. 6, n. 178.

G

George A. Fuller Co., Natkin & Co. v.

H

Heat Exchangers, Inc., 1963 BCA ¶ 3881 (1963) — Ch. 4, n. 98.
H. E. Cook, Inc. v. United States, 270 U.S. 4, 46 S. Ct. 184, 70 L. Ed. 438 (1926) — Ch. 1, n. 5.
Henry Ericsson Co. v. United States, 62 F. Supp. 312 (Ct. Cl. 1945) — Ch. 4, n. 137.
Hi-Way Elec. Co., Pathman Constr. Co. v.
Howard Foley Co., United States v.
Hunkin-Conkey Constr. Co., Brooks Tower Corp. v.

I

Iowa Southern Util. Co., Peter Kiewit Sons' Co. v.

J

J. A. Jones Constr. Co. v. Dover, 372 A.2d 540 (Del. 1977) — Ch. 4, nn. 88, 125.

TABLE OF CASES

Joseph E. Bennett Co., 72-1 BCA ¶ 9364 (1972) — Ch. 4, nn. 103, 104.
Joseph Rugo, Inc., Drew Brown, Ltd. v.
Jos. Schlitz Co., Pearl Brewing Co. v.

K

Koppers Co., E. C. Ernst, Inc. v.
Kroeger v. Franchise Equities, Inc., 212 N.W.2d 348 (Neb. 1973) — Ch. 4, n. 141.

L

Lane-Verdugo, 73-2 BCA ¶ 10,271 (1973) — Ch. 4, nn. 55, 56, 108, 109, 129, 151, 152, Ch. 6, nn. 171, 172.

M

Manhattan Constr. Co., E. C. Ernst, Inc. v.
Minmar Builders, Inc., 72-2 BCA ¶ 9599 (1972) — Ch. 4, nn. 43, 44.
M. Morrin & Son Co., Burgess Constr. Co. v.
Montgomery-Marci Co. & Western Line Constr. Co., 1963 BCA ¶ 3819 (1963) — Ch. 4, n. 95.

N

Natkin & Co. v. George A. Fuller Co., 347 F. Supp. 17 (W.D. Mo. 1972) — Ch. 4, nn. 33, 42, 63, 97, 116, 127, 142.
New Jersey, American Sanitary Sales Co. v.

P

Pathman Constr. Co. v. Hi-Way Elec. Co., 382 N.E.2d 453 (Ill. 1978) — Ch. 4, nn. 49, 74-76, 131, 132.
Pearl Brewing Co. v. Jos. Schlitz Co., 415 F. Supp. 1122 (D.C. Texas 1976) — Ch. 6, nn. 181, 187.
Peter Kiewit Sons' Co. v. Iowa Southern Util. Co., 355 F. Supp. 376 (S.D. Iowa 1973) — Ch. 4, nn. 38, 39, 60, 61, 66, 67, 68.
Prepakt Concrete Co., Steenberg Constr. Co. v.

R

R. F. Ball Constr. Co., Southern Fireproofing Co. v.
Rice, United States v.

TABLE OF CASES

Rochester, Vanderlinde Elec. Corp. v.
Rugo, Brown v.
Rutgers, Dobson v.

S

Seib, Transport Indem. Co. v.
Southern Fireproofing Co. v. R. F. Ball Constr. Co., 334 F.2d 122 (8th Cir. 1964) — Ch. 4, nn. 69-72.
Steenberg Constr. Co. v. Prepakt Concrete Co., 381 F.2d 768 (10th Cir. 1967) — Ch. 4, nn. 62, 124.

T

Transport Indem. Co. v. Seib, 178 Neb. 253, 132 N.W.2d 871 (1965) — Ch. 6, n. 189.
Turnbull, Inc. v. United States, 389 F.2d 1007 (Ct. Cl. 1967) — Ch. 4, nn. 139, 140.

U

United States, Chouteau v.
United States, Frye v.
United States, H. E. Cook, Inc. v.
United States, Henry Ericsson Co. v.
United States v. Howard Foley Co., 329 U.S. 64, 67 S. Ct. 154, 91 L. Ed. 44 (1946) — Ch. 1, n. 6.
United States v. Rice, 317 U.S. 61, 63 S. Ct. 120, 87 L. Ed. 53 (1942) — Ch. 1, n. 3.
United States, Turnbull, Inc. v.

V

Vanderlinde Elec. Corp. v. Rochester, 54 A.D.2d 155 (N.Y. 1976) — Ch. 4, n. 153.
Vermont Marble Co. v. Baltimore Contractors, Inc., 520 F. Supp. 922 (D.C.D.C. 1981) — Ch. 4, nn. 146-148.

W

William Passalacqua Builders, Inc., 77-1 BCA ¶ 12,406 (1977) — Ch. 4, nn. 110-112.

INDEX

A

Acceleration, ch. 5.
Activities, ch. 1, ch. 2, §§ 2-1, 2-2, 2-3, 4-1, 4-7, 4-12, ch. 5.
  Amount of, §§ 2-1, 4-2.
  Descriptions, §§ 2-1, 4-7.
  Numbering, § 2-1.
AIA, ch. 3, § 4-13, ch. 5.
Arbitration, ch. 1, § 4-1, ch. 5.
Architects, ch. 1, ch. 2, §§ 2-1, 4-6, 4-8, 4-11, ch. 5.
Argonaut Realty, ch. 1.
ASPR, ch. 3, § 4-13.
A201, ch. 3, § 4-13, ch. 5.

B

Backward Pass, §§ 2-1, 4-6, ch. 5.
Bar Charts, ch. 1, ch. 2, §§ 2-3, 4-1, 4-3, 4-4, 4-5, 4-7, 4-9, ch. 5, 6-2.
Belmont House, § 4-11.
Benota, ch. 1.
Best Evidence Rule, § 6-2.
Black & Veatch, §§ 4-4, 4-5.
Board of Contract Appeals, ch. 1, §§ 4-3, 4-6, 4-7, 4-10, 4-13, 6-2.
Booze, Allen and Hamilton, § 2-4.
Broadway Maintenance Corporation, § 4-2.
Bureau of Reclamation, §§ 4-5, 4-9.
Business Records Exception, §§ 6-2, 6-5.

C

Cathgart, Lloyd, ch. 1.
Changes, ch. 1, ch. 2, §§ 4-1, 4-5, 4-6, 4-7, 4-10, 4-11, 4-13, ch. 5.
Charles H. McCawley Associates, § 4-6.
Chief of Engineers, ch. 5.
Claims, §§ 4-1, 4-6, 4-11, ch. 5.
College of Medicine and Dentistry of New Jersey, § 4-2.
Computers, ch. 1, §§ 2-1, 2-3, 6-2, 6-4.

INDEX

Construction Manager, §§ 4-4, 4-5.
Corps of Engineers, §§ 4-1, 4-3, 4-5, 4-6, 4-11, 4-12, ch. 5.
Correspondence, ch. 5.
Cost Control, § 2-4, ch. 5.
Courts, ch. 1, ch. 3, §§ 4-1, 4-2, 4-5, 4-10, 4-13, 6-4.
CPM, ch. 1, §§ 2-1, 2-3, 2-5, 4-1, 4-2, 4-3, 4-5, 4-7, 4-9, 4-10, 4-11, 4-12, 4-13, ch. 5, §§ 6-1, 6-2, 6-5.
Craig, J. David, § 2-2.
Critical Path, §§ 2-1, 2-3, 2-4, 4-1, 4-6, 4-7, 4-10, ch. 5, § 6-5.
Cross Examination, § 6-5.

D

Dams, §§ 4-5, 4-9, 4-11.
Delay, ch. 1, §§ 2-1, 4-1, 4-2, 4-5, 4-6, 4-7, 4-9, 4-10, 4-11, 4-12, 4-13, ch. 5, § 6-2.
Department of Energy, § 4-13.
Design-Build, § 4-5.
Designers, ch. 2, ch. 3, §§ 4-4, 4-6, 4-8, 4-9, 4-12.
deVos, Bill, ch. 1.
Differing Site Conditions, §§ 2-5, 4-9, 4-13.
Discovery, §§ 4-1, 6-4, 6-5.
Disputes, ch. 1, §§ 4-1, 4-11, ch. 5.
Dummies, §§ 2-1, 2-2, 4-7, 4-10.
Durations, ch. 2, §§ 2-1, 2-2, 2-3, 4-7, 4-10, 4-13, ch. 5.

E

Early Finish Dates, §§ 2-1, 2-2, 4-6, ch. 5.
Early Start Dates, §§ 2-1, 2-2, 4-6, ch. 5.
E.I. Dupont de Nemours, ch. 1.
Engineers, ch. 1, ch. 2, §§ 2-1, 4-5, 4-6, 4-8.
Errors, ch. 3, §§ 4-7, 4-12, 4-13, ch. 5, § 6-5.
Everett M. Dirksen Senate Office Building, § 4-11.
Experimental Evidence, § 6-5.
Experts, §§ 4-1, 4-4, 4-7, 4-11, 6-2, 6-3, 6-4, 6-5.

F

Federal Procurement Regulations, § 4-13.
Float, §§ 2-1, 2-5, 4-6, 4-7, 4-10, 4-13, ch. 5.
Ford, ch. 1.

INDEX

Forward Pass, §§ 2-1, 4-6, ch. 5.
Free Float, §§ 2-1, 4-6.

G

Gantt Charts, ch. 2, § 2-3.
General Electric, § 4-9.
General Motors, ch. 1.

H

Hearsay, §§ 6-2, 6-5.
Hohns, H. Murray, § 4-6.
Holiday Inns, ch. 3.

I

IBM, ch. 1, § 2-2.
IJ, §§ 2-1, 2-2, 2-3, ch. 5.
Impacting, ch. 5.
Internet, ch. 2.

J

Jones and Laughlin Steel Corp., § 4-5.
Julia C. Lathrop Homes, § 4-11.

K

Kelley, James E., Jr., ch. 1.

L

Lap and Lag, §§ 2-1, 2-2.
Late Finish Dates, §§ 2-1, 4-6, ch. 5.
Late Start Dates, §§ 2-1, 4-7, ch. 5.
Liquidated Damages, §§ 4-1, 4-7.
Lockheed Aircraft Corporation, § 2-4.
Logic, ch. 2, §§ 2-1, 4-7, 4-12, ch. 5, § 6-2.
Longhorn Ordinance Works, § 4-11.

M

Manloading, ch. 2, §§ 2-1, 4-5.
Mauchly Associates, ch. 1.
Mauchly, John W., ch. 1.

INDEX

Milestone Dates, §§ 2-1, 4-4, 4-11, 4-13.
MIT, ch. 1.
Model Procurement Code, § 4-13.
Multiple Prime Contractors, §§ 4-1, 4-2, 4-5, 4-9.

N

Narrative, ch. 5.
Navy, § 2-4.
Network Analysis System, ch. 3.
Nodes, §§ 2-1, 2-2.
Notice, § 4-12.

O

Out-of-Sequence Work, §§ 4-2, 4-5, 4-11, ch. 5, § 6-1.
Overlap, §§ 2-1, 2-2.
Owners, ch. 1, ch. 2, § 2-1, ch. 3, §§ 4-1, 4-6, 4-7, 4-9, 4-11, 4-13.

P

PDM, ch. 2, §§ 2-1, 2-2.
Perini-Canada, ch. 1.
PERT, ch. 2, §§ 2-4, 4-5.
Polaris Missile Program, § 2-4.
Port-Mann Bridge, ch. 1.
Pre-bid Schedule, §§ 4-5, 4-8.
Printout, ch. 5, §§ 6-2, 6-5.
Progress Meeting Minutes, ch. 5.
Progress Photos, ch. 5.
Project Management Institute, ch. 2.
Providence Hospital of Mobile, § 4-6.

R

Remington Rand, ch. 1.
Rescheduling, §§ 2-5, 4-11.
Rescission, § 4-11.
Restraints, ch. 2, §§ 2-1, 2-2, 4-7, 4-10.
Rice Doctrine, ch. 1.
Rules of Civil Procedure, § 6-5.

INDEX

S

Schedules.
  Approval of, §§ 4-2, 4-9, 4-13.
  As-built, §§ 4-1, 4-3, 4-5, ch. 5.
  As evidence, §§ 4-3, 4-5, 4-12, 6-1, 6-5.
  Clauses for, ch. 1, ch. 3, §§ 4-1, 4-2, 4-5, 4-7, 4-11, 4-12.
  Completion of, § 4-2.
  Dates in, ch. 2, § 2-3, ch. 3, §§ 4-5, 4-13, ch. 5, § 6-2.
  Definition of, ch. 1, ch. 2, §§ 4-1, 4-3, 4-5, 4-13, 6-5.
  Flexibility of, §§ 4-5, 4-6, 4-12.
  History of, ch. 1.
  Interpretation of, ch. 1, ch. 3, § 4-5.
  Preparation of, ch. 2, § 2-1, ch. 3, §§ 4-1, 4-2, 4-4.
Scheduling Consultant, §§ 2-1, 4-1, 4-2, 4-4, 4-5, 4-7, 6-2.
Scientific Evidence, §§ 6-1, 6-3, 6-5.
Sequence, ch. 1, § 2-1, ch. 3, §§ 4-3, 4-5, 4-6, 4-13, ch. 5.
Shop Drawings, §§ 4-9, 4-11.
Specifications, ch. 1, § 2-1, ch. 3, §§ 4-2, 4-5, 4-8, 4-11, 4-12.
Subcontractors, ch. 2, §§ 2-1, 4-5, 4-6, 4-9, 4-10, 4-11, 4-13, ch. 5.
Succeedence § 2-2.
Suppliers, §§ 2-1, 4-4, 4-9.
Suspension of Work, §§ 4-5, 4-11, 4-12, 4-13, ch. 5.

T

Termination, § 4-11.
Time Extensions, §§ 4-1, 4-5, 4-6, 4-10, 4-12, ch. 5.
Time Float, §§ 2-1, 4-6.
Time Scale, §§ 2-1, ch. 5.

U

United States Public Works Administration, § 4-11.
UNIVAC Applications Research Center, ch. 1.
Updates, ch. 2, §§ 2-2, 2-5, 4-2, 4-5, 4-10, 4-12, ch. 5, § 6-2.

V

Veterans Administration, §§ 2-1, 2-5, ch. 3, ch. 5.
Voluminous Writing Exception, § 6-2.

INDEX

W

Wagner, William B., ch. 1, § 4-7.
Waldron, A. James, ch. 1.
Walker, Morgan, ch. 1.
Walter Reed Hospital, § 4-11.
Western Electric Co., §§ 4-5, 4-11.
Westinghouse, § 4-9.
Winter Weather, §§ 4-9, 4-11.

Z

Zink, Dwight, ch. 1.